Creative art of
Knitting

Joan Fisher

HAMLYN
London · New York · Sydney · Toronto

Consultant editor **Louise Daniels**

Published by
The Hamlyn Publishing Group Limited
London · New York · Sydney · Toronto
Astronaut House, Feltham, Middlesex, England

© Copyright The Hamlyn Publishing Group Limited 1974
ISBN 0 600 31797 8

Contents

Introduction   4

Tools and materials   5

First steps   12

Working methods   26

Fancy stitch patterns   29

Aran knitting   40

Colour work   46

Circular knitting   56

Details that count   62

Machine knitting   75

The patterns   80

Glossary of terms   170

Index   175

Introduction

Knitting, as well as being one of the oldest crafts known to us, is one of the most versatile. Indeed, with the constant introduction of new yarns and materials, its scope seems to broaden with every age. At one time, mothers knitted for their children, and worked underclothes and socks for the family—and that was about the limit of the craft's usefulness. Nowadays it is usual for couturiers to introduce knitted garments into their ranges, and to interpret the latest fashion ideas in knitted fabrics; and we can buy patterns for knitting everything from top coats to tea-cosies.

Knitting needs hardly any equipment—just a pair of knitting needles and a ball of wool. It can be worked almost anywhere—on a train, on a bus, while you watch television—and it has so many facets that every woman can find some type of work to suit and please her: delicate lacy designs for tablecloths and household accessories, intricate colour patternings, chunky Aran stitches. And the diversity of designs available means that no one need ever be bored with what she is making.

Nor should the economics of the matter be overlooked: it is frequently very much cheaper to make something yourself than to buy it ready-made, and in addition you have the satisfaction of choosing exactly the style you want, in the colour that suits you best. Not least, the actual process of knitting is relaxing and soothing: one of the most rewarding handicrafts a woman can enjoy.

This book is designed to take the beginner from the first stage, when she knows virtually nothing of the craft, through to doing complex colour work and advanced patterns. By the time she reaches the pattern section at the end of the book, she should be able not only to tackle any pattern given there, but any other pattern she chooses to try.

I hope, too, that the already experienced knitter will find pleasure and instruction in this book. A number of fascinating stitch patterns, both traditional and modern, have been illustrated, and it may be that some of these will be new and valuable additions to the repertoire that every knitter endeavours to build up.

Knitting, in fact, is such a varied craft that perhaps no one is ever an expert, since we are all learning continuously. Certainly knitting is one of the most fascinating of hobbies, one which does not stale with time and experience, and which provides tangible rewards as well as the pleasure and satisfaction which always come from making something rather than buying it.

Tools and materials

A pair of needles and some yarn are all that are necessary to begin to knit. This sounds simple, and indeed it is, but to the beginner the enormous range of different types and weights of yarn available, and the many different sizes of needles, are bewildering.

Yarns used for knitting fall into two main groups: natural and synthetic. Both types are available in many different forms, to suit different purposes. Usually, however, most yarns are marked according to the 'ply' and this term needs to be understood.

The term 'ply' means the number of threads which are twisted together to make the finished yarn. Usually two-ply is finer than four-ply but this does not have to be so, since two heavy plies can be twisted together to form a very thick yarn indeed. In general terms, however, two-ply is very fine and used mainly for shawls, the finest underwear and baby clothes; three-ply is for light sweaters, socks, first size vests, dresses and so on; four-ply is used for medium-weight knitwear of all kinds, dresses, sweaters, socks, children's wear and school-wear; double knit is heavier, and is used for everything from sweaters to top coats. As it knits up quickly and is comfortable to work and to wear, double knit yarn has become tremendously popular over the past few years, and it is probably the most rewarding type of yarn for a beginner to use.

SPECIAL YARN TYPES

Woollen yarns are available in all the weights mentioned above, and sometimes, if fashion dictates it, in exceptionally heavy qualities as well. Wool has the great advantage of being easy to knit, comfortable and warm to wear and, provided that it is well treated and carefully washed, it lasts for years. Different weights and types will supply most needs: botany wool is generally used for baby wear (and anyone with a sensitive skin may prefer it for sweaters); crossbred yarns are a little less soft than botany but are strong and hardwearing.

Crêpe yarns are available in both wool and synthetics. They are twisted in a special way to give a flatter, rather less hairy surface than ordinary woollen yarns and they knit up into a surface which is slightly crinkled and which has a flatter appearance than usual. Pilling—the condition which occurs when knitwear rubs into little balls on the surface of the yarn—is less likely to occur with crêpe yarns, and for this reason it is often a good idea to use them for garments which have to withstand constant wear and tear—such as schoolwear.

Mohair, angora and cashmere are luxury yarns, and generally expensive, but as they are very light in weight—and sometimes very fine as well—the quality of yarn in each ball is usually greater than for a comparable weight of a heavier yarn. For

Two pretty party dresses for a little girl, both knitted in a random-dyed mohair yarn.

instance, a one-ounce ball of cashmere will go a lot further than a one-ounce ball of four-ply wool, so you will therefore need fewer balls of yarn for your garment and the cost will come down accordingly. Cashmere is exceptionally soft and fine, angora has the traditional fluffy surface and mohair is spun with a long, shaggy pile. Each yarn is made to a thickness roughly equivalent to one of the standard plies—angora usually works like a four-ply, for instance. It is not wise, however, in a given pattern, to substitute any of these special yarns for a conventional yarn even if it is of a similar weight. Patterns are carefully worked out to suit specific yarns, and satisfactory results cannot be guaranteed if a different yarn is used.

Glitter yarns have become very popular in the last few years for evening tops, dresses and party accessories. Usually these yarns consist of a thread of glitter twisted with a basic yarn, but some are entirely of metallic construction. They need special patterns and careful handling, as they must not be split or pulled in work, but they give a splendid effect for all kinds of glamorous party wear.

Bouclé yarns are usually in wool, although some cotton versions are produced. They have little bobbles set at irregular intervals along the length of the thread, and when knitted up produce a tweedy effect which is especially appropriate to suits. They do not flow as smoothly as plain yarns, but it is easy to get used to working with them. Bouclé yarns are generally equivalent to a four-ply weight.

Cotton yarns are also available in different thicknesses, and are good for summer tops, dresses and beachwear. Cotton is simple and rewarding to knit.

Synthetics cover a very wide range of yarns. Nylon, Orlon, Courtelle, Acrilan and Tricel are all spun into knitting yarn, either by themselves or in combination with other fibres. They have great advantages: people who find wool irritating to wear usually have no trouble with synthetics; these yarns also wash extremely well and because of their special construction, they take dyes which are sharp and fast—the colour range in synthetics is always excellent, and the whites, in particular, are hard and brilliant.

Synthetic yarns dry quickly and, if the washing is correctly done, garments in synthetics keep their shape and wear very well. They, too, are made in two-, three- and four-ply weights, and in double knitting. Often a pattern will give you the choice of a woollen or synthetic yarn.

Mixtures – usually in three-ply and four-ply weights – have a lot to recommend them as well. Usually the yarns consist of wool with a thread or two of synthetic twisted in them. They are good for school knitwear, socks and children's trousers, which need to be laundered often and which take a lot of hard wear.

Washing qualities are very important in garments which have to go into the tub frequently, and so it is always as well to ask before you buy a new yarn, in case you spoil the finished garment by washing it in the wrong way. In fact, virtually every yarn produced for hand-knitting is washable, and many wools can even be washed by machine. Hand-knits should never be allowed to get really dirty, because rubbing will impair the fabric; it is much better to wash frequently by squeezing them gently through mild suds and hand-hot water.

So high is the general standard of yarns produced today that you can be sure, if you buy a reputable brand of yarn, that you will get a big colour choice, good washing performance, long wear and fast dyes.

However, it is a mistake to think that because A is a good make of knitting yarn and you have a pattern produced by B, another good firm, that you can use A's wool for B's pattern. You cannot. Every pattern you buy stresses the importance of using only the yarn specified by that pattern, and there is a very good reason for this. No two spinners produce a yarn which is identical. They may look and feel alike, but in fact one may be infinitesimally thinner and lighter than the other. It will follow, then, that the thinner yarn will give you a slightly different tension (see page 21) from the heavier one, and that you will get rather more length of yarn to the ball. So if you use a heavier yarn on a pattern designed for the finer one, you will end up with a garment which is a different size (and it may not be *your* size) and will need more yarn than the quantity specified.

If you absolutely cannot get the specified yarn, then buy the nearest to it (the sales assistant will help you) and buy just one ball; take it home, test your tension and if necessary make such adjustments as you need to the size—perhaps by working a different size from the one you had originally chosen. But this is for the experienced knitter; the beginner would do better to buy the right pattern for the right yarn, since that pattern has already been tested by the maker.

When you buy yarn for a garment, try to buy the complete quantity at once. When yarn is dyed, it goes into the dye in

For evening elegance—skinny rib tops knitted in a glitter yarn.

batches called 'lots' and each lot is given a number (you will find this on the band round the yarn you buy). No matter how hard the yarn manufacturer tries to keep all dyes identical, it is impossible to do this and sometimes there is a tiny variation between one dye lot and another.

You may not even notice the difference when the two resulting yarns are put in front of you, but if you knit them both in the same garment you will most probably get an uneven patchiness—and this is as true of white and black as of any colour. So make sure you are buying *all* the yarn from the same dye lot.

KNITTING NEEDLES

Knitting needles are made in lightweight, strong alloys, in wood, bone and plastic, but the alloys are the most widely used today. Whichever type of needle you use, however, and whether you are buying pairs, sets of four double-pointed needles, or single circular needles, all are sized according to the same system. In the UK, the thicker the needle the smaller the size—size 3, for instance, is a very thick needle, and size 12 a fine one. In the USA, this sizing system is reversed and a high number denotes a thick needle, a low number a fine one. UK size 8 (USA size 6) is most commonly used for double knitting yarns, UK size 10 (USA size 3) for four-ply.

Needles vary in length, and which length you use (except with circular needles) depends very much on personal preference and the type of work to be done. It is a good plan to build up a stock of various lengths on each size. Some knitters like a long needle, which takes the work comfortably; others like a shorter one and find it easier to manipulate. Within the limits of good sense—since obviously a very big, bulky sweater should not be crammed on a short needle—it is a matter of personal taste. Very short needles are made for children, and they can be useful to the adult knitter as well for small pieces of work such as pockets, ties or edgings for buttonhole trims.

Sets of four needles, each needle pointed at both ends, are used for socks, polo collars, gloves and so on, because by using them you produce a seamless tube. If you want a similar effect on a larger garment—a dress or a skirt—then a circular needle is used. This is a long needle, with a flexible centre section and each end rigid and pointed like a conventional knitting needle; various lengths are available. It is important to use the right length of needle for the number of stitches you will be working with—ideally the minimum number of stitches used in the pattern should reach from point to point on the needle without stretching. Circular knitting is just as easy as the two-needle method, and experienced knitters sometimes prefer to work the front and back of a sweater all in one on a circular needle as far as the armholes, so as to avoid side seams (a very important point when knitting a skirt as well).

Needles should be kept together in a box, so that they are not damaged. If you find that you bend needles in work (some people grasp their knitting very firmly and manage to distort even the toughest needle) you must replace them from time to time. A bent needle does not produce even work.

Similarly, if you damage or scratch the point of the needle throw it away, otherwise it will tear the yarn with every stitch

Top to bottom: maxi wooden needle, medium wooden needle, size 1 (bone), then sizes 6, 7, 9, 10 and 12, all in alloy (all UK sizes).

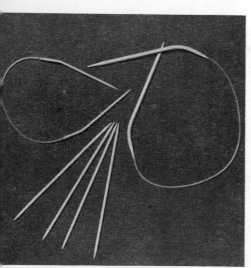

Circular needles and a set of four double-pointed needles, for knitting 'in the round'.

you make. Most needles are marked by having the size number stamped on the side or top, but if this is not the case, keep the needles together and marked by twisting an elastic band round them and slipping in a piece of paper on which the size is clearly written. Never use a needle because you think it looks about the right size—always make certain the needle *is* the correct size, or the tension of your work will suffer.

OTHER EQUIPMENT

There are a few more items of equipment which every knitter will need at some time or other:

Cable needles. These are short needles, usually sold in sets, with a point at each end. Cable patterns look like twisted ropes, and when working them a small group of stitches has to be put at the back or the front of the work. A cable needle is used for this, and it is helpful if the needle is the same size as those being used for the main work, or as near to the size as possible.

Stitch holders. In many patterns, a group of stitches will sometimes be left on the needle to be worked at a later stage— perhaps at the back of the neck to be knitted up later for a collar, or at the top of a sleeve. The pattern will sometimes instruct 'leave stitches on a spare needle' but this is very unwise, since the stitches are almost certain to slip off. If you have only a few spare stitches, then slip them on to a large safety pin; if a larger number of stitches is left then a stitch holder is essential. There are several shapes to choose from, all of them efficient. Some are like outsize safety pins, others have a wire fixed to a rigid bar so that the holder can be closed and there is no risk of stitches being lost.

Row counters. These, too, come in several designs, although the most popular is probably the small light cylinder which slips on to the end of the needle itself. If the pattern specifies that you must increase on every seventh row, or make a repeat of the pattern every eighth row (and sometimes both at once) it is important to know which row you are on. A row counter will keep a reliable check on this.

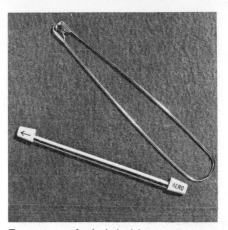

Two types of stitch holders.

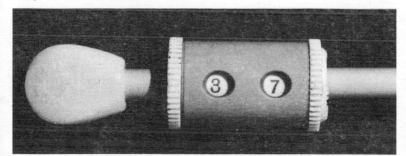

Needle gauge. If you are not certain of the size of a needle you can measure it on a gauge; these are usually metal with slots, ridges or holes in which to check different sizes of needles.

Tape measure. A good tape measure is essential, not only for use during work but also for checking tension before you begin. Do not use a fabric measure as these are inclined to stretch; plastic measures are excellent, and are unlikely to change size. If the measure has a small metal end, so much the better, since this can be used for accurate marking over small spaces—if you have to make buttonholes at $1\frac{1}{4}$-inch intervals, for instance.

Workbag and cloth. Knitting should always be put away in a bag to keep it clean. And it is important to have a plain, clean piece of cloth to spread over your lap while you work, as—when the knitting gets long—it will dangle against your clothes, and constant movement against material will dirty the work. An old pillowcase is the ideal solution since you can spread it over your lap in work and wrap the knitting up in it when you put it away. Of course, hands should always be perfectly clean when you start to knit—particularly if you are working with pale colours or white. If the weather is warm, and your hands tend to perspire, use talc lightly to dry them. Nails and the skin at finger and thumb tips should be kept as smooth as possible, particularly if you are working with synthetic yarns.

Crochet hook. A medium-sized crochet hook is useful in many ways. It can be used for picking up dropped stitches or picking up stitches along an edge, and so on. Also, a crochet edging or trimming on a knitted garment can look most attractive.

Pattern holders. These are transparent envelopes for holding patterns, and keeping them clean and flat. It is important that a pattern remains uncreased (since frequent folding will destroy the print at the fold) and if you are going to build up a stock of patterns, then the better their condition the easier it will be to use them repeatedly. If you find during work that you need to alter the pattern slightly for your individual requirements (perhaps you prefer the sleeve an inch longer or shorter) then mark the pattern clearly for the next time.

COMPARATIVE SIZES OF KNITTING NEEDLES

British	Continental	American
14	2	0
13	—	—
12	2·50	1
11	3·00	2
10	3·25	3
—	3·50	4
9	4·00	5
8	4·50	6
7	4·75	7
6	5·00	8
5	5·50	9
4	6·00	10
3	7·00	$10\frac{1}{2}$
2	8·00	11
1	9·25	13

USEFUL FACTS AND FIGURES

Some knitting yarns are sold in ounce quantities, some are sold in gram balls. If it is wished to convert an ounce quantity into the appropriate gram measure, or vice versa, follow the simple conversion tables below.

Weights

1 oz.	= 28·35 grams	1 lb.	= 454·0 grams
4 oz.	= 113·4 grams	2 lb. 3 oz.	= 1 kilogram
8 oz.	= 226·8 grams	(approx.)	

Note. When buying knitting yarn, a 25-gram ball of yarn will very approximately equal a 1-oz. ball. But as 1 oz. equals slightly over 25 grams, for larger quantities increase the number of gram balls—e.g. if 12 oz. of yarn is required, buy fourteen 25-gram balls, and if 20 oz. is required, buy twenty-three 25-gram balls.

Linear measures

1 inch	=2·54 centimetres
6 inches	=15·2 centimetres
1 foot (12 in.)	=30·48 centimetres
1 yard	=0·914 metre (just over 91 centimetres)
1 yard 4 in. (approx.)	=1 metre

ABBREVIATIONS

The following are the abbreviations used in the stitch patterns and designs to make throughout this book. If a pattern involves a complicated stitch formation, this will be described and the appropriate abbreviation given within the pattern. Colour abbreviations will also be given in individual patterns.

alt., alternate

beg., beginning

ch., chain

cont., continue

d.c., double crochet

dec., decreas(e)(ed)(ing)

foll., following

g.st., garter stitch

in., inch(es)

inc., increas(e)(ed)(ing)

k., knit

m.1, make one stitch (by working into front and back of stitch, or as otherwise specified in pattern)

m.st., moss stitch

p., purl

patt., pattern

p.s.s.o., pass slipped stitch over

rem., remain(ing)

rep., repeat

sl., slip

s.s. or **sl.st.**, slip stitch

st(s)., stitch(es)

st.st., stocking stitch

t.b.l., through back of loop(s)

tog., together

tr., treble

y.b., yarn back

y.f. or **y.fwd.**, yarn forward

y.o.n., yarn on needle

y.r.n., yarn round needle

Size note

Instructions in every pattern are given in size order, with larger sizes in brackets. Where only one set of figures occurs this refers to all sizes.

First steps

The creation of knitted fabric is a very simple process. A needle filled with stitches is held in the left hand. The needle in the right hand is used to work into those stitches and to transfer them to the right-hand needle, by the forming of a row of loops. The filled needle is then transferred to the left hand and the process is repeated.

There are only two stitches, called knit and purl (sometimes plain and purl) and there are dozens of combinations of these which will produce fabric that is plain or patterned, flat or surfaced, solid or lacy.

HOLDING THE WORK

As with most forms of needlecraft, there are as many ways of working as there are workers—so it is not possible to lay down hard and fast rules about technique. But in general, knitting should be held in the following way: keep your hands relaxed and put one needle into your left hand with the fingers and thumb above the needle, so that it is braced against the palm. The other needle rests on the division between thumb and fore-finger of the right hand and is controlled by the first two fingers and the thumb. Hold the needles comfortably, and try not to grip too tightly.

To control the yarn smoothly—and this is important because smooth, evenly-running yarn not only makes for even work but for speed in working—the accepted method is to pass the yarn round the little finger of the right hand, take it under the third and middle fingers and out over the first finger. In this way the yarn slips through the channel of palm and fingers and you should not need to keep stopping to pull a length free from the ball.

You may well evolve a method of working which suits you better than this one and it is safe to say that provided any method produces regular work, and is not tiring in the performance, then it is acceptable.

Practise working as smoothly and rapidly as possible without removing the right hand from the needle; this is a habit that beginners often succumb to, and it slows down work.

When you begin to knit, and to try the techniques outlined in this chapter, use a fairly short medium-sized needle and a double knitting yarn in a light colour. This is an easy weight of yarn to handle, and you will see your stitch formation clearly as you go.

If you are left-handed . . .

Then merely reverse the instructions given for right-handed workers. The left hand will control the yarn, and the right hand will control the stitches. Throughout instructions for stitches and techniques, for each reference to right-hand needle read left-hand needle, and vice versa.

CASTING ON (see three diagrams, right)

Casting on is the technical term given to the process of actually putting the first set of stitches on the left-hand needle. There are several methods of doing this and sometimes a pattern will actually specify one of them, so it is wise to master them all.

Every method begins with a slip loop which becomes the first stitch. Make it in this way: holding the yarn between thumb and forefinger of the left hand, take hold of the end in the right hand and make a loop in a clockwise direction round the first two fingers of the left hand.

Hold that loop in place with the left thumb. Now take a needle in the right hand and slip it through the loop working from front to back, and with the point draw through a length of yarn, thus forming a loop in the needle. Pull gently on the hanging ends of the yarn and you will tighten the loop on the needle. This is the first stitch, and whichever type of casting on method you go on to employ, this is the way the first stitch is always formed.

The thumb method (see two diagrams below)

This is probably the most popular method of casting on as it is suitable for virtually every edge. It forms a firm, springy base. Unwind a length of yarn from the ball (allow about a yard of yarn for every seventy stitches required). Now make a slip loop as described above. You will therefore have a loop on the needle some way along the length of the yarn.

Put the needle with the loop on it into your right hand, and take the shorter length of yarn in your left. Using this length, make a loop round your left thumb, working clockwise (hold the yarn into your palm with the last two fingers of the left hand and twist your thumb round the yarn). Now slip the point of the right-hand needle through the loop formed on your thumb, working from front to back, and with your right hand wrap the yarn which is attached to the main ball round the point of the needle, from back to front. Using the point of the needle, draw the yarn through the needle and slip the stitch thus formed off your thumb. Pull the shorter end of the yarn gently to make a taut stitch. Continue in this way to make the number of stitches required.

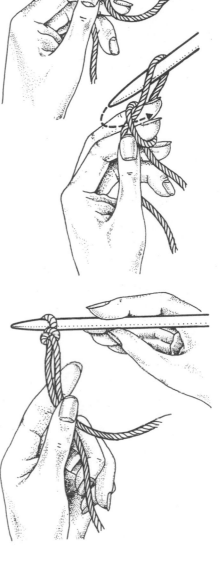

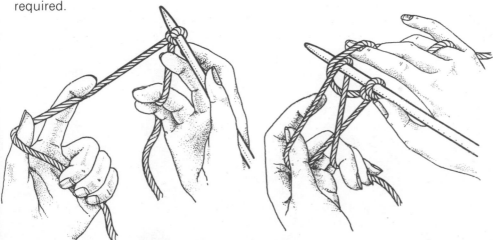

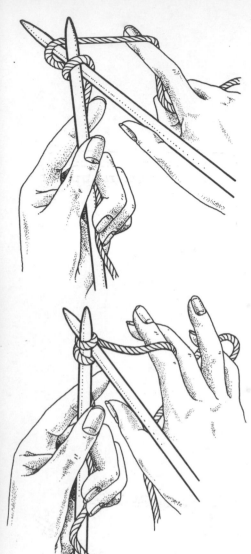

If you use this casting on method you can begin to work at once. The first row is usually a bit tricky, so go carefully. Once a few rows have been worked and you have a little piece of work to hold on to it is easier to manipulate. If the end of the yarn used for casting on is too long, cut it about five inches from the needle. Never leave a too-short end, as it might unravel.

Two-needle method

This method produces a much looser edging than the thumb method, and has pronounced loops. This can be an advantage (later you will learn how to use these loops to pick up a hem and sometimes a pattern allows for fringing to be knotted through hem loops). However, for ordinary knitting it is advisable to work all the stitches in the first row into the back rather than the front of the stitch, to give the necessary firm edging.

Make a slip loop on the needle (see page 13), within a few inches of the end of the yarn. Put the needle into your left hand. Now with the right-hand needle, slip the point through the first stitch, from front to back, and take the yarn in the right hand. Bring the yarn from the back of the needles to the front, passing it between the two needles, then bend the right-hand needle slightly towards you, drawing the yarn through the loop to make a stitch. Transfer this stitch from the right-hand to the left-hand needle, which will now have two stitches on it. Withdraw the right-hand needle, slip it through the second stitch just made, and repeat the process. Continue in this way to make required number of stitches.

Between-stitch method

This is suitable for most edges and gives a twisted, springy edge. It is usually better to work the first row into the back of the stitches, as for the two-needle method. Between-stitch casting on is very useful if you have to widen work suddenly (perhaps by adding a few stitches at the beginning of a row).

Make a slip loop on the needle (see page 13) and then, working as for two-needle method, make a stitch. You now have two stitches on the left-hand needle. Put the right-hand needle between the two stitches on the left-hand needle, and make a stitch in the same way as you did for the second one, transferring it to the left-hand needle when it is completed. Withdraw the right-hand needle, slip it between the second and third stitches and repeat the process to form another stitch. Continue in this way to make number of stitches required.

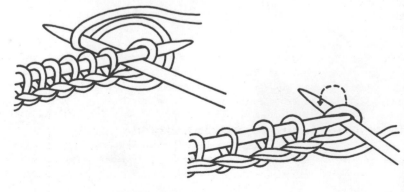

Invisible method

This gives a looped edge which is useful if you want to add a fringing round a shawl, for instance. Make a slip loop (see page 13) and put both needles through it, points facing in the same direction. Take a length of yarn in a contrast colour and hold it along the length of the two needles. Now, using the main yarn, wrap that yarn round both needles and the contrast yarn, each turn of the yarn standing for one stitch.

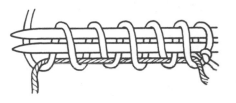

When you have wound on the number of 'stitches' required, slip one needle out of the work and put the remaining needle with the loops into your left hand, with the other needle in your right hand. With the main yarn, work the first row as follows: put the point of the right-hand needle from front to back through the first loop, bring the yarn from front to back between the needles and using the point of the right-hand needle, bring the yarn through the loop to form a stitch.

Repeat this all along the row, ending by working into the original loop. After one or two rows you can pull out the contrast thread, leaving a row of loops which can be used for picking up and working a decorative edge, or as the basis for fringing, whichever is desired.

Important note. The cast-on edge of a garment—usually at the bottom of a sweater or cuff, or the edge of a skirt—takes a great deal of strain every time the garment is put on or taken off. For this reason it is important that this edge should be flexible. If you are a fairly tight knitter, use a needle a couple of sizes larger than the size specified in the pattern when you cast on and off (this is equally important because if you finish a neckline too tightly you will have a struggle every time it has to go over your head).

Casting on for four-needle knitting

Knitting with two needles produces a flat piece of fabric. But it is possible to work a seamless tube (usually for socks or gloves) if you use four needles. What happens is that the stitches are divided among three needles which form a triangle in work. The fourth needle knits off the stitches of the first needle, which is then free and used to knit off the stitches of the second needle, and so on. Every time the stitches have been taken off the complete set of three needles you have worked a 'round' rather than a 'row'.

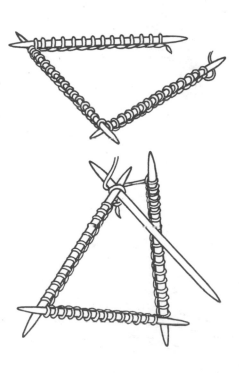

Cast on for four-needle work as you would for any two-needle method: that is, if you are instructed to put 16 stitches on each needle, it is easier if you cast on 48 stitches on one needle and then divide them up. Be careful to work the first linking stitch (which completes the first round) tightly, to give a good edge.

If you have difficulty with stitches twisting, work the first couple of rows on two needles and then divide them up; you can always stitch the two edges together from the wrong side when the garment is finished.

Casting on for circular needle knitting

Another way to produce a seamless tube of knitting is by using one circular needle, which is made like a flexible tube with a point at each end (see note on page 8). Such needles are

useful for producing a larger piece of work than four needles can usually make. Stitches are cast on to the circular needle by any of the two-needle methods. You then bend the needle into a circle and with the right-hand point work into the last stitch which was cast on. It is usually safer to thread a piece of contrast coloured yarn through this stitch, to mark the beginning of the round, and to carry this thread up your work every time you arrive at it. In this way you will always know when a round is completed.

Casting on with this type of needle can be difficult, especially if the yarn is fine, because the stitches can get twisted. It is sometimes preferable to work the first two or three rows to and fro in the usual way, and then join into a ring when you have a few rows worked.

THE BASIC STITCHES

Now the stitches are on the needle, you can begin to make the two basic stitches—knit and purl—which are used for all pattern permutations. Concentrate on the knit stitch until you can do it easily, and then go on to the purl.

The knit stitch

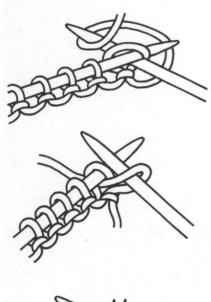

This stitch, usually referred to as 'k.' in pattern abbreviations, is worked with the yarn kept at the *back* of the work, and brought forward with every stitch made.

Cast on the number of stitches required and put the needle with the stitches into your left hand. Insert the point of the right-hand needle into the first loop from front to back, and draw the yarn, with your right hand, forward between the two needles. With the point of the right-hand needle draw the yarn through the stitch, by turning the needle slightly towards you. There will now be a loop on the right-hand needle. Let the loop on the left-hand needle drop, and draw the yarn gently taut so that the stitch on the right-hand needle is firm. Now work the next and all subsequent stitches in a similar way. When you have reached the end of the row, the filled needle in your right hand should be transferred to your left hand, and the empty needle transferred to your right. You are now ready to work the next row.

The purl stitch

For this stitch, usually referred to as 'p.' in patterns, the yarn is kept at the *front* of the work.

Cast on stitches as before and hold the needle with stitches in your left hand. See that the yarn is lying towards the front of the work, then slip the needle in your right hand through the *front* of the first stitch, working in a right-to-left direction. Wrap the yarn in a clockwise direction round the point of the right-hand needle, keeping it at the front when you have completed the loop. Turn the right-hand needle slightly away from you and with the point draw through the loop of yarn you have just made. Slip this stitch on to the right-hand needle, and let the loop on the left-hand needle drop. Repeat this action with all subsequent stitches.

CASTING OFF

When a piece of work has been completed, the stitches have to

Top picture: a selection of modern yarns and wools. Above: all-over diamond colour pattern (see page 51).

Above: fancy diamond colour pattern (see page 52).

Easy-to-wear zip-up jacket knitted in one of the newest yarns—a tweedy look mixture.

be finished off in such a way that they will not come undone. This is called casting off.

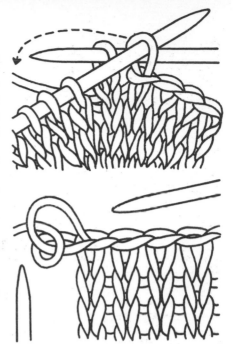

Knit the first two stitches from the left-hand needle on to the right-hand needle. With the point of the left-hand needle, draw the first stitch knitted over the second, and let it drop. You now have only one stitch on the right-hand needle. Knit the next stitch from the left-hand needle, and repeat the process. In this way you will work along the row, always with one stitch left on the right-hand needle.

At the end of the row, when only one stitch is left, pull on it gently to enlarge it, cut the yarn a few inches from the work and pass the cut end through the loop. Draw on this cut end and the stitch will tighten. This loose end can be run into the work with a sewing needle or taken into the seam when the work is completed.

If you are casting off while working a rib pattern, then continue the pattern—that is, knit the knit stitches and purl the purl stitches, so that the continuity of the work is unbroken. Always cast off loosely and, if you are a tight worker, use a larger needle for this last row.

Casting off four-needle knitting
Follow the method given above, emptying first one needle, then the next and so on, taking great care to work bridging stitches at the ends of the needles fairly tightly.

Casting off circular needle knitting
This must be done with an extra needle; the spare needle is used in the right hand and the stitches are worked off the circular needle as for the two-needle method given above.

SHAPING WORK
Once you are proficient at casting on, knitting, purling and casting off, you are ready to begin work on an actual design. Most beginners work first on a straight piece of knitting which presents no problems—a child's scarf is a good start—and eventually progress to more sophisticated designs. For these, it is necessary to produce *shape* in work. For instance, a sleeve widens from the cuff up to the underarm, and then narrows to form the sleeve head, or a skirt will start wide, and narrow down towards the waistline.

To achieve the necessary shape, increasing and decreasing techniques are employed, which either remove stitches or put them on, depending on how the basic shape is to be altered.

Increasing
There are several ways to widen work by increasing the number of stitches on your needle. Which method you use will depend on the type of shape alteration needed, and the position of the increase (either within the body of the work or at each end of it).

Method 1. Working twice into the same stitch. This is done as follows: knit the stitch in the usual way, but do not slip it off the left-hand needle. Put the point of the needle into the back of the stitch and knit into the stitch a second time. This time take the two stitches off the needle at once. It is also possible to purl into the front and back of the stitch, of course,

if this suits the pattern better. This increase is usually worked at the end or beginning of a row and to avoid the slight 'step' it creates at the end of the fabric, is best worked on the second stitch in from the edge rather than the first.

Method 2. Working into the base of the next stitch. Put the right-hand needle into the fabric *below* the stitch which is next to be worked, putting the needle right through the fabric. Work a stitch in the usual way, and then continue with the stitch above. This type of increase is virtually invisible, so is very good for shaping within the body of the fabric.

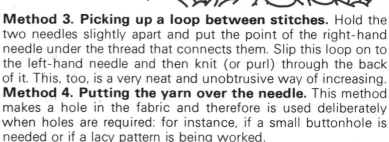

Method 3. Picking up a loop between stitches. Hold the two needles slightly apart and put the point of the right-hand needle under the thread that connects them. Slip this loop on to the left-hand needle and then knit (or purl) through the back of it. This, too, is a very neat and unobtrusive way of increasing.

Method 4. Putting the yarn over the needle. This method makes a hole in the fabric and therefore is used deliberately when holes are required: for instance, if a small buttonhole is needed or if a lacy pattern is being worked.

Between two knit stitches the yarn is brought from the back to the front of work between the stitches and then taken over the top of the right-hand needle so it is ready for the next stitch to be worked in the usual way. This is called **'yarn forward'** (diagram A).

Between two purl stitches it is necessary to wind the yarn round the needle, in an anti-clockwise direction. This is called **'yarn round needle'** (diagram B).

Between a knit and a purl stitch (when the yarn would ordinarily be brought forward between the needles anyway) it is brought forward *over* the needle, before the purl stitch is worked (C). This is **'yarn on needle'**. Between a purl and a knit stitch the yarn is taken back over the needle in a similar way (D). In every case a small hole is made in the fabric by the addition of the extra stitch.

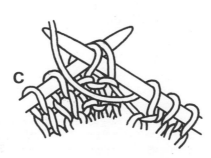

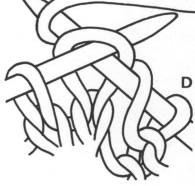

Method 5. Casting on. It frequently happens that the work has to widen suddenly and several stitches at once have to be added at either end. In this case, the two-needle or between-stitch method of casting on may be used; with either method it is best to work into the back of the new stitches on the first row.

Decreasing

As with increasing, there are several methods by which the width of your work may be reduced by decreasing the number of stitches on the needle.

Method 1. Taking two or three stitches together. This is the easiest way in which to lose one or two stitches in one movement (more than this is rarely possible except in some fancy stitch patterns). Put the needle through the next two or three stitches together and work them in the usual way, slipping them off the needle together. Two stitches knitted together will lose one stitch, three stitches knitted together will lose two. This can be done with purled stitches as well. Sometimes the pattern will specify that you knit 'through the back of the loops'. This is because the decreased stitches will lean in a certain direction in the fabric according to whether they are knitted together in the ordinary way, or through the back of the loops, or passed over a stitch already knitted (see next method).

Method 2. Passing a slipped stitch over. The first stitch on the left-hand needle is slipped on to the right without being worked. Then the next two stitches are knitted (or purled) together and worked on to the right-hand needle in the usual way. With the point of the left-hand needle pick up the slipped stitch and pass it over the stitch just made. It is then dropped.

It frequently happens that this type of decreasing is used for raglan shaping and as it creates a fashioning line, it is set a few stitches inside the edge of the garment. For instance, you may be instructed to knit five stitches, then work a decrease, then work to last seven stitches, take two together and knit to the end. In subsequent rows the decreasings will be set at the same point so that a continuous line is created—usually by the 'pass slipped stitch over' method at one end and the 'take two together' method at the other, as the two lines will run at opposing angles.

Method 3. Casting off. If a group of stitches has to be taken off all together, for instance during shoulder shaping, then the stitches are cast off in the usual way at the beginning of the row, and you continue to knit or purl the rest of the row. Be sure to cast off knit stitches knitwise, and purl stitches purlwise so the pattern is not interrupted.

WHAT IS TENSION?

Tension is the measurement of the number of stitches and rows which are produced to the inch when a certain yarn is knitted on a certain size of needle. In other words, the number of rows and stitches to the inch determine the finished size of the garment, and it is impossible therefore to emphasise too strongly how important it is to get the tension right.

For example: the designer is working out a pattern for a child's jersey. By experiment with double knitting yarn she finds that if she uses size 8 needles (USA size 6) she produces

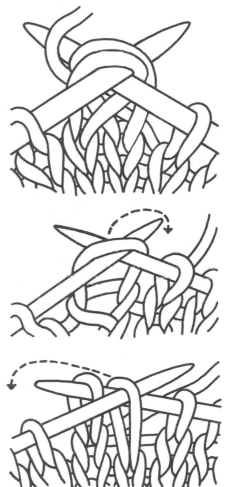

fabric with $5\frac{1}{2}$ stitches to the inch, and $7\frac{1}{2}$ rows to the inch. The child's jersey is intended to fit an 18-inch chest—so the front and back should each measure 10 inches across to allow ease of fit. This means that you will need 55 stitches to produce a 10-inch width, and the designer will base her pattern on this calculation.

Now if you are a loose knitter you may produce only 5 stitches to the inch, using the same needles. Therefore, your 55 stitches will work out to a piece 11 inches wide, and the jersey will measure 22 inches when it is made up. The bigger stitch probably will not work out at $7\frac{1}{2}$ rows to the inch either, but more likely to 7 rows. So the shaping, which depends on the number of rows involved, will be too short. In other words you will have worked long hours to turn out a garment that does not fit, and may well be completely useless.

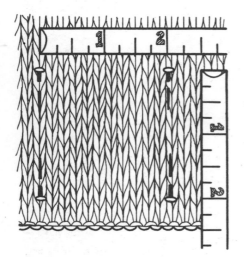

Most patterns give a tension measurement, and it is essential before you embark on any pattern that you check your tension against the measurement given. To do this work a square of three or four inches in the stitch specified by the pattern, and with the yarn and needle size quoted. Now press the square lightly and give it time to settle back to its normal shape. Working from the middle, mark off a two-inch square, using pins to outline the square, and keeping to the tension the pattern gives as correct. For example, if you are working on $5\frac{1}{2}$ stitches and $7\frac{1}{2}$ rows to one square inch, count across 11 stitches and put a pin at each end, then count down 15 rows and put pins at top and bottom. Measure the square you have formed. If it is two inches in both directions your tension is correct and you can go ahead and make the garment. If the square is smaller than two inches, make another piece using a size larger needle. If it is too large, use a smaller size needle. Continue in this way to work sample squares using different size needles until you achieve the correct tension measurement.

After some experience, many knitters get to know that they always need a size smaller or larger needle than is quoted in the pattern because their tension deviates a little from the norm. If you find, after repeated experiment, that you cannot get both stitches and rows to agree to the number given for the correct tension, concentrate on getting the number of stitches accurate. In this way the garment will always be the right width, and, as so many patterns are based on measurement rather than number of rows, you can knit to the correct length and your pattern should still work out well.

Working methods

Although there are only two basic stitches in knitting, the combinations into which these two stitches can be worked are endless. There are, however, a handful of 'classic' stitch patterns which every knitter must master, because they occur so frequently. Practise working squares or lengths of each stitch pattern until you know them thoroughly.

GARTER STITCH

Every beginner should start with this pattern—so called because it was originally used for stocking tops. Every row is worked in knit stitches. This produces a ridged fabric, with two rows forming one ridge (so this is not a fast-growing stitch). If you were to purl every stitch on all rows you would achieve the same result.

STOCKING STITCH

Cast on the required number of stitches.
1st row: k. (every stitch knitted).
2nd row: p. (every stitch purled).
These two rows are repeated throughout, resulting in a fabric which is flat and smooth on one side, and ridged on the other. It is probably the most frequently used stitch but, because it is so simple and flat, it unfortunately shows every imperfection; good stocking stitch is the hallmark of a good kr tter.

REVERSED STOCKING STITCH

This is worked in the same way as stocking stitch, except that the design calls for the wrong side—i.e. the ridged side—to show in wear. Work as for ordinary stocking stitch, but remember that the purl rows are the right-side rows. The narrow ridging of reversed stocking stitch is a very pleasant fabric, which many people prefer for casual clothes to flatter, conventional stocking stitch.

CONTINENTAL STOCKING STITCH

This, too, produces a flat surface very similar to ordinary stocking stitch but it has a slight twist to the knitted stitches, which gives it rather more interest.
Cast on the required number of stitches.
1st row: k., but work into the back of every stitch (i.e. pass the needle from front to back of the back part of the loop on the left-hand needle and then knit the stitch off in the ordinary way)
2nd row: p.
Repeat these two rows throughout.

RIB PATTERNS

Ribs of various widths can be produced by the alternation of

Garter stitch.

Stocking stitch.

Reversed stocking stitch.

Continental stocking stitch.

knit and purl stitches. Rib patterns usually have the effect of drawing the fabric into a narrower width than would be provided by the same number of stitches used for a flat stitch, although in wear they will stretch out. For this reason ribs are used for edges that need to fit closely: polo collars, cuffs, anklets, hems of jerseys. It is also customary to work them on a finer needle than will be used for the main part of the garment.

You will probably have noticed by now that when a stitch is worked knit it looks purl on the reverse side and that you must purl that stitch when you reach the next row if you want to produce a flat surface on the right side. In most rib patterns, where you are working with an even number of stitches, the same rule is followed: on each row you knit the purl stitch of the previous row, and purl the knit stitch of the previous row. The resultant rib will therefore look the same from either side.

The following are a few variants on ribbing.

Single rib
The most commonly used rib for edgings on gloves, socks, sweaters, jackets and necklines.
Cast on an even number of stitches.
1st row: * k.1, p.1; rep. from * to end (i.e. knit the first stitch, purl the second stitch, knit the next, purl the next, and so on all along the row).
Repeat this row throughout.

Double rib
Another very popular rib, often used for an entire garment when a skinny rib style is desired.
Cast on a number of stitches divisible by four.
1st row: * k.2, p.2; rep. from * to the end (i.e. knit two stitches, purl two stitches, knit the next two, purl the next two, and so on all along the row).
Repeat this row throughout.
Of course, if it suits the pattern to have an even number which is *not* divisible by four (e.g. 22) then it is still possible to use double rib; care must be taken however to see that on the reverse side row knit stitches are purled and vice versa—'right' side and 'wrong' side instructions will not be the same.

Wide rib
The wider spaced the ribs are, the less springy will be the fabric, and some wide ribs are used as the main stitch of a garment, as they break the surface and are more interesting than a flat stitch. Here is one example of a wide rib pattern:
Cast on a number of stitches divisible by eight.
1st row: * p.3, k.5; repeat from * to end.
2nd row: * p.5, k.3; repeat from * to end.
Repeat these two rows throughout.
You will see that, because the number of knitted and purled stitches are not identical, the ribs are not equally wide and this rib pattern looks different on the reverse side (you may well prefer the look of the reverse side and there is no reason why this could not be used equally well).

MOSS STITCH
This is a flat stitch with a textured surface, which is worked in a

similar way to a rib but with an uneven number of stitches. This is a stitch where you do in fact knit the knit stitch of the previous row and purl the purl stitch of the previous row.

Cast on an uneven number of stitches.

1st row: * k.1, p.1; repeat from * to the last stitch, k.1 (i.e. knit the first stitch, purl the second, knit the next and purl the next all along the row until the last stitch is reached, then knit that). Repeat this row throughout.

CHOOSING AND FOLLOWING A PATTERN

Now that you have mastered the arts of casting on and off, knitting and purling, and working increases and decreases, you are ready to make a complete garment.

Before you choose a pattern and dash out to buy yarn there are one or two points to consider, however. Any beginner will get tired of a very long and complicated pattern which is a struggle all the way through. Choose a small garment if you can (something for a baby or child is ideal) or a simple sweater. It will be made quickly and you will then want to go on and try something new.

Look for a simple pattern but not, if possible, one entirely in stocking stitch. Every fault shows up in this stitch, so it is not one for a beginner. Moreover, although it is quick and easy, it is not interesting to do. Try to find a stitch with a small variation which gives surface interest without too much complexity—a broken rib, perhaps.

Next, take a look at the sizing. Most good patterns are made in several sizes. Jackets, jumpers and sweaters, including men's and children's, are sized on the bust or chest measurement, and other measurements—such as sleeve length and length from top to bottom of the garment—are also usually given. If in doubt—and many people, children especially, do not fit all these measurements exactly—then go by the chest or bust size. You can adjust the length in work.

Some patterns specifically say that the finished garment measures 34 in. across the chest, so if you are a 34-in. bust size you may prefer to knit the 36-in. size to give extra ease in wear. Other patterns will say 'to fit bust size 34 in.' which probably means that the actual size of the garment will be about 36 in. If you are in any doubt, do a simple mathematical calculation. Look through the pattern and find out how many stitches are used for the widest part of the back and the front: let us suppose 120 on each. Now look at the tension measurement. If there should be 7 sts. to the inch, then the back of the garment is going to measure 18 inches across, and so will the front. In other words, the garment made up will measure 36 in., so if that is your bust measurement, then you would be wise to make the next size up, to give enough ease in fit.

Having established the correct bust or chest size, look at the other measurements. Sleeves are measured from cuff to armhole along the underarm seam; garment length (for a sweater) from shoulder to waist, or sometimes from centre back neck to waist. Lengthening or shortening can therefore be done between cuff and armhole, or welt and armhole. If on the back you are instructed to 'continue until the work is 14 inches to the armhole', and you want to lose an inch off the length, then work for 13 inches only to this point. Never attempt to alter armhole measurements until you are much more experienced, since these are mathematically worked out and if you do not understand the principles involved, you will not be able to alter the top of the sleeve proportionately.

If you are going to alter the length of back or sleeve, mark the pattern accordingly and remember, if you are lengthening, that you may need more than the quantity of yarn than is specified on the pattern.

Before you begin, read the pattern carefully, and be sure that you understand the abbreviations listed at the beginning. In addition to these, there are two marks which are constantly used in patterns to save space: brackets and asterisks.

Brackets

These are generally used when more than one size is shown on the pattern. For instance, if a jersey is for bust sizes 32, 34 and 36 in., there will be often three sets of figures for each instruction, e.g. 'work for 9 (10, 11) in.' or 'cast on 100 (108, 116) sts.' The first figure (outside brackets) will refer to the 32-in. size, the other two figures (inside brackets) will refer to the 34 and 36-in. sizes, in size order. Consequently if you are making the second size you follow the first set of instructions inside the brackets throughout. If only one set of figures is given, this will mean that the instruction applies to all sizes.

Brackets are also sometimes used to save writing out instructions more than once: e.g. '(k.3, p.3) twice' is a quick way of saying 'k.3, p.3, k.3, p.3'.

Asterisks

These are used as space-savers as well. In most cases, the back and front of a jersey or sweater will be worked in exactly the same way as far as the start of armhole shaping. It is therefore a waste of space to print the instructions twice, so an asterisk or sometimes a pair of asterisks are inserted at the beginning and end of the section which is common to both parts of the garment. The instructions for the front would then read: 'Work as for the back from ** to **'.

Asterisks are also used with a very complex pattern; some Aran patterns have as many as twenty-four different rows making up one whole section of the design and it is obviously absurd to print them repeatedly. The pattern will therefore read: 'repeat the pattern from ** to ** 3 times' or whatever is needed.

Checking the tension

Before you begin any pattern *check your tension* by the method outlined on page 22. The importance of doing this cannot be overstressed. The tension measurement should be clearly stated at the beginning of the pattern and you must be sure that your work corresponds to this measurement otherwise your garment will not look as it should and your labours will have been a waste of time. Checking tension may seem a bore: it is also the foundation of all successful knitting. Even if you have made up a particular pattern before, always re-check your tension each time you use it again—it is possible your knitting may have become very slightly slacker or tighter, or even the yarn itself may be of a marginally different quality.

Order of working

Most sweater patterns usually give the instructions for the back of the garment first, then for the front, then for the sleeves and finally such trimmings as neck edgings or buttonhole bands. To begin with at least it is wise to work in the suggested order. As has already been explained, the back may be fully written out and other pieces keyed to that, in which case you must work the back first in order to understand the pattern. The back may also contain explicit instructions for a complicated pattern which is repeated or adapted on other parts of the garment.

MEASURING YOUR WORK

Measurements on knitting must be taken carefully and must on different pieces be exactly the same. For instance, in dressmaking when you cut out fabric for a dress you usually cut the sleeves together, so they will be identical, or you will cut from two pieces of a paper pattern which have been exactly sized. In knitting, however, each piece is individually made, and it is easy to stretch the work a bit (especially if you are impatient!) or perhaps to knit a few rows too many, and then when you put front to back you will have unequal seams to join.

To avoid this, it is best to keep a careful check on the number of rows knitted. For instance, if your pattern instructs you to 'work 3 in. of rib' and you find when you have completed the three inches that you have worked thirty rows, then work thirty rows for the matching piece.

Similarly, if you have to make one cardigan front so many inches deep, work the first one and measure it accurately. When you work the second front work the identical number of rows and there should be no possibility of error.

It is possible to work two sleeves at the same time, which does not save time but does cut out the risk of unequal sleeve lengths. To do this, cast on the required number of stitches for one sleeve and then, using a separate ball of yarn, cast on the same number again on the same needle. Now work the first set of stitches on to your right-hand needle, and then the second set, and continue in this way right through the pattern.

Experienced knitters can employ this technique with cardigan or jacket fronts as well, working shapings at one end for the left front and at the other for the right front.

COPING WITH TECHNICAL PROBLEMS
Joining in new yarn

If it is at all possible never join in a new ball of yarn in the middle of the row. If you are getting near the end of the ball, then measure the remaining yarn against the length of the row. If it is about four times the length of the row it will probably be enough to work the complete row. If you are in any doubt, break or cut the yarn about five inches from the work and join in a new ball. You can keep the odd length for sewing up later.

To join at the end of the row, loosely tie the new yarn round the hanging thread and gently draw it up until it is in position to be used for the next row. When you come to sew up you can undo the knot if you wish and run the ends in separately, or the ends can be taken into the seam.

It sometimes happens that yarn has to be joined in the middle

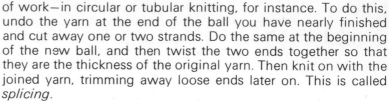

of work—in circular or tubular knitting, for instance. To do this, undo the yarn at the end of the ball you have nearly finished and cut away one or two strands. Do the same at the beginning of the new ball, and then twist the two ends together so that they are the thickness of the original yarn. Then knit on with the joined yarn, trimming away loose ends later on. This is called *splicing*.

You may occasionally find that there is a knot or lump in the yarn. If you notice early enough you can cut the yarn and join it afresh at the beginning of the row. Failing that, splice the two ends on either side of the knot when it has been cut away.

Picking up dropped stitches

Everyone drops a stitch occasionally, and if it happens there is no need to panic! Nor is it always necessary to pull the needles out and rip out the work right down to the point of the dropped stitch (although this is usually the best method to use if you are working a lacy pattern).

Using a crochet hook or the point of the right-hand needle, secure the dropped loop, and then pick it up the fabric by working as if it had been knitted in the usual way. For a knit stitch, draw the horizontal thread through the stitch from back to front, keeping the stitch in front of the thread, and repeat this action up every row. For a purl stitch, put the stitch behind the thread, reverse the work and pick up in the same way. Alternating knit and purl stitches (which may have been worked above each other on successive rows) will have to be picked up by the alternating methods to preserve continuity of the pattern.

By using this method, it is possible to undo one or more stitches that have been worked incorrectly. If you notice a wrong stitch a few rows down the fabric, work to a point exactly above the offending stitch, slip the corresponding stitch off the needle and let the stitch run down to the incorrect point. It can then be picked up correctly.

Undoing stitches

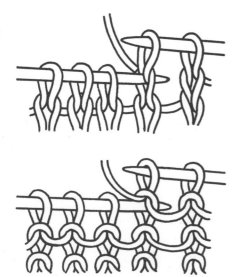

Sometimes several stitches are knitted incorrectly on to the right-hand needle, and have to be undone so they may be correctly worked. Undo them in this way: insert the left-hand needle into the base of the first stitch on the right-hand needle, working from front to back, and take the whole stitch off needle, pulling gently on the yarn, so that the stitch is transferred to the left-hand needle. Make sure that the stitch is not twisted in the wrong direction on the left-hand needle.

As many stitches as necessary—a whole row if need be—can be undone by this method. It is much safer than pulling out the needle, undoing the yarn and slipping all the stitches back on to the needle.

However, if this method *is* employed, be careful that the number of stitches picked up is accurate, and that they are all lying in the same—and the correct—direction.

Fancy stitch patterns

Cable patterns are used in many traditional styles of knitting, including these Guernsey seamen's sweaters.

All the stitch patterns which have been created so far are basically flat—that is, they produce a smooth, relatively plain fabric. Now we come to some variants which will give chunky or lacy surfaces and which, when contrasted with the plain stitches already learned, can produce interesting and attractive results.

CABLE KNITTING

Cable stitch was originally devised by fisherfolk and indeed a traditional cable pattern looks like a rope: it is twisted and it stands away from the ground surface of the knitting. Cable patterns are much favoured for sporting styles—cricket sweaters, boys' jerseys and so on—but there are plenty of ways in which cables can be used on fashion garments too.

In its simplest form, the cable consists of a group of stitches

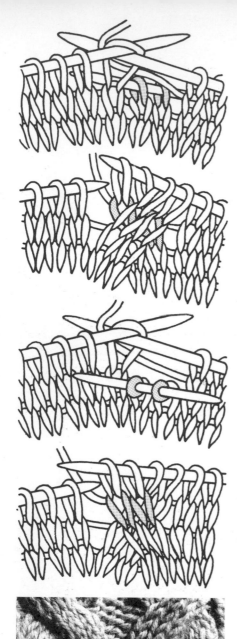

which are twisted in one direction at a regular interval, but there are dozens of variations, several of which can be combined in the same design if desired.

Cabling is done with the use of an extra needle—a short cable needle. Cable needles can be bought in packets, usually with two or three sizes included. Two or three stitches are slipped off the left-hand needle, before they are knitted, on to the cable needle and this short needle is then put to the back or front of the work, depending on the direction in which the 'rope' is to twist. The next two or three stitches on the left-hand needle are knitted in the usual way and then the short needle is brought back into line with the main knitting and the stitches are knitted off this needle. In this way, a small group of stitches is taken behind or in front of the main body of work.

The stitches are nearly always equally divided: three are slipped on to the cable needle, three knitted and then the three knitted from the cable needle. Usually the pattern will call this 'cable six front (C.6F.) —i.e. cable six stitches, taking the first three to the front of the work; or 'cable six back (C.6B.)'—i.e. cable six stitches, taking the first three to the back of the work. In a cable eight pattern, the first four stitches are slipped on to a cable needle, and put to the back or front of the work. Cable patterns are rarely worked over more than eight stitches.

It should be realised that the action of cabling makes the fabric fairly rigid so it is customary to work cable-patterned garments with more stitches than for a similar sized flat stitch pattern. If you want to introduce cabling into a plain pattern then it is advisable to adjust the number of stitches accordingly.

Cables are usually set against purl stitches so that they stand out by contrast.

Simple cable

This is the basic cable rib, with both directions worked, so that you can clearly see the contrast.
Cast on a number of stitches divisible by 11 plus 3 (e.g. 47).
1st row: * p.3, k.8; rep. from * to last 3 sts., p.3.
2nd row: * k.3, p.8; rep. from * to last 3 sts., k.3.
3rd row: * p.3, C.8B. (i.e. slip 4 sts. on to cable needle and put to back of work, k.4 then k. sts. from cable needle), p.3, C.8F. (i.e. as for C.8B. but put sts. to *front* of work); rep. from * to last 3 sts., p.3.
4th row: as 2nd row.
Now repeat first and 2nd rows 3 times.
11th row: as 3rd row.
12th row: as 2nd row.
Continue in this way, working a cable row on every 8th row. As a variation on this simple cable, try using only 6 sts. for the basic cable, putting 4 sts. between each cable and working the cable on every 10th row. A quite different effect will be produced.

Alternating cable

This is an interesting variant on the traditional cable, with the twists set in alternating directions.
Cast on a multiple of 9 sts. plus 3 (e.g. 30).
1st row: * p.3, k.6; rep. from * to last 3 sts., p.3.
2nd row: * k.3, p.6; rep. from * to last 3 sts., k.3.

3rd row: * p.3, slip 2 sts. on cable needle and put to back of work, k.2, k.2 sts. from cable needle, k.2; rep. from * to last 3 sts., p.3.

4th row: as 2nd row.

5th row: * p.3, k.2, slip 2 sts. on cable needle and put to front of work, k.2, k.2 sts. from cable needle; rep. from * to last 3 sts., p.3.

6th row: as 2nd row.

Now repeat the pattern working from rows 3 to 6 inclusive.

Wheatear cable

This is a wider, fanning rib, where the cable is not closed.

Cast on a multiple of 16 sts. plus 3 (e.g. 35).

1st row: * p.3, k.13; rep. from * to last 3 sts., p.3.

2nd row: * k.3, p.13; rep. from * to last 3 sts., k.3.

3rd row: * p.3, C.6B., k.1, C.6F.; rep. from * to last 3 sts., k.3.

4th row: as 2nd row.

The pattern is produced by repeating these 4 rows throughout.

Open cable

Another stitch where the cable 'grows' out of itself without being closed at the top.

Cast on a multiple of 11 sts. plus 3 (e.g. 36).

1st row: * p.3, k.8; rep. from * to last 3 sts., p.3.

2nd row: * k.3, p.8; rep. from * to last 3 sts., k.3.

3rd row: * p.3, C.4B., C.4F.; rep. from * to last 3 sts., p.3.

4th row: as 2nd row.

Now rep. first and 2nd rows twice.

9th row: as 3rd row.

Continue in this way, working a cabling row on every 5th row.

Medallions

This produces an attractive circular panel as the cables are closed at the top.

Cast on a multiple of 19 sts. plus 3 (e.g. 41).

1st row: * p.3, k.16; rep. from * to last 3 sts., p.3.

2nd row: * k.3, p.16; rep. from * to last 3 sts., k.3.

3rd row: * p.3, C.8B., C.8F.; rep. from * to last 3 sts., p.3.

4th row: as 2nd row.

Rep. first and 2nd rows 4 times.

13th row: * p.3, C.8F., C.8B.; rep. from * to last 3 sts., p.3.

14th row: as 2nd row.

The next medallion can be worked straight away (i.e. starting again at the first row) or at any desired interval. If the medallion is 8 or 12 sts. wide, then 5 or 7 rows of plain work should be knitted between each one, instead of 9 as here.

Honeycomb

This is not strictly a cable stitch, but rather one in which cabling as a technique is used, and it is very effective used by itself or interspersed with bars of plain or ribbed knitting.

Cast on a multiple of 8 sts. (e.g. 32).

1st row: k.

2nd row: p.

3rd row: * C.4B., C.4F.; rep. from * to end.

4th row: as 2nd row.

Now rep. first and 2nd rows once.

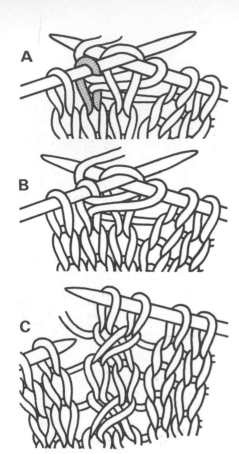

Twisted cable rib.

Diamonds.

7th row: * C.4F., C.4B.; rep. from * to end.
8th row: as 2nd row.
Repeat these 8 rows throughout for pattern.

TWISTED STITCHES

The principle of twisting stitches (that is, knitting them out of order) is often used to give a similar effect to true cabling, but no third needle is necessary.

To twist a stitch to the left on a knit row, put the right-hand needle to the back of the work, put it through to the front between the first and second stitches on the left-hand needle, and knit the second stitch from the front in the usual way, then pulling the yarn through gently, knit the first stitch in the usual way and take both stitches off the left-hand needle at the same time (A).

To twist a stitch to the right on a knit row, knit the *second* stitch on your left-hand needle, passing in front of the first stitch, then knit the first stitch and take the two off the left-hand needle at the same time (B and C).

If the pattern instructs you to work twisted stitches on a purl row, it is possible to do this but to twist to the left you will have to slip the first left-hand needle stitch on to a cable needle, hold it at the front of work, and then purl the second. To twist to the right, however, it is possible to purl the second stitch first, working from the front of the work (D).

The following are a few stitch patterns using the twisted stitch technique.

Twisted cable rib

This makes a very narrow twisted line which looks as though it has been cabled.
Cast on a multiple of 5 sts. plus 3 (e.g. 23).
1st row: * p.3, k.2; rep. from * to last 3 sts., p.3.
2nd row: * k.3, p.2; rep. from * to last 3 sts., k.3.
Repeat first and 2nd rows once.
5th row: * p.3, cross 2R. (i.e. k. 2nd st. from the front, then k. first st. and take both sts. off needle together); rep. from * to last 3 sts., p.3.
6th row: as 2nd row.
Repeat rows 3 to 6 inclusive.

Diamonds

This is a most effective raised stitch, the crossing used this time to outline a pattern on the surface of the fabric.
Cast on a multiple of 6 sts. plus 3 (e.g. 27).
1st row: * cross 2L. (i.e. k. the 2nd stitch from the back, then k. the first st. and take both sts. off needle together), k.4; rep. from * to last 3 sts., cross 2L., k.1.
2nd and alternate rows: p.
3rd row: k.1, cross 2L., * k.2, cross 2R., cross 2L.; rep. from * to end.
5th row: * k.2, cross 2L., cross 2R.; rep. from * to last 3 sts., k.3.
7th row: * k.3, cross 2L., k.1; rep. from * to last 3 sts., k.3.
9th row: * k.2, cross 2R., cross 2L.; rep. from * to last 3 sts., k.3.
11th row: k.1, * cross 2R., k.2, cross 2L.; rep. from * to last 2

sts., cross 2R.
12th row: as 2nd row.
Repeat these 12 rows throughout.

Wide twisted rib (see two diagrams, right)
Once the principle of twisting stitches has been grasped, it will be seen that a greater number than two stitches can be involved—for you can knit the fourth stitch from the left-hand needle, then the third, then the second and finally the first, slipping them all off the needle together. Here is a stitch which uses this method, working with three stitches.
Cast on a multiple of 8 sts. plus 2 (e.g. 26).
1st row: * k.2, (cross 2R.) 3 times; rep. from * to last 2 sts., k.2.
2nd row: p.
3rd row: * k.2, (k. 3rd st. from the front, then the 2nd then the first and slip all sts. off needle together) twice; rep. from * to last 2 sts., k.2.
4th row: p.
These 4 rows form the pattern.

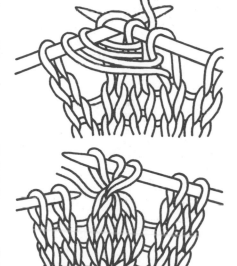

CLUSTERS
Another way of adding surface interest to a design is to use the principle of the cluster stitch; by this, the same group of stitches is worked over several times so that the stitches stand away from the basic fabric. This is fairly slow work but it is extremely effective.

Bobble stitch
In this, the bobbles can be of varying sizes, depending on the number of stitches involved. To make the bobble, work into one stitch 3, 4 or 5 times and then, turning the work round each time, work 2, 4 or 6 rows stocking stitch respectively across those sts. Then using the point of the left-hand needle, slip the 2nd stitch over the first, then the next and so on until one stitch only is left.

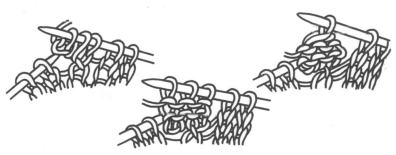

Cast on a multiple of 6 sts. plus 3 (e.g. 27).
1st row: * k.5, make bobble (i.e. k. 4 times into next st., then work 4 rows of st.st. on these 4 sts., then take the 2nd, then the 3rd, then the 4th st. in turn over the first st.); rep. from * to last 3 sts., k.3.
2nd row: p.
3rd row: k.
Rep. 2nd and 3rd rows once, then the 2nd row again.
7th row: * k.1, make bobble (as in first row), k.4; rep. from * to

last 3 sts., k.1, make bobble, k.1.
Rep. 2nd and 3rd rows twice, then the 2nd row again.
These 12 rows form the pattern.

Petal stitch

This is a variation on the cluster theme.
Cast on a multiple of 6 sts. plus 2 (e.g. 26).
1st row (wrong side): k.1, * p.5 tog., (k.1, p.1, k.1, p.1, k.1) all into next st.; rep. from * to last st., k.1.
2nd and 4th rows: p.
3rd row: k.1, (k.1, p.1, k.1, p.1, k.1) all into next st., p.5 tog.; rep. from * to last st., k.1.
5th row: k., winding the yarn three times round the needle when every stitch is made.
6th row: p., letting the extra loops formed on the 5th row drop off the needle.
These 6 rows form the pattern.

LACY PATTERNS

Another way to vary the texture of knitted fabric is by making lacy patterns, which can either spread all over the entire surface of the fabric, or be confined to small areas of it (for instance, between bands of ribbing or in lattice shapes).

Lacy patterns need not be confined to fine yarns or delicate garments such as baby clothes or traditional tablecloths; open stitches in double knitting weights can be very effective as well. It is an interesting exercise to work a lacy stitch pattern using size 8 needles (USA size 6) and double knitting yarn, and then to work the same pattern on size 12 needles (USA size 1) using a three-ply. The resulting fabrics are totally different.

A pretty summer cardigan knitted in a lacy stitch pattern, with stocking stitch yoke, button bands and edgings.

Lacy-patterned cotton sweater for brother and sister (see page 102 for instructions).

Two-piece suit for a little boy, worked in a simple wide rib pattern (see page 93).

The holes in lacy patterns are made by the 'over' principle as explained in increasing method 4 (see page 20). By this method the yarn is passed over the needle so that it creates an extra stitch and therefore a hole in the fabric. The extra stitch is then eliminated either by working two stitches together somewhere along the same row or immediately above the increase on a subsequent row. That is why you should not be alarmed if you find that you have more stitches on the needle in one row than you started out with! This will be corrected on a subsequent row. On the other hand, if you make a mistake in your work, this increasing technique makes undoing lacy work difficult for the beginner, so these open stitches are best attempted when you have had a fair amount of experience. It is not in fact always easy for an expert to see where she has gone wrong in a very complicated pattern, and never simple to put such errors right.

A selection of open stitches have been included in this chapter which are appropriate for heavy and light yarns; some of these stitch patterns are very simple indeed but still extremely effective.

Net stitch

This is probably the simplest open design of all, consisting of rows of holes; it can be somewhat stretchy and so is usually placed between bands of stocking stitch to prevent the fabric stretching out of shape.

Cast on a multiple of 2 sts. (e.g. 24).

1st row: k.1, * y.fwd. (see page 20), k.2 tog.; rep. from * to last st., k.1.

2nd row: p.

3rd row: k.2, * y.fwd., k.2 tog.; rep. from * to end.

4th row: p.

Repeat these 4 rows throughout.

Butterfly stitch

In this pattern, small openwork motifs are placed on a stocking stitch ground—it is a good pattern for a party sweater or a baby's dress.

Cast on a multiple of 10 sts. (e.g. 30).

1st row: * k.2 tog., y.fwd., k.1, y.fwd., sl.1, k.1, p.s.s.o., k.5; rep. from * to end.

2nd and 4th rows: * p.7, sl.1 purlwise, p.2; rep. from * to end.

3rd row: as first row.

5th row: k.

6th row: p.

7th row: * k.5, k.2 tog., y.fwd., k.1, y.fwd., sl.1, k.1, p.s.s.o.; rep. from * to end.

8th and 10th rows: * p.2, sl.1 purlwise, p.7; rep. from * to end.

11th row: as 5th row.

12th row: as 6th row.

Repeat these 12 rows throughout.

Vandyke stitch

Used mostly on skirts (for children's or women's dresses) because it forms attractive scallop shapes which can be used as a decorative edging. Garter stitch forms an effective border.

Cast on a multiple of 12 sts. plus 1 (e.g. 25).

1st row: * k.1, y.fwd., k.4, sl. 1, k.2 tog.; p.s.s.o., k.4, y.fwd.;

rep. from * to last st., k.1.
2nd row: p.
Repeat these 2 rows throughout.

Diamond lattice

This gives a regular open shaping of diamonds and looks as good on heavy-weight yarns as on fine ones.
Cast on a multiple of 10 sts. plus 1 (e.g. 31) — the extra stitch is an edge stitch which is used in the 15th row.

1st row: k.1, * y.fwd., sl.1, k.1, p.s.s.o., k.5, k.2 tog., y.fwd., k.1; rep. from * to end.
2nd and alternate rows: p.
3rd row: k.1, * k.1, y.fwd., sl.1, k.1, p.s.s.o., k.3, k.2 tog., k.2; rep. from * to end.
5th row: k.1, * k.2, y.fwd., sl.1, k.1, p.s.s.o., k.1, k.2 tog., y.fwd., k.3; rep. from * to end.
7th row: k.1, * k.3, y.fwd., sl.1, k.2 tog., p.s.s.o., y.fwd., k.4; rep. from * to end.
9th row: k.1, * k.2, k.2 tog., y.fwd., k.1, y.fwd., sl.1, k.1, p.s.s.o., k.3; rep. from * to end.
11th row: k.1, * k.1, k.2 tog., y.fwd., k.3, y.fwd., sl.1, k.1, p.s.s.o., k.2; rep. from * to end.
13th row: k.1, * k.2 tog., y.fwd., k.5, y.fwd., sl.1, k.1, p.s.s.o., k.1; rep. from * to end.
15th row: k.2 tog. (one of these sts. is the edge st.), * y.fwd., k.7, y.fwd., sl.1, k.2 tog., p.s.s.o.; rep. from * ending with sl.1, k.1, p.s.s.o.
16th row: p.
Repeat these 16 rows throughout.

Chevron lace stitch

In this pattern openwork in vertical bars is set between solid bands of stocking stitch. This is an effective stitch used down the fronts of a cardigan or on a child's skirt. Cast on a multiple of 6 sts. plus 4 (e.g. 28).

1st row: k.1, * y.fwd., k.2, k.2 tog., k.2; rep. from * to last st., k.1.
2nd and 4th rows: p. (including the made sts. of first row).
3rd row: k.1, * k.2, k.2 tog., k.2, y.fwd.; rep. from * to last st., k.1.
Repeat these 4 rows throughout.

Curving openwork stitch

This is a delicate-looking pattern, to be used primarily on light yarns and for such items as shawls, stoles, evening wear and so on. It is extremely effective worked in a glitter yarn. To purl through the back of loop, put the point of the right-hand needle through the back of stitch, from left to right, then purl in the usual way. To purl through the back of two stitches, put needle through the second then the first stitches on left-hand needle.
Cast on a multiple of 8 sts. plus 2 (e.g. 34).

1st row: k.1, * y.fwd., k.1 t.b.l. (through back of loop), y.fwd., sl.1, k.1, p.s.s.o., k.5; rep. from * to last st., k.1.
2nd row: k.1, * p.4, p.2 tog. t.b.l., p.3; rep. from * to last st., k.1.
3rd row: k.1, * y.fwd., k.1 t.b.l., y.fwd., k.2, sl.1, k.1, p.s.s.o., k.3; rep. from * to last st., k.1.
4th row: k.1, * p.2, p.2 tog. t.b.l., p.5; rep. from * to last st., k.1.
5th row: k.1, * k.1 t.b.l., y.fwd., k.4, sl.1, k.1, p.s.s.o., k.1,

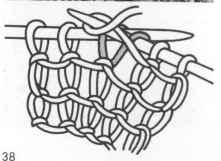

y.fwd.; rep. from * to last st., k.1.

6th row: k.1, * p.1, p.2 tog. t.b.l., p.6; rep. from * to last st., k.1.

7th row: k.1, * k.5, k.2 tog., y.fwd., k.1 t.b.l., y.fwd.; rep. from * to last st., k.1.

8th row: k.1, * p.3, p.2 tog., p.4; rep. from * to last st., k.1.

9th row: k.1, * k.3, k.2 tog., k.2, y.fwd., k.1 t.b.l., y.fwd.; rep. from * to last st., k.1.

10th row: k.1, * p.5, p.2 tog., p.2; rep. from * to last st., k.1.

11th row: k.1, * y.fwd., k.1, k.2 tog., k.4, y.fwd., k.1 t.b.l.; rep. from * to last st., k.1.

12th row: k.1, * p.6, p.2 tog., p.1; rep. from * to last st., k.1.

Eyelet stitch

Although open, this is a much more tailored stitch pattern than the previous one, and could be used on very heavy yarn, even for men's wear.

Cast on a multiple of 7 sts. plus 6 (e.g. 34).

1st row: k.2, * p.2, k.2 tog., y.fwd., k.1, y.fwd., k.2 tog. t.b.l.; rep. from * to last 4 sts., p.2, k.2.

2nd row: p.2, * k.2, p.5; rep. from * to last 4 sts., k.2, p.2.

3rd row: k.2, * p.2, k.5; rep. from * to last 4 sts., p.2, k.2.

4th row: p.2, * k.2, p.5; rep. from * to last 4 sts., k.2, p.2.

Snowdrop stitch

Regularly repeating motifs form a delicate overall look in this pattern.

Cast on a multiple of 8 sts. plus 5 (e.g. 29).

1st and 3rd rows: k.1, * y.r.n. (see page 20), sl.1 purlwise, k.2 tog., p.s.s.o., y.fwd., k.5; rep. from * to last 4 sts., y. fwd., sl.1, k.2 tog., p.s.s.o., y.fwd., k.1.

2nd and alternate rows: p.

5th row: k.1, * k.3, y.fwd., sl.1, k.1, p.s.s.o., k.1, k.2 tog., y.fwd.; rep. from * to last 4 sts., k.4.

7th row: k.1, * y.fwd., sl.1, k.2 tog., p.s.s.o., y.fwd., k.1; rep. from * to last 4 sts., y.fwd., sl.1, k.2 tog., p.s.s.o., y.fwd., k.1.

8th row: p.

Repeat these 8 rows throughout.

EDGE STITCHES

It will be noticed that many of these patterns include an edge stitch at each end. Edges are dealt with more fully in the chapter beginning on page 62, but at this point it should be mentioned that one or two 'odd' stitches at each end—especially on open patterns—are essential as a firm basis for the seams afterwards. When the garment is put together these are used for the actual stitching, so that the pattern itself is not distorted.

Aran knitting

To the west of Ireland, off the coast of Connemara, lie the Aran Islands, a region of great beauty and loneliness where a living is culled from the sea by fishermen whose families have followed the same pattern of life for generations. Running strongly through this daily life is a deep religious faith, and evidence of these two main influences appears in the traditional Aran knitting: crisp, creamy and rich with intricate cabling. The stitches are used to chronicle the pattern of living in the area.

The traditional wool for knitting Aran garments is Bainin (pronounced Baw-neen) which is actually the Irish word for 'white', but has gradually evolved into a name for the wool itself, which can be dyed to any other colour wished.

The Aran stitches originated approximately 500 years ago, when knitting was done with goose quills by the menfolk from wool spun by their women. This does not seem so strange, when one considers the dexterity required to make fishing nets—they simply used this skill instead to produce clothing for themselves. Each family had its own design; each man his own pattern, and it was a matter of pride that a family should be known by its own variations on the traditional stitches, much in the way that a Scottish clansman is identified by his tartan.

The stitches have remained virtually unchanged through the centuries, but the most usual way to employ them in modern knitting is repeated in panels down the whole length of the garment, each featuring several different stitches. Each of these stitches has a meaning: some being of religious significance while others relate to the sea or the characteristics of the countryside.

THE TRADITIONAL STITCH PATTERNS
Cable
There are many variations of this stitch, and all are said to represent the fisherman's ropes.

Ladder of life
Purl or twist stitches are worked to form the poles and rungs of the ladder, against a plain knitted background. The ladder is considered to represent a man's earthly climb to eternal happiness.

Lobster claw
Lobsters are plentiful off the Irish coast and it is from these that we get this type of cable stitch.

Zigzag
This stitch is said to represent the cliff paths which twist along the coastline.

Diamond (or diamond cable)

This symbolises success, wealth or treasures, and is sometimes combined with the cable which, as the fisherman's rope, is essential to any sort of prosperity in a fishing community.

Trinity stitch (also known as blackberry stitch and popcorn stitch)

Made by making three from one, and one from three. A very popular stitch in many Aran patterns.

Honeycomb

This stitch recalls the honey earned by the hardworking bee, and is made by twisting stitches forward and back across the panel.

Tree of life

Worked by knit or twist stitches against a purl background, this stitch should ensure the wearer a long life, and strong sons to help with the fishing gear.

Basket stitch

This refers to the fisherman's basket symbolising a large and profitable catch.

Blarney kiss

This recalls the famous stone in the battlements of Blarney Castle. Those who kiss the Blarney Stone it is said, enjoy for ever the gift of a persuasive tongue.

Spoon

As the name suggests, this stitch indicates that the family will be well fed and healthy and not suffer from droughts and famines, and will have good catches of fish.

Trellis

This is said to represent the small fields enclosed by stone walls which are such a familiar part of the west of Ireland landscape.

ABBREVIATIONS USED IN ARAN STITCH SAMPLES

See general abbreviations on page 11; F., front; B., back; R., right; L., left; C., cable; c.n., cable needle; l.h.n., left-hand needle; T., twist; Cr., cross; k.b. or p.b., k. or p. into the back of the number of sts. stated; C.4B., sl. next 2 sts. on c.n. at back, k.2, then k.2 from c.n.; C.4F., as C.4B. but leave the 2 sts. at front; C.6B. or F., as C.4B. or F. but sl. 3 sts. on c.n. and k. next 3 sts.; T.2F., sl. next st. on c.n. at front, p.1 then k.b.1 from c.n.; T.2B., sl. next st. on c.n. at back, k.b.1 then p.1 from c.n.; Cr.2F., take needle in front of first st. on l.h.n. and k.2nd st. then p. first st. and sl. both sts. off l.h.n. tog.; Cr.2B., take needle behind first st. on l.h.n. and p. 2nd st. then k. first st. and sl. both sts. off l.h.n. tog.; Cr.2P., take needle behind first st. on l.h.n. and p. 2nd st., then p. first st. and sl. both sts. off l.h.n. tog.; C.6L., sl. next 2 sts. on c.n. at front, sl. next 2 sts. on 2nd c.n. at back, k.2 from l.h.n., p.2 from back c.n., k.2 from front c.n.; C.3R., sl. next st. on c.n. at back, k.2 then p.1 from c.n.; C.3L., sl. next 2 sts. on c.n. at front, p.1, then k.2 from c.n.; M.B., make bobble on next st. as follows: k. into front, back, front, back, front of next st., turn, p.5, turn, k.5, turn, p.5, turn, sl. 2nd, 3rd and 4th sts. over first st. and k. first and 5th sts. tog. through back of loops.

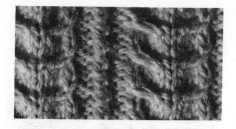

LOBSTER CLAW AND TWISTED RIB
Cast on a multiple of 14 sts. plus 5 (e.g. 33).
1st row: p.2, k.b.1, p.2, * k.9, p.2, k.b.1, p.2; rep. from * to end.
2nd row: k.2, p.b.1, k.2, * p.9, k.2, p.b.1, k.2; rep. from * to end.
3rd row: p.2, k.b.1, p.2, * sl. next 3 sts. on c.n. at back, k.1, then k.3 from c.n., k.1, sl. next st. on c.n. at front, then k.3, then k.1 from c.n., p.2, k.b.1, p.2; rep. from * to end.
4th row: as 2nd row.
These 4 rows form the patt.

CORK CABLE AND SMALL MOCK CABLES
Cast on a multiple of 16 sts. plus 6 (e.g. 38).
1st row: p.2, k. into front of 2nd st. on l.h.n. then k. first st. and sl. both off (this will be called Twist 2), p.2, * (k.2, p.2) 3 times, Twist 2, p.2; rep. from * to end.
2nd row: k.2, p.2, k.2, * (p.2, k.2) 8 times; rep. from * to end.
3rd row: p.2, Twist 2, p.2, * C.6L., p.2, k.2, p.2, Twist 2, p.2; rep. from * to end.
4th row: as 2nd row.
5th to 8th rows: rep. first and 2nd rows twice.
9th row: p.2, Twist 2, p.2, * k.2, p.2, C.6L., p.2, Twist 2, p.2; rep. from * to end.
10th row: as 2nd row.
11th and 12th rows: rep. first and 2nd rows.
These 12 rows form the patt.

BLARNEY KISS AND CROSS-STITCH RIB
Cast on a multiple of 12 sts. plus 4 (e.g. 52).
1st row: p.1, put point of needle through first st. on l.h.n., k. into front of 2nd st. and sl. off, then k. into back of first st. and sl. off (this will be called Cross 2), p.1, * k.8, p.1, Cross 2, p.1; rep. from * to end.
2nd row: k.1, p.2, k.1, * p.8, k.1, p.2, k.1; rep. from * to end.
3rd row: p.1, Cross 2, p.1, * C.4F., C.4B., p.1, Cross 2, p.1; rep. from * to end.
4th row: as 2nd row.
5th to 10th rows: rep. rows 1 to 4 then first and 2nd rows again.
11th row: p.1, Cross 2, p.1, * C.4B., C.4F., p.1, Cross 2, p.1; rep. from * to end.
12th row: as 2nd row.
13th and 14th rows: rep. first and 2nd rows.
15th row: as 11th row.
16th row: as 2nd row.
These 16 rows form the patt.

TRELLIS
Cast on a multiple of 6 sts. plus 4 (e.g. 40).
Foundation row: p.4, * k.2, p.4; rep. from * to end.
1st row (wrong side): k.4, * Cr.2P., k.4; rep. from * to end.
2nd row: p.3, * Cr.2F., Cr.2B., p.2; rep. from * to last st., p.1.
3rd row: k.3, * p.1, k.2; rep. from * to last st., k.1.

4th row: p.2, * Cr. 2F., p.2, Cr.2B.; rep. from * to last 2 sts., p.2.

5th row: k.2, p.1, k.4, * Cr.2P., k.4; rep. from * to last 3 sts., p.1, k.2.

6th row: p.2, * Cr. 2B., p.2, Cr.2F; rep. from * to last 2 sts., p.2.

7th row: as 3rd row.

8th row: p.3, * Cr.2B., Cr.2F., p.2; rep. from * to last st., p.1.

These 8 rows form the patt.

HONEYCOMB

Cast on a multiple of 8 sts. plus 2 edge sts. at each side (e.g. 44).

1st row: p.2, k. to last 2 sts., p.2.

2nd row: k.2, p. to last 2 sts., k.2.

3rd row: p.2, * C.4B., C.4F.; rep. from * to last 2 sts., p.2.

4th row: as 2nd row.

5th and 6th rows: rep. first and 2nd rows.

7th row: p.2, * C.4F., C.4B.; rep. from * to last 2 sts., p.2.

8th row: as 2nd row.

These 8 rows form the patt.

LATTICE CABLE

Cast on a multiple of 8 sts. plus 2 (e.g. 42).

1st row: p.2, * k.2, p.2; rep. from * to end.

2nd row: k.2, * p.2, k.2; rep. from * to end.

3rd row: p.2, * sl. next 3 sts. on c.n. at front, k.2, p.1 then p.1, k.2 from c.n., p.2; rep. from * to end.

4th row: as 2nd row.

5th to 8th rows: rep. first and 2nd rows twice.

9th row: p.2, k.2, * p.2, sl. next 3 sts. on c.n. at back, k.2, p.1 then p.1, k.2 from c.n.; rep. from * to last 6 sts., p.2, k.2, p.2.

10th row: as 2nd row.

11th and 12th rows: rep. first and 2nd rows.

These 12 rows form the patt.

DOUBLE DIAMOND WITH PLAIT CABLES

Cast on a multiple of 22 plus 10 (e.g. 54).

1st row: p.2, * k.6, p.4, T.2B. twice, T.2F. twice, p.4; rep. from * to last 8 sts., k.6, p.2.

2nd row: k.2, * p.6, k.4, (p.b.1, k.1) twice, (k.1, p.b.1) twice, k.4; rep. from * to last 8 sts., p.6, k.2.

3rd row: p.2, * C.4B., k.2, p.3, T.2B. twice, p.2, T.2F. twice, p.3; rep. from * to last 8 sts., C.4B., k.2, p.2.

4th row: k.2, * p.6, k.3, (p.b.1, k.1) twice, k.2, (k.1, p.b.1) twice, k.3; rep. from * to last 8 sts., p.6, k.2.

5th row: p.2, * k.6, p.2, T.2B. twice, p.4, T.2F. twice, p.2; rep. from * to last 8 sts., k.6, p.2.

6th row: k.2, * p.6, k.2, (p.b.1, k.1) twice, k.4, (k.1, p.b.1) twice, k.2; rep. from * to last 8 sts., p.6, k.2.

7th row: p.2, * k.2, C.4F., p.1, T.2B. twice, p.6, T.2F. twice, p.1; rep. from * to last 8 sts., k.2, C.4F., p.2.

8th row: k.2, * p.6, k.1, (p.b.1, k.1) twice, k.6, (k.1, p.b.1) twice, k.1; rep. from * to last 8 sts., p.6, k.2.

9th row: p.2, * k.6, p.1, T.2F. twice, p.6, T.2B. twice, p.1; rep. from * to last 8 sts., k.6, p.2.

10th row: k.2, * p.6, k.1, (k.1, p.b.1) twice, k.6, (p.b.1, k.1) twice, k.1; rep. from * to last 8 sts., p.6, k.2.

11th row: p.2, * C.4B., k.2, p.2, T.2F. twice, p.4, T.2B. twice,

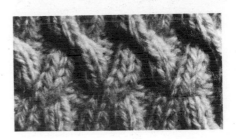

p.2; rep. from * to last 8 sts., C.4B., k.2, p.2.
12th row: k.2, * p.6, k.2, (k.1, p.b.1) twice, k.4, (p.b.1, k.1) twice, k.2; rep. from * to last 8 sts., p.6, k.2.
13th row: p.2, * k.6, p.3, T.2F. twice, p.2, T.2B. twice, p.3; rep. from * to last 8 sts., k.6, p.2.
14th row: k.2, * p.6, k.3, (k.1, p.b.1) twice, k.2, (p.b.1, k.1) twice, k.3; rep. from * to last 8 sts., p.6, k.2.
15th row: p.2, * k.2, C.4F., p.4, T.2F. twice, T.2B. twice, p.4; rep. from * to last 8 sts., k.2, C.4F., p.2.
16th row: k.2, * p.6, k.5, p.b.1, k.1, p. into back of 2nd st. on l.h.n., then into back of first st. and sl. both off, k.1, p.b.1, k.5; rep. from * to last 8 sts., p.6, k.2. These 16 rows form the patt.

TREE OF LIFE WITH TWISTED RIB PANELS

Cast on a multiple of 22 plus 6 (e.g. 50).
1st row: * (p.1, k.b.1) 3 times, p.6, k.b.4, p.6; rep. from * to last 6 sts., (k.b.1, p.1) 3 times.
2nd row: * (k.1, p.b.1) 3 times, k.6, p.b.4, k.6; rep. from * to last 6 sts., (p.b.1, k.1) 3 times.
These 2 rows form the patt. of the twisted rib panels to be referred to as rib 6.
3rd row: * rib 6, p.5, T.2B., k.b.2, T.2F., p.5; rep. from * to last 6 sts., rib 6.
4th row: * rib 6, k.5, p.b.1, k.1, p.b.2, k.1, p.b.1, k.5; rep. from * to last 6 sts., rib 6.
5th row: * rib 6, p.4, T.2B., p.1, k.b.2, p.1, T.2F., p.4; rep. from * to last 6 sts., rib 6.
6th row: * rib 6, k.4, p.b.1, k.2, p.b.2, k.2, p.b.1, k.4; rep. from * to last 6 sts., rib 6.
7th row: * rib 6, p.3, T.2B., p.2, k.b.2, p.2, T.2F., p.3; rep. from * to last 6 sts., rib 6.
8th row: * rib 6, k.3, p.b.1, k.3, p.b.2, k.3, p.b.1, k.3; rep. from * to last 6 sts., rib 6.
9th row: * rib 6, p.2, T.2B., p.3, k.b.2, p.3, T.2F., p.2; rep. from * to last 6 sts., rib 6.
10th row: * rib 6, k.2, p.b.1, k.4, p.b.2, k.4, p.b.1, k.2; rep. from * to last 6 sts., rib 6.
11th row: * rib 6, p.1, T.2B., p.4, k.b.2, p.4, T.2F., p.1; rep. from * to last 6 sts., rib 6.
12th row: * rib 6, k.1, p.b.1, k.5, p.b.2, k.5, p.b.1, k.1; rep. from * to last 6 sts., rib 6. These 12 rows form the patt.

ZIGZAGS ON DOUBLE MOSS STITCH GROUND

Cast on a multiple of 20 sts. plus 3 (e.g. 43).
Foundation row (wrong side): k.2, * (p.1, k.1) twice, (p.b.1, k.1) 5 times, p.b.1, (k.1, p.1) twice, k.1; rep. from * to last st., k.1.
1st row: k.2, * p.1, k.1, p.1, (T.2B.) 3 times, k.1, (T.2F.) 3 times, (p.1, k.1) twice; rep. from * to last st., k.1.
2nd row: k.1, p.1, * k.1, p.1, k.1, (p.b.1, k.1) 3 times, p.1, (k.1, p.b.1) 3 times, (k.1, p.1) twice; rep. from * to last st., k.1.
3rd row: k.1, p.1, * k.1, p.1, (T.2B.) 3 times, k.1, p.1, k.1, (T.2F.) 3 times, p.1, k.1, p.1; rep. from * to last st., k.1.
4th row: k.2, * p.1, k.1, (p.b.1, k.1) 3 times, p.1, k.1, p.1, (k.1, p.b.1) 3 times, k.1, p.1, k.1; rep. from * to last st., k.1.
5th row: k.2, * p.1, (T.2B.) 3 times, (k.1, p.1) twice, k.1, (T.2F.) 3 times, p.1, k.1; rep. from * to last st., k.1.

6th row: k.1, p.1, * k.1, (p.b.1, k.1) 3 times, (p.1, k.1) twice, p.1, (k.1, p.b.1) 3 times, k.1, p.1; rep. from * to last st., k.1.

7th row: k.1, p.1, * (T.2B.) 3 times, (k.1, p.1) 3 times, k.1, (T.2F.) 3 times, p.1; rep. from * to last st., k.1.

8th row: k.2, * (p.b.1, k.1) 3 times, (p.1, k.1) 3 times, p.1, (k.1, p.b.1) 3 times, k.1; rep. from * to last st., k.1.

9th row: k.2, * (T.2F.) 3 times, (p.1, k.1) 3 times, p.1, (T.2B.) 3 times, k.1; rep. from * to last st., k.1.

10th row: k.1, p.1, * k.1, (p.b.1, k.1) 3 times, (p.1, k.1) twice, p.1, (k.1, p.b.1) 3 times, k.1, p.1; rep. from * to last st., k.1.

11th row: k.1, p.1, * k.1, (T.2F.) 3 times, (p.1, k.1) twice, p.1, (T.2B) 3 times, k.1, p.1; rep. from * to last st., k.1.

12th row: k.2, * p.1, k.1, (p.b.1, k.1) 3 times, p.1, k.1, p.1, (k.1, p.b.1) 3 times, k.1, p.1, k.1; rep. from * to last st., k.1.

13th row: k.2, * p.1, k.1, (T.2F.) 3 times, p.1, k.1, p.1, (T.2B.) 3 times, k.1, p.1, k.1; rep. from * to last st., k.1.

14th row: k.1, p.1, * k.1, p.1, k.1, (p.b.1, k.1) 3 times, p.1, (k.1, p.b.1) 3 times, (k.1, p.1) twice; rep. from * to last st., k.1.

15th row: k.1, p.1, * k.1, p.1, k.1, (T.2F.) 3 times, p.1, (T.2B.) 3 times, (k.1, p.1) twice; rep. from * to last st., k.1.

16th row: k.2, * (p.1, k.1) twice, (p.b.1, k.1) 5 times, p.b.1., (k.1, p.1) twice, k.1; rep. from * to last st., k.1.

These 16 rows form the patt.

ZIGZAGS WITH BOBBLES AND SMALL CABLES

Cast on a multiple of 23 sts. plus 8 (e.g. 54).

1st row: p.2, * k.4, p.5, C.3R., p.3, C.3L., p.5; rep. from * to last 6 sts., k.4, p.2. **2nd row:** k.2, * p.4, k.5, p.2, k.5, p.2, k.5; rep. from * to last 6 sts., p.4, k.2.

3rd row: p.2, * C.4B., p.4, C.3R., p.2, M.B., p.2, C.3L., p.4; rep. from * to last 6 sts., C.4B., p.2.

4th row: k.2, * p.4, k.4, p.2, k.7, p.2, k.4; rep. from * to last 6 sts., p.4, k.2.

5th row: p.2, * k.4, p.3, C.3R., p.7, C.3L., p.3; rep. from * to last 6 sts., k.4, p.2.

6th row: k.2, * p.4, k.3, p.2, k.9, p.2, k.3; rep. from * to last 6 sts., p.4, k.2.

7th row: p.2, * C.4B., p.2, C.3R., p.2, M.B., p.3, M.B., p.2, C.3L., p.2; rep. from * to last 6 sts., C.4B., p.2.

8th row: k.2, * p.4, k.2, p.2, k.11, p.2, k.2; rep. from * to last 6 sts., p.4, k.2.

9th row: p.2, * k.4, p.2, C.3L., p.9, C.3R., p.2; rep. from * to last 6 sts., k.4, p.2.

10th row: k.2, * p.4, k.3, p.2, k.9, p.2, k.3; rep. from * to last 6 sts., p.4, k.2.

11th row: p.2, * C.4B., p.3, C.3L., p.3, M.B., p.3, C.3R., p.3; rep. from * to last 6 sts., C.4B., p.2.

12th row: k.2, * p.4, k.4, p.2, k.7, p.2, k.4; rep. from * to last 6 sts., p.4, k.2.

13th row: p.2, * k.4, p.4, C.3L., p.5, C.3R., p.4; rep. from * to last 6 sts., k.4, p.2.

14th row: k.2, * p.4, k.5, p.2, k.5, p.2, k.5; rep. from * to last 6 sts., p.4, k.2.

15th row: p.2, * C.4B., p.5, C.3L., p.3, C.3R., p.5; rep. from * to last 6 sts., C.4B., p.2.

16th row: k.2, * p.4, k.6, p.2, k.3, p.2, k.6; rep. from * to last 6 sts., p.4, k.2. These 16 rows form the patt.

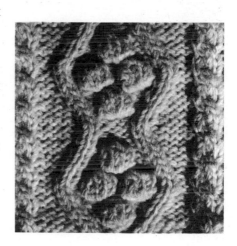

Colour work

A modern slipover worked in a traditional Fair Isle pattern.

Working with more than one colour of yarn opens up a whole new dimension in knitting. The simplest piece of stocking stitch is transformed once it is striped (in as many colours as you like) and the effects produced by putting in one extra colour in a basically plain piece of fabric—either in stripes, checks or motifs—are infinite.

It is essential when you are using more than one colour to use yarns of a similar type; a double knitting yarn, for instance, cannot be worked with a four-ply as the tension will go wrong and an uneven fabric will be produced. It is also wise to use only top-quality yarn for colour work, since hours of hard work can be wasted in seconds if the dyes are not fast—one immersion in water may ruin a garment knitted in non-colourfast yarns.

There are certain techniques to be mastered in working with several colours, but to begin with try some of the stitches already familiar to you, varying them with the introduction of as many colours as you like.

SIMPLE STRIPES

This is the easiest of all. Working in stocking stitch, work two rows in one colour. Then join in a second colour without breaking the first off. Work two rows in the second colour. Now drop this yarn and pick up the first, taking it up past the two rows already worked (be careful not to drag it) and then work with that for two rows. Continue like this all the way up the piece of knitting. If you are working in garter stitch, you will produce very fine stripes, since two rows of knitting form only one ridge of garter stitch. Try striping across ribbing—this is equally effective.

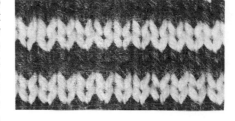

When you cast off, cut the yarn from the previous stripe about eight inches from the fabric. This end is then run into the fabric (remember to run it into a stripe of its own colour) or taken into the seam when the garment is sewn up.

STRANDING AND WEAVING

Stripes are the simplest way of using a number of colours on plain knitting. If you want to progress to blocks of colour, or complex Fair Isle types of patterning, two techniques have to be learned and practised: stranding and weaving.

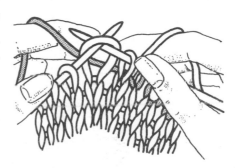

Multi-coloured—or bi-coloured—patterns are made up by having groups of stitches knitted in different colours, and every row may be different. For instance, on one row you may need to work five green stitches and then twelve white all along. On the next you will want one green and six white repeated all along. These two colours have to be carried along behind the work so that the correct colour is always ready when you need it, and this is where weaving and stranding come in.

If the colour changes come frequently and repeatedly—e.g. three white, two blue, all along the row—then you can *strand* the two colours. This technique is safe if you are not using blocks of more than five or six stitches. To do this, you knit your three stitches in white, then take the blue yarn, carry it loosely across the back of the three white stitches and knit two stitches with it. Then the blue is left, and the white picked up again, taken across the back of the blue stitches, and used for the next three stitches— and so on all along the row. For this type of work, it is much easier to hold one colour yarn in one hand and the second in the other. Then the interchange is easily made.

It will be seen that if you pull the stranded yarns at the back too tightly, you will pucker the resulting fabric, and the tension will go wrong, quite apart from the fact that the work will look uneven. So practise stranding so that the yarn taken across the back is loose enough to cross the intervening stitches easily (and to allow for them to give in wear) but not so slack that loops hang at the back of the work and the stitches are too loose. It is not easy to begin with, but time and practice will produce the right effect.

Weaving is rather more complex. It is used when you need to take the yarn across a large number of stitches. For instance, suppose you have a white sweater with two or three vertical bands of yellow set at intervals across it. You might perhaps work fifteen stitches in white, then a block of yellow, then

fifteen stitches of white and so on. Stranding is no good for this type of operation, because the loops will be too large.

To weave, the yarn not in use is taken round the yarn that is being used. On the first stitch you make in white, say, take the yellow yarn *over* the white before you make the stitch. On the next stitch, take the yellow yarn *under* the white before you make the stitch. If the row is a purl row, the procedure is just the same except that the yarn not in use will, of course, be at the front of the work instead of behind it. Be careful not to weave too much if you are using a dark colour behind a white one: for instance, small sections of black set on a white ground. If you take too much black behind white you may find that it will show through, or at least darken the ground fabric.

In this case, where the black work to be done is only a few stitches across, it is better to join in the black only a few stitches before you get to the black section and then, by stranding or weaving, bring it into play for the black section only. If there are two or three widely-spaced black sections it is still possible to do this, if you attach a separate small ball of yarn to each section.

This technique is also used if you want to work stripes vertically—perhaps a vertical strip of yellow running up the centre of a blue sweater. Join in the yellow a few stitches before the stripe, be careful to twist it round the blue yarn when you get to the yellow stitches, so there is no looseness in the work, and strand or weave the blue while you are working the yellow. You then strand or weave the yellow for a few stitches beyond the stripe, so that it is waiting for you in the correct place on the next row.

This principle is followed as well if you are working one colour spot—perhaps a central motif on a sweater. There is no need to carry the contrasting colour right across the fabric; in fact, it is much better not to weave or strand any more than you have to, because both processes tend to make the basic fabric a little more rigid than usual.

To prevent confusion if you are using two or three balls of yarn, be sure to untwist the threads at the end of each row. Many workers like to keep each ball in a separate container, spaced well away from each other on the floor (small cardboard boxes will do) and it is certainly safer than holding them all on your lap where they may well tangle.

COLOUR PATTERNS

There are two ways of writing colour patterns. The simplest types are written rather like an ordinary plain pattern, with the addition of letters for colours, but the more complex patterns are usually followed from a chart.

A pattern with a regular repeat, such as checks, can be written as a plain pattern, except that an extra symbol is used for the colour. For example, if checks in stocking stitch are worked in yellow and blue blocks of four stitches and four rows each, the pattern may be written thus (B. = blue; Y. = yellow):

1st row: * k.4B., k.4Y.; rep. from * to end (i.e. four knit stitches of each colour).
2nd row: * p.4Y., p.4B; rep. from * to end (i.e. four purl stitches of each colour). Rep. first two rows once.
5th row: * k.4Y., k.4B.; rep. from * to end (colours reversed), and so on.

Alternatively the pattern may be written throughout in this style:

1st row: k. * 4B., 4Y.; rep. from * to end (showing that all stitches in that row are knitted, and worked in blocks of four blue and four yellow each).

Occasionally the pattern will use the symbols 'L.' and 'D.' for light and dark colours, if the actual shades are not specified, but the appropriate symbols will be given in the abbreviations list at the beginning of the pattern, and should present no difficulty.

FAIR ISLE AND SCANDINAVIAN WORK

These colour patterns are more complex, and are best worked from a chart. The Fair Isle patternings, which were originally brought to Scotland from Spain, and which were then adapted and modified by the native workers, are traditionally worked in as many colours as are desired on a neutral (white, grey, brown or oatmeal) background. Today not everyone chooses traditional colourings.

Scandinavian designs—often used for ski sweaters, caps, boys' sweaters and so on—owe much for their inspiration to the trading exchanges between Norwegian and Scottish fishermen, and are often very similar to Fair Isle patterns. What the two kinds of design have in common is that they can be very detailed, with every row different and as many as twenty or thirty rows in a design.

It would take an inordinate amount of space to keep on writing out all these rows, so instead of a written pattern, instructions are often given in the form of a chart. Although these look frightening to the uninitiated, they are simple enough to follow, once the basic principles are understood.

On the chart, each *square* represents one *stitch* and each horizontal line of squares represents one *row*. So a chart fifteen squares wide and ten squares deep represents a piece of knitting made up of fifteen stitches worked for ten rows. In a stocking stitch pattern, all the knit rows on the chart are worked from right to left, and the purl rows are worked from left to right.

Since the design is probably repeated several times, the chart will give only the basic design—fifteen stitches—with the probable addition of one, for the end stitch. Thus your pattern might be, say, for sixty-one stitches, which means that you work the design on the chart four times, ending each knit row with the odd edge stitch, and beginning each purl row with the odd edge stitch. It may be that the depth of the pattern is repeated as well—that is, as soon as you have finished the tenth row you begin again with the first.

Each colour used will be differentiated on the chart. The ground shade is usually shown by squares left blank, and there are various ways of marking the squares to denote colour. For instance, a square with a spot in the middle of it may represent blue, a square divided into two halves diagonally with one shaded may represent green, and one with a cross marked on it may represent red. There will be a key beside the chart to indicate which symbols represent which colours. If you are using different colours from those on the chart (perhaps preferring to use three shades of blue on a white ground) then it is advisable for you to mark the pattern chart accordingly, so that you do not get confused.

A new look for Fair Isle—knitted beach set with a Fair Isle top and matching plain-coloured shorts.

These traditional multi-coloured designs are nearly always worked in stocking stitch, so you do not have to worry about a complicated stitch pattern and a colour chart at the same time!

Colour work is not as quick as plain colour knitting but it is fascinating to see the designs develop—and when you are more expert you can devise your own. The variations are infinite—you may like to work a single flower or an initial on an otherwise plain sweater or cap, or use up balls of yarn (as long as they are of the same weight) on attractive cushions and so on. Heavily patterned sweaters and dresses never lose their appeal, and the extra work is worth while.

As with other patterns, do not embark on a vastly complicated piece of work before you have had some practice. Try the stitches illustrated here, be sure that you can strand and weave without distorting the basic work, and then have a go at a small simple pattern. From that you can progress to the all-over designs that have made the Scottish Isles so famous for this craft.

Here are a few two-colour and multi-colour patterns for you to try, and also some simple charts.

Checks

Using dark (D.) and light (L.) yarn.
Cast on a multiple of 8 sts. plus 4 (e.g. 28), using D. (dark).
1st row: k. * 4D., 4L. (light); rep. from * to last 4 sts., 4D.
2nd row: p. * 4D., 4L.; rep. from * to last 4 sts., 4D.
Rep. these 2 rows once.
5th row: k. * 4L., 4D.; rep. from * to last 4 sts., 4L.
6th row: p. * 4L., 4D.; rep. from * to last 4 sts., 4L.
Rep. these 2 rows once.
These 8 rows are repeated throughout.

Houndstooth

Using light and dark yarn. A most popular pattern for men's sports knitwear.
Cast on a multiple of 4 sts. (e.g. 24), using D.
1st row: k. 2L., * 1D., 3L.; rep. from * to last 2 sts., 1D., 1L.
2nd row: p. * 1L., 3D.; rep. from * to end.
3rd row: k. * 1L., 3D.; rep. from * to end.
4th row: p. 2L., * 1D., 3L.; rep. from * to last 2 sts., 1D., 1L.
These 4 rows are repeated throughout.

Diamonds

Using dark and light yarn, another excellent stitch for sportswear.
Cast on a multiple of 8 sts. plus 7 (e.g. 31), using D.
1st row: k. 3L., * 1D., 7L.; rep. from * to last 4 sts., 1D., 3L.
2nd and alternate rows: p. working colours as for previous row.
3rd row: k. 2L., * 3D., 5L.; rep. from * to last 5 sts., 3D., 2L.
5th row: k. 1L., * 5D., 3L.; rep. from * to last 6 sts., 5D., 1L.
7th row: k. * 7D., 1L.; rep. from * to last 7 sts., 7D.
9th row: k. D.
11th row: as 7th row.
13th row: as 5th row.
15th row: as 3rd row.
16th row: as 2nd row.

These 16 rows form the basic shape and should be repeated throughout, ending, if desired, with a complete diamond in whichever colour is preferred.

Fleur de lys

In light and dark. One of the most popular of all motifs. This pattern produces the fleur de lys shape when the finished knitting is reversed.

Cast on a multiple of 6 sts. plus 3 (e.g. 21), using D.

1st row: k. 3D., * 1L., 5D.; rep. from * to end.
2nd row: p. 1L., * 3D., 3L.; rep. from * to last 2 sts., 2D.
3rd row: as first row.
4th row: p. 2D., * 1L., 5D.; rep. from * to last st., 1L.
5th row: k. 2L., * 3D., 3L.; rep. from * to last st., 1D.
6th row: as 4th row.

These 6 rows are repeated throughout.

Mock checks

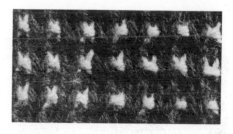

In dark and light colours. This pattern is really a fake, since the effect of checks is given without the yarn being stranded or woven.

Cast on a multiple of 2 sts. plus 1 (e.g. 23) using either colour.

1st row: k. in first colour.
2nd row: p. in first colour. Join in second colour.
3rd row: with second colour, * k.1, sl.1 purlwise; rep. from * to last st., k.1.
4th row: with second colour * k.1, y.fwd., sl.1 purlwise, y.b.; rep. from * to last st., k.1.

Repeat these 4 rows throughout.

This looks equally effective with the dark shade either as the main check or the inner spot; it can also be worked with two colours of equal strength.

Border strip

There are a great number of these designs—worked in a contrast colour on plain ground shade—which are used as edgings or above cuffs and welts, or across yokes. Stripes of the contrast colour are often placed above and below the strips, to mark them off.

Cast on a multiple of 6 sts. plus 1 (e.g. 25), using the ground shade.

1st row: k. * 1C. (contrast), 2G. (ground); rep. from * to last st., 1C.
2nd row: p. 1G., * 1C., 3G., 1C., 1G.; rep. from * to end.
3rd row: k. * 2G., (1C., 1G.) twice; rep. from * to last st., 1G.
4th row: p. * 1C., 2G.; rep. from * to last st., 1C.
5th row: as 3rd row.
6th row: as 2nd row.
7th row: as first row.

This is the basic design and forms a narrow band. If you wish to make the band deeper, repeat from rows 2 to 7 inclusive.

All-over diamonds _illustrated in colour on page 17_

Using light and dark yarn. This is a repeating pattern with a sporty look.

Cast on a multiple of 5 sts. (e.g. 25), using D.

1st row: k. * 2L., 1D., 2L.; rep. from * to end.

2nd row: p. * 1L., 3D., 1L.; rep. from * to end.
3rd row: k. in D., stranding light colour behind work.
4th row: p. * 1L., 3D., 1L.; rep. from * to end.
5th row: k. * 2L., 1D., 2L.; rep. from * to end.
6th row: p. * 2L., 1D., 2L.; rep. from * to end.
7th row: k. * 1L., 3D., 1L.; rep. from * to end.
8th row: p. in D., stranding light colour behind work.
9th row: k. * 1L., 3D., 1L.; rep. from * to end.
10th row: p. * 2L., 1D., 2L.; rep. from * to end.
These 10 rows are repeated throughout.

Fancy diamonds *illustrated in colour on page 17*
Using light and dark yarn. This forms a regular all-over design of enclosed diamonds.
Cast on a multiple of 10 sts. plus 1 (e.g. 31), using D.
1st row: k. * 1L., 2D., 2L., 1D., 2L., 2D.; rep. from * to last st., 1L.
2nd row: p. * 2D., 2L., 1D., 1L., 1D., 2L., 1D.; rep. from * to last st., 1D.
3rd row: k. * 1D., 2L., 1D., 3L., 1D., 2L.; rep. from * to last st., 1D.
4th row: p. * (2L., 1D.) 3 times, 1L.; rep. from * to last st., 1L.
5th row: k. * 1L., 1D., 2L., 3D., 2L., 1D.; rep. from * to last st., 1L.
6th row: p. * 1D., 2L., 2D., 1L., 2D., 2L.; rep. from * to last st., 1D.
7th row: as 5th row.
8th row: as 4th row.
9th row: as 3rd row.
10th row: as 2nd row.
These 10 rows are repeated throughout.

WORKING FROM A CHART

The following designs are worked from a chart. Study first the Fair Isle design below, and you will see how the chart works. This design is in four colours: yellow, black, red and green, and is worked over a 22 stitch repeat. The 23rd stitch is used at the end of the knitting (i.e. if you work to a three-pattern repeat you would have 66 stitches and one extra for the end stitch). In the instructions, written out in full below, this last stitch is not included. You will see that work is in stocking stitch, with every knit row worked from right to left, and every purl row from left to right. Borders have been worked in the illustration to make a framework for the design; these are not included in the instructions. In the instructions: Y., yellow; R., red; B., black; G., green. *Sample is illustrated in colour on page 54.*
Cast on 22 sts. in Y. and, if wished, work an even number of rows in stocking stitch.
1st row: k. 1R., 6Y., 9R., 6Y.
2nd row: p. 1R., 4Y., 11R., 4Y., 2R.
3rd row: k. 2B., 4G., 11B., 4G., 1B.
4th row: p. 5G., 11B., 5G., 1B.
5th row: k. 5G., 2B., 1G., 2B., 1G., 1B., 1G., 2B., 1G., 2B., 4G.
6th row: p. 3G., 1B., 2G., 1B., 3G., 1B., 3G., 1B., 2G., 1B., 4G.
7th row: k. 3G., 1B., 3G., 1B., 2G., 1B., 1G., 1B., 2G., 1B., 3G., 1B., 2G.
8th row: p. 1Y., 3R., 2Y., 1R., 3Y., 1R., 3Y., 1R., 2Y., 3R., 2Y.

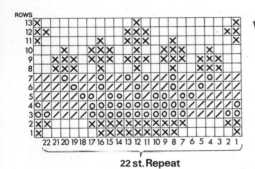

22 st. Repeat

⊠ RED
☐ YELLOW
◙ BLACK
▨ GREEN

Roll-collar dress for a little girl is worked in stocking stitch, with broad bands of two-colour patterning (see page 100).

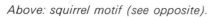

Above: squirrel motif (see opposite).

Above, right: Argyll-type colour pattern (see opposite).

Right: Greek key pattern (see opposite).

Below, right: Fair Isle pattern (see page 52).

9th row: k. 2Y., 3R., 1Y., 3R., 1Y., 3R., 1Y., 3R., 1Y., 3R., 1Y.
10th row: p. 2Y., 1R., 2Y., 3R., 2Y., 1R., 2Y., 3R., 2Y., 1R., 3Y.
11th row: k. 1R., 6Y., 1R., 2Y., 3R., 2Y., 1R., 6Y.
12th row: p. 1R., 8Y., 3R., 8Y., 2R.
13th row: k. 1R., 10Y., 1R., 10Y.
Work a few rows in st.st. in Y. if wished.

Greek key pattern *illustrated opposite*

The pattern is repeated over 18 sts. and 26 rows, so cast on a multiple of 18.

Work in st.st. following chart, right, for colour pattern. Each square on the chart represents one stitch, and each horizontal row of squares represents one row in the pattern. The colour pattern is repeated from stitch 1–18 inclusive across work.

Squirrel motif *illustrated opposite*

The motif itself is worked over 15 sts. and 25 rows and can have any number of border sts. on either side as wished. Our sample shows a border of 5 sts. at each side of the motif. Cast on 15 sts., plus number of border sts. required (e.g. for our sample you would cast on 25 sts.).

Work in st.st., following chart for motif colour pattern. Each square on the chart represents one stitch, and each horizontal row of squares represents one row of the motif pattern. A number of rows may be worked in white only before beginning colour motif, if wished.

Argyll-type colour pattern *illustrated opposite*

The pattern is repeated over 16 sts. and 16 rows, so cast on a multiple of 16 sts.

Work in st.st., following chart for colour pattern. Each square on the chart represents one stitch, and each horizontal row of squares represent one row in the pattern. The colour pattern is repeated from stitch 1–16 inclusive across work.

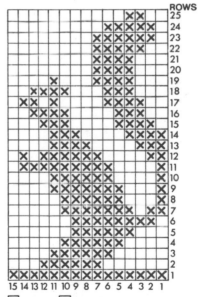

18st. Repeat

⊙ RED   ☐ WHITE
Greek key pattern

⊠ BLUE ☐ WHITE
Squirrel motif

⊠ RED
⊙ WHITE
⬤ BLACK
☐ GREEN

16st. Repeat

Circular knitting

Conventional two-needle knitting produces a flat fabric with two sides—a 'wrong' and a 'right'. It sometimes happens that a pattern is identical on each side (usually a rib) but usually the technique is to work the first (right-side) row, then to turn the work and reverse the stitches (knitting purl stitches and purling knitted stitches), or arranging them in such a way that the continuity of the pattern on the right side is maintained. It therefore follows that in most two-needle patterns wrong-side rows are usually different from right-side rows.

With circular work, however, the principle is different. The knitter works round and round to produce a seamless tube. As the work is never turned in the reverse direction, the side facing the knitter is always the right side. Patterns and stitches for this type of work have often to be specially adapted, but there is virtually no type of stitch or patterning that cannot be used in circular knitting. It is, in fact, a very valuable extension of the knitter's craft.

The advantages of circular knitting are many: being able to produce a seamless tube makes sock or glove-making a simple matter; it is also important to be able to pick stitches up round a neckline and work a polo collar, or a decorative edging, without any unsightly seam. Skirts and the skirt section of dresses usually hang much better in wear if they are made without side seams (since the joining of those seams, even if only slightly faulty, can spoil the overall appearance). When you are experienced in working with a circular needle, you may well prefer to make jerseys, cardigans and so on with no side seams, and this is perfectly possible. You simply combine the pattern instructions given for the back and front of the garment and work both sections concurrently on a circular needle.

Circular knitting is achieved in either of two ways: with the use of a set of four needles, or with a long circular needle (see page 8). The four-needle method is used for smaller tubes, such as socks, gloves or collars because, although sets of needles are made in a choice of sizes, the needles themselves are usually fairly short.

For a much larger number of stitches—for a skirt, perhaps, or a jersey—you need a circular needle. This will be available in a choice of lengths, and it is important to use the right length of needle for the number of stitches you will be working with. The minimum number of stitches used in the pattern should reach from point to point on the needle without stretching.

Usually a pattern for a circular needle design will specify which length of needle will be required. If this length is not given, or if you are adapting a two-needle pattern to work on a single circular needle then you will need to check right through the pattern to find out what the minimum number of stitches will be, and then choose the correct length of needle, according to the chart below. Each length of needle will normally hold up to four times more than the minimum number of stitches.

Tension Stitches to 1 inch	Lengths of circular needles and minimum number of stitches required				
	16 in.	24 in.	30 in.	36 in.	42 in.
5	80	120	150	180	210
$5\frac{1}{2}$	88	132	165	198	230
6	96	144	180	216	250
$6\frac{1}{2}$	104	156	195	234	270
7	112	168	210	252	294
$7\frac{1}{2}$	120	180	225	270	315
8	128	192	240	288	336
$8\frac{1}{2}$	136	204	255	306	357
9	144	216	270	324	378

For example, if you are working a pattern in which the minimum number of stitches in use at any time is 180 stitches, and you are working to a tension of $7\frac{1}{2}$ stitches to 1 inch, then you would require a circular needle not exceeding 24 in. in length. Provided the maximum number of stitches in the pattern never exceeds 720, then this one needle may be used throughout. If by any remote chance you did have to work with more than 720 stitches, then you would be advised to change to a longer circular needle for this section in the pattern.

Although circular needles are primarily for use in seamless knitting, many people prefer to use them for ordinary flat knitting as well. In this case, the circular needle is used in exactly the same way as a pair of knitting needles. Cast on stitches in the usual way, then begin knitting from the left-hand point on to the right-hand point. When the last cast-on stitch has been worked, transfer the point with the stitches on from the right hand to the left hand. Knit off stitches from the left to right point, turn round and repeat as if you were using a pair of needles. Working in this way is more compact than working with two needles, and also the weight of the work as it grows is evenly distributed round the needle all the time.

Sometimes if a circular needle has been coiled up in a pack or drawer for any length of time, the flexible central nylon section becomes rather tightly twisted. This twist may easily be removed by immersing the needle in fairly warm water for at least one minute, and then drawing the nylon section straight out between finger and thumb until the nylon lies naturally and inert in a gradual curve.

Circular and sets of four needles are sized in the same way as for pairs of needles, so it is advisable to build up a stock of them, in various lengths for different uses.

Casting on and off for circular work has been explained on pages 15 and 19; the actual methods employed (thumb method, two-needle method and so on) are precisely as for two-needle knitting. The only problem is that until a few rounds have been worked, and there is a piece of knitted fabric to take hold of, there is a danger of the first round being twisted and the stitches lying in the wrong direction. This can be overcome by working back and forth over the stitches on two needles for two or three rows and then joining into the round.

A complete circle of stitches on the circular needle, or three sets of stitches (one set on each needle) when working with a set of four needles, is called a round rather than a row, although the round is, of course, the equivalent of one row of flat knitting. It is essential to have some kind of marker at the beginning of each round so you will know when a round has been completed. With the four-needle method if you leave the casting-on thread hanging this is usually a clear enough marker. For a circular needle, it is best to use a coloured thread which is tied to the first stitch and then carried up the work by being knitted into the stitch above when each round is completed and the coloured marker is reached.

When you are making a circular tube of knitting, the right side of the fabric is always towards you. If you want to make stocking stitch, then every round is *knitted*. If you want reverse stocking stitch, then every round is *purled*. If you want garter stitch, then rounds are alternately *knitted* and *purled*. If you are *ribbing*, then work knit stitches above knit stitches and purl stitches above purl stitches. The finished stitch patterns will then be exactly similar to those worked on two needles.

COLOUR WORK

Multi-coloured patterns in circular knitting are worked in a similar way as for two-needle knitting. The second colour is joined in at the back of the work (i.e. inside the tube) and woven or stranded by the methods described for flat knitting (see page 47). Similarly, stripes or checks can be worked in circular knitting, but take special care if you are knitting in stripes to finish at exactly the end of every round and make the change of colour then.

ADAPTING TWO-NEEDLE PATTERNS

This section is *not* for the beginner, but the more experienced knitter may well want to try her skill at changing two-needle patterns and stitches so that complete finished garments can be made without seams.

For instance, a jersey can be made on a circular needle up to armhole level by working the back and the front together in a continuous round. The sleeves, likewise, can be knitted on a small round needle or on a set of four needles so that there is no seam up to the armhole. At armhole level, the back and front stitches have to be divided into two and the yoke worked, first for the back and then the front; similarly the sleeves will be worked as flat knitting when the shaping begins.

If you want to take this process a stage further you can graft shoulder seam stitches together (see page 68) and have a virtually seamless garment. The improved comfort and fit of the garment make the extra effort involved in adapting the pattern well worth while.

If your pattern is in stocking stitch, then the conversion from the two-needle to circular technique is not difficult: you simply work every row as a knit round.

If the pattern is in a fancy stitch, however, the adaptation is a little more complicated: wrong-side rows have to be converted into right-side rows since there is no wrong side in circular knitting. All knit and purl stitches on wrong-side rows must be reversed: i.e. knit stitches must be purled and purl stitches knitted. A wrong-side purl row is simply worked as a round of knitted stitches. If on the wrong side, a stitch is slipped with yarn to the front, then in circular knitting you must slip it with the yarn to the back and vice versa.

If you are knitting a front and a back together as one piece check carefully to find out if the pattern has edge stitches (e.g. one knitted stitch at beginning and end of each row). If it has, you can omit these edge stitches, unless you want a line of plain stitches to run down where a seam would normally be.

If the design is a fancy one, with an irregular number of stitches before the asterisk in any one row (e.g. 'k.3, * p.2, k.9; rep. from *' on one row, and 'k.2, * p.2, k.10; rep. from *' on the next) you must work out in advance which the edge stitches are. If there is one at each end, you work k.2 at the beginning of the first row and k.1 at the beginning of the next—in other words, omit the knit edge stitches on each row.

Take particular care with all wrong-side rows; if the row is symmetrical (i.e. reading the same both ways) then you can work it exactly as it stands, remembering only to substitute knit stitches for purl, and vice versa. However, if the pattern is not symmetrical, then it must be reversed, since this would normally be knitted from right to left seen from the right side, and all circular knitting is done in continuous rounds from right to left.

Once these basic rules have been understood it is possible to work any pattern you choose by the circular-knit technique.

CIRCULAR STITCH PATTERNS

Although, as we have seen, any pattern can be incorporated into circular work, there are a few stitches which are especially appropriate to this technique, and are traditionally associated with it. Many of the stitches form spirals, and a continuously-knitted spiral looks effective. Originally many stitches of this type were used for socks, but there is no reason why they should not be used for larger items if wished. The finer, ribbed spiral stitches are popular with the type of fine sock, or bedsocks, which have no heel knitted into them; the spiral stitch is close enough for the sock to cling without having any special shaping worked into it.

Stepped diagonal rib
Cast on a multiple of 6 sts. (e.g. 48).
1st round: * p.3, k.3; rep. from * to end.
2nd and alt. rounds: k. all the k. sts. and p. the p. sts. of previous round.
3rd round: p.2, * k.3, p.3; rep. from * to last 4 sts., k.3, p.1.
5th round: p.1, * k.3, p.3; rep. from * to last 5 sts., k.3, p.2.
7th round: * k.3, p.3; rep. from * to end.
9th round: k.2, * p.3, k.3; rep. from * to last 4 sts., p.3, k.1.
11th round: k.1, * p.3, k.3; rep. from * to last 5 sts., p.3, k.2.
12th round: as second round.
Now repeat from rounds 1 to 12 inclusive.

Wide-set rib
Cast on a multiple of 11 sts. (e.g. 55).

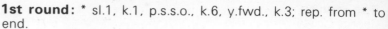

1st round: * sl.1, k.1, p.s.s.o., k.6, y.fwd., k.3; rep. from * to end.
2nd round: k.
These 2 rounds are repeated throughout.

Spiral openwork

Cast on a multiple of 12 sts. (e.g. 48).
1st round: * p.3, y.o.n., k.4, k.2 tog., k.3; rep. from * to end.
2nd round: * p.3, k.1, y.fwd., k.4, k.2 tog., k.2; rep. from * to end.
3rd round: * p.3, k.2, y.fwd., k.4, k.2 tog., k.1; rep. from * to end of row.
4th round: * p.3, k.3, y.fwd., k.4, k.2 tog.; rep. from * to end.
These 4 rounds are repeated throughout.

Note. If you are knitting on four needles (i.e. with stitches divided among three of the needles) you may find that you will not manage an exact set of pattern on each needle. For instance, if the pattern is 'k.2, p.4' repeated all along and you have 17 stitches on one needle you will have to break the continuity of the pattern. This may also happen in a 'travelling' stitch such as those given above, where the pattern moves round the needles. There is no need to worry about this, but the continuity of the pattern must be maintained. If you come to the point where you must knit two together, and one stitch is the last on one needle and the other the first on the next, then slip the last stitch on to the next needle and work the decrease. The stitch can be returned on the next round.

MEDALLION KNITTING

This is a technique whereby various geometric shapes are worked with four needles or more—for instance, circle, square, pentagon, hexagon and so on. These individual motifs are ideal for patchwork, as they can be easily stitched together to form an attractive fabric. Used separately, and depending on the thickness of the yarn employed, the motifs can be used for teapot stands or fine table-mats. You will need two sets of four needles, pointed at each end.

The circle

Cast on 2 sts. on each of four needles and work with the fifth needle.
1st round: k.
2nd round: inc. in every st. (so 16 sts.).
3rd to 5th rounds: k.
6th round: inc. in every st. (so 32 sts.).
7th to 9th rounds: k.
10th round: inc. in every 2nd st. (so 48 sts.).
11th to 13th rounds: k.
14th round: inc. in every 3rd st.
You should now have 64 sts.
Continue in this way until the circle is the size required, working three rounds plain and then an increase round. Each time the increase round will move 'upwards' by one stitch: that is, on the next increase round, work increase in every 4th st., in the following increase round, work increase in every 5th st., and so on.

The square

Cast on 2 sts. on each of four needles and work with the fifth needle.

1st round: inc. in every st. (so 16 sts.).

2nd round: k.

3rd round: inc. in first st. on first needle, knit to last st. on first needle and inc. in that st.; rep. on each of the other three needles.

The last 2 rounds are repeated until the square is the desired size, that is, working alternate rounds plain and inc. in the first and last st. on each needle on the intervening rounds.

(*Note.* It is, of course, very easy to knit a square simply by casting on and working the necessary number of rows, but by using this medallion method you can work stripes (as in the illustration) following the line of the square, and this is an attractive variant for patchwork, cushions and so on.

The hexagon

This is made in a similar way as for the square, except that stitches are put on to six needles (2 sts. on each) and a seventh needle is used for working.

Similarly, you put 2 sts. on each of five needles for a *pentagon*, and on eight needles for an *octagon*, always using an extra needle for working.

TUBULAR KNITTING

This is a special technique used in two-needle knitting which makes a flat double fabric. Most often it is used for scarves, but there are times when a double band of knitting is needed (perhaps for a hem) and this is useful.

Cast on an even number of stitches, using two needles.

1st row: * k.1, y.fwd., sl.1 purlwise, y.b.; rep. from * to end.

This row is repeated throughout, knitting the slipped stitches and slipping the knitted stitches of each previous row. This produces stocking stitch. If you want reversed stocking stitch, then the yarn should be kept at the back of the work all the time.

Details that count

It is worth spending time and trouble on the finishing details of your knitting. Often such details are laborious, time-consuming and even tedious but attending to them correctly makes all the difference between a well-fitting, professional garment and an inexact 'amateurish' one.

The hints which follow should help you not only with the all-important process of making up a knitted garment—that is, the assembling of the various individual knitted pieces into their finished form—but also how to cope with the 'technical problems' which frequently occur in the course of work. A few finishing techniques and tricks of the trade are given as well . . . All designed to give your knitting that extra couture look.

MAKING UP A GARMENT

Most sweaters and dresses are made in four main pieces: back, front and the two sleeves. Once these major pieces are knitted it is usual to sew them together to form the basic garment. And then at this stage neck edgings, pockets and trimmings are frequently added.

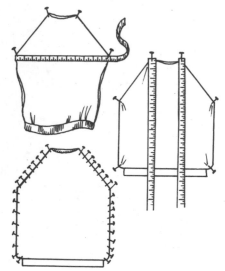

Before any sewing up is done, however, every individual piece of knitting should be *blocked*, to set its shape. Blocking is done in the following way: spread a thick, soft cloth (a folded blanket topped by a piece of sheeting is ideal) over the table or ironing board, and lay on it the first piece of knitting, wrong side uppermost. Spread it flat with your hands, and—using steel pins—fix it to the cloth by placing pins closely together all round the outer edge of the knitted piece. Do not stretch it, but gently ease it to the correct size and shape: use a tape measure to check measurements as you work. Your pattern should quote the correct measurements for the garment—follow this as your guide.

If the yarn used is wool, and the stitch pattern is a flat one, lay a damp cloth over the knitting and press lightly with a warm iron, omitting any ribbing. If the stitch pattern is a raised one, give it the lightest possible press across the main part of the piece, and concentrate on the edges, otherwise you will flatten the design and spoil its appearance. Remove the damp cloth, leave the knitting until completely dry, and then remove the pins, and repeat the blocking process with the next section.

Take care when blocking work to keep stitches and rows running in straight lines. Plenty of pins should always be used, and these should be inserted from the outer edge towards the centre of the work: the closer the pins are, the straighter the pressed edge will be.

If the yarn used is a synthetic, it will probably not need pressing—your pattern should recommend whether or not pressing is required—but the individual pieces of work should still be blocked. Pin out in a similar way as described above, then lay a damp cloth over the fabric, and leave until the cloth is completely dry. This takes time but it is worth while, for your finished garment will fit better and look neater. It is sometimes possible to iron synthetic yarns if the iron is very cool, and you are quick, but this is not generally recommended: if the iron is even a shade too warm the work can be stretched.

Sewing pieces together

After the individual pieces of your work have been thoroughly blocked and pressed, then they are stitched together. First make sure all loose ends are neatly darned in to the wrong side of the knitted pieces. Ideally the yarn which was used for the main knitting should also be used for the sewing together. If a double knitting yarn was used, it is sometimes possible to strand it (i.e. pull it apart) and to use a single strand of the yarn for the sewing.

Alternatively, many yarn manufacturers make their three-ply, four-ply and double knittings in the same range of colours, so it may be possible to buy one ball of a fine yarn to match the thicker yarn you used for knitting, and use the fine yarn for sewing. If you have used a tweedy yarn which cannot be stranded, or a bouclé yarn, then use a flat yarn for sewing, in a colour to match or blend with the knitted yarn.

There are two principal seams used for sewing knitted garments together: **backstitch seam**, which should be used for edges where there will be extra pull or strain, such as side, shoulder and sleeve seams; and **flat seam**, which should be used to join front bands to the main garment, or to join two pieces of ribbing. Instructions for stitching these two seams are given below. A tapestry needle is the best needle to use for either seam, as its blunt tip should not split or damage the yarn.

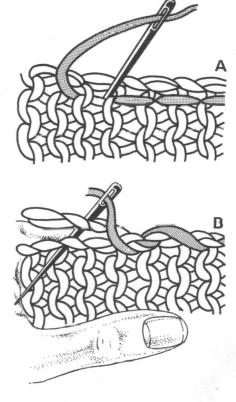

After the main seams of the garment are stitched, they should be lightly pressed again on the wrong side, with a warm iron over a damp cloth. Do not press too heavily: the object is merely to neaten the join made by the seam and to eliminate any ridges in the fabric.

Ideally, seams should be stitched in the following order: shoulders; set in sleeves; sleeve and sides all in one. Edgings, pockets and trimmings are stitched on last of all.

Backstitch seam (A). Put two pieces of work together, right sides facing, and pin carefully along edges so the edges match exactly. Work from right to left. Put the sewing needle into the work, and draw it out about a quarter of an inch along. Keeping close to the edge of the fabric, put the needle back into the fabric at the point where it was originally inserted, and draw it out about half an inch further on. Now insert it about a quarter of an inch back, and draw it out about half an inch further on. Continue in this way until edges are stitched together along entire length of seam. Try to keep the stitches as close to the edge of the fabric as possible. Finish with a couple of secure stitches.

Flat seam (B). With right sides facing, place two pieces of work together, edge to edge. Place the forefinger of your left hand just between these edges. Using an overcasting stitch draw the edges together over your finger. Move finger along as work proceeds.

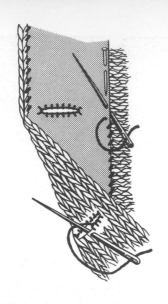

Button bands

A cardigan or jacket can be given extra life, and a neat finished appearance, by strengthening the button and buttonhole bands down the centre front. Use petersham ribbon, as near to the main colour of the knitting as possible, and the width of the knitted band. Cut two strips of petersham, the correct length with enough over to allow for a small turning at top and bottom.

Sew the petersham strips to the back of the band where the buttons will be, and also to the back of the band with the buttonholes. Be careful not to stretch the knitting as you stitch, otherwise it may wrinkle.

With a very sharp small pair of scissors cut a vertical slit in the ribbon a fraction wider than each buttonhole, and exactly over it. Turn in the edges of the ribbon and neaten them without sewing them entirely to the knitting. It should be sufficient to catch the two buttonholes (knitted and ribbon) together at the corners.

These petersham strips will hold the fronts of the garment absolutely firm and will preserve the shape, as well as preventing the buttonholes from being stretched.

Waistbands

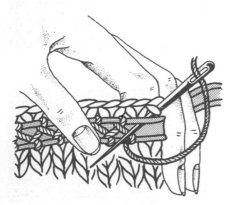

Skirts, shorts and trousers can have their waistbands stayed with petersham ribbon, in a similar way as for fabric skirts and trousers, provided the garment has a side zip closing.

Alternatively, if it is not wished to have a side opening, then side seams may be stitched for their entire length, and a length of elastic inserted round waistband. In this way the garment can be simply pulled on over the hips.

To make an elastic waistband: cut a length of elastic to fit comfortably and firmly round your waist, plus half an inch. Overlap the two short ends by half an inch, and stitch together to form an elastic ring. Put this ring inside the skirt waistband and, working over the elastic, attach it to the knitting with a casing of herringbone stitches (see diagram left).

Zip fasteners

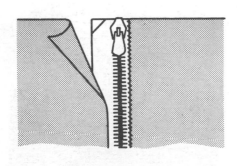

Care must be taken when stitching a zip fastener into a knitted garment to prevent the knitted fabric from wrinkling. Choose the length of the fastener carefully to fit the opening left in the garment, and use cotton thread for sewing in a colour to match knitting as closely as possible. There are two methods of stitching zips in place, depending on whether you wish the zip to be invisible from the right side or not.

Visible method. The zip should fit easily in the opening into which it is to be inserted—it is in fact an advantage if there is a little allowance for easing the edge of the opening on to the zip when stitching. On no account should the edge be stretched to fit the zip—this will cause the zip to buckle. Mitre the zip tapes at the top, folding them back on to the right side. Place the zip —closed—at the back of the opening, right side of zip to wrong side of opening, so that the slider is just below the top edge and the end of the zip teeth exactly level with the point of the opening. Baste in position, using soft cotton thread. Neatly oversew edge of the opening—on the right side—to the tape of the zip, just clear of the zip teeth. Finally, on the wrong side lightly oversew the outer edges of the zip tape.

Concealed method. With thin binding tape neatly face the wrong side of the opening to which the zip is to be sewn. Mitre the zip tapes at the top, folding them back on to the right side. Place the zip and baste in position as described for the visible method, above, the bound edges of the opening meeting along the centre of the zip. Finally, on the wrong side, lightly oversew the edges of the zip tape. This method is very neat, and facilitates easy running of the zip.

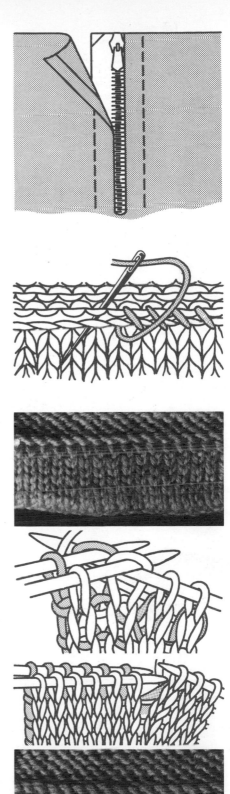

HEMS AND EDGES
Hems

The lower edges of jerseys and cardigans are usually ribbed to ensure a snug fit at the waist, but skirts and dresses need some kind of a hem to give a firm edge and the necessary weight. Hems are generally worked in stocking stitch, and may either be folded back and sewn into position after the garment is completed, or else knitted into position as you work.

Sewn hem. The usual method is to work a few rows of stocking stitch, perhaps with needles one or two sizes finer than for the main body of the work, ending with a knitted row. Then the next row, which would normally be purled, is knitted. This produces a ridge on the right side of the fabric which forms a neat edge as well as a useful guide line. When the garment is ready for finishing the hem is turned back with this ridged line forming the bottom edge of the skirt. The hem should then be slipstitched lightly into place all along.

Knitted hem. Cast on with the two-needle method. Begin knitting at once, without working into the back of the stitches, and you will produce a piece of work with a looped edge, each loop representing a stitch. A number of rows are then worked to give hem of required depth, followed by a ridge row as for the sewn hem method above, and then the same number of rows which were worked for the hem are worked again, ending with a purl row. Fold the hem back along the ridge row and with the right-hand needle knit the first stitch on the left-hand needle in the usual way but at the same time put the point of the needle through the first loop of the hem edge. Knit the two together and slip them off the needle. Continue in this way all along the row, and then continue work in the usual way. The hem is now knitted into position and is absolutely accurate.

This method gives a very neat finished appearance, but of course once knitted in, a hem cannot then be altered without ripping out a fairly major part of the garment. It is also very important to match every stitch exactly with its opposite loop, so that the hem is straight when it is completed.

Picot hem. This is an attractive variation of the plain hem, which is made with a series of holes in the fabric; when the hem is turned back a scallop-shaped hem is formed. This is particularly effective on baby clothes and children's party dresses. The hem may be sewn or knitted in, but is worked in the following way:

Cast on an uneven number of stitches, and work a few rows of stocking stitch, ending with a purl row (the number of rows worked determines the depth of the hem). **

Next row: * k.1, y.fwd., k.2 tog.; rep. from * to end.
Next row: p.

Now work the same number of rows in stocking stitch as you

did up to **, then either knit the hem into position, or leave it to be sewn into position afterwards.

Picking up stitches for borders

Frequently after the main parts of a garment have been knitted, these are sewn together, then the stitches are picked up round the neckline edge and a collar or ribbed border is worked on the stitches. Similarly, stitches can be picked up round a sleeve or armhole edge for a decorative edging or border, or stitches may be picked up down the centre front opening edge of a cardigan, and the front band worked on the picked-up stitches.

For the beginner, it is easier to pick up stitches round an edge with a fine crochet hook. The hook is put right through the knitted fabric, as close to the edge as possible, the yarn is wrapped round the hook at the back of the work, and then pulled through to the front. The resulting stitch is then slipped on to a knitting needle. Continue in this way along the edge. When you reach the end, you will have a row of stitches on the knitting needle, and the edging, collar or border is worked on these stitches.

It is important that stitches are picked up evenly along the length of the fabric, with no gaps or bunching. The best way to do this is to mark the length of the edge into even sections, and then to pick up the same number of stitches in each section.

For instance, if you have to pick up 100 stitches down a cardigan front, measure the front (or count the rows). Assuming the edge is 20 in. long, then with pins mark off the halfway point (10 in.) first, then divide each half into two. You will now have four sections, each 5 in. long, and you will therefore pick up 25 stitches in each section. By working in this way you will be able to see at once if you are over-estimating or being too skimpy in the picking-up.

To pick up stitches round a neck edge, mark the neckline at centre front, at shoulder seams, and at centre back (depending on the type of design being worked) and follow a similar technique.

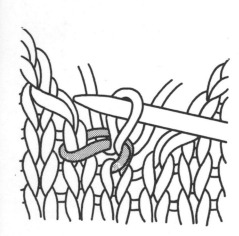

V-necked pullovers usually have a stitch in the centre front of the neck edge, and the decreases during the neck ribbing, which forms the shape of the neck, are worked on each side of this stitch. It is therefore essential that you pick up the exact central stitch, otherwise the whole neckline will be out of true.

When picking the stitches up, try always to work through the firm parts of the knitted fabric, rather than through the loose threads which sometimes occur between rows or on the slope or a shaped edge, so there are no holes in the fabric when the edging is made. If you cannot avoid picking up through a long or loose thread, then slip the stitch on to the left-hand needle and knit into the back of it.

An additional way to ensure a neat, fine line of picked-up stitches is to pick them up with a needle or crochet hook which is somewhat finer than the needle size you will use to work the edging or border.

Necklines

Instead of working a ribbed edging to a neckline, it is possible to finish necklines with a turned-back hem, either plain or

picot. Pick up the stitches round the neck edge, as described above, then work the edging in whatever pattern you wish. Follow this with a ridge or picot row, as described for hem finishes on page 65, then work a few more rows of stocking stitch for the turn-back. When the stitches are cast off, the neckline is doubled back along the ridge or picot row, and the hem is slipstitched into position.

This type of neckline, however, has no elasticity, so is not suitable for necklines without a zipped or buttoned opening.

Selvedges

The selvedge, which is really a term more strictly applicable to woven cloths, is the firm edge down each side of a piece of knitted fabric. Seams are usually made along the selvedges, so it is important that the edges are firm and stable in order to give a neat, flat seam.

If you are working a lacy pattern, then the edges must be reasonably solid so you can sew them together. Sometimes even a plain fabric will have a tendency to curl at the edges which can make seaming difficult. There are two ways in which neat edgings can be formed. These are: by slipping the first stitch of every row; by knitting the first and last stitches of every row.

In the first method, slipping the first stitch of every row forms a chain up the side of the work, and stitching can be made through this. In the second method, a narrow garter stitch edging is made, and if the ridges are kept exactly together when the seam is made, then the seams will match identically.

Often a pattern will allow for an edging, and when you read through the instructions you will see that the first and last stitches are knitted on each row, or that slipped stitches are recommended. If an edging is not 'built in' to the pattern you are using, then it is a relatively simple matter to adjust the pattern yourself to include edging stitches. Sometimes these stitches are referred to as the 'pip edge'.

Opening edges

A narrow band of garter stitch makes an excellent flat edging for a zip fastener opening, and makes the actual stitching of the zip much easier.

When you reach the point in the pattern where stitches are divided into two groups, and each group is worked separately to allow for the zip opening, then you simply work three stitches in garter stitch on either side of the centre opening. For instance, suppose you are working with a total of forty stitches; you will then be instructed to work twenty stitches, to turn and work on these stitches only for the right side. Simply knit three stitches, then pattern the remaining seventeen. On the next row, pattern seventeen, knit three. Continue in this way, keeping a three-stitch garter stitch edging until that half is completed. Rejoin yarn to remaining stitches, knit three stitches, and pattern to the end. Continue to work this side to match the first side.

Centre front open edges—on cardigans or jackets, for instance—are often finished with a ribbed facing band, which is knitted upwards from the hem and sewn on separately or worked from stitches picked up all along the length of the front. An alternative method is to work an extra few stitches on the row at the front edge—six stitches will give a reasonable width of facing. On every row slip the stitch immediately before these six, then work them in the pattern. When the work is finished, the edging band is turned back neatly along the line formed by the slipped stitches, and can be slipstitched lightly in place.

GRAFTING

This is the term given to the technique of joining two pieces of knitting without first casting off. There is no visible seam, since the join is created by using a needle to 'sew' in a new row of 'knitting' between the two pieces of knitted fabric. Not only is this very comfortable for a garment—on a sock toe, for instance—but it is neat as well. Some knitters prefer to work a sweater on a circular needle in order to avoid side seams, and then graft the shoulder seams together, and work the sleeves on a set of four needles. In this way, there will be seaming only where the sleeves are sewn into the armholes.

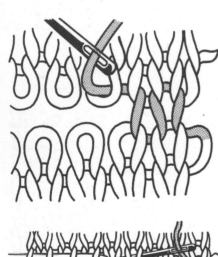

A tapestry needle, which has a blunt end and will not split the yarn, is the best needle to use for grafting. Leave an end of yarn equal to four times the width of the row to be worked. Arrange the stitches to be joined equally on two needles, and place the needles together so the wrong sides of the knitted fabrics are facing. Both needle points should be at the right, and the end of yarn should be coming from the front needle.

Thread the yarn end on to the tapestry needle and work as follows: * insert needle into first stitch on front needle as if to knit it, draw yarn through and slip stitch off needle. Insert needle into next stitch on front needle as if to purl, draw yarn through and leave stitch on needle. Insert needle into first stitch on back needle as if to purl it, draw yarn through and slip stitch off needle. Insert needle into next stitch on back needle as if to knit, draw yarn through and leave stitch on needle. Repeat from * until all stitches are joined. Fasten off securely.

This method should be used for joining two pieces of fabric worked in stocking stitch. Once the principles of grafting are understood, it is possible to apply the rules to suit various stitch patterns of knitted fabric.

BUTTONHOLES

Buttonholes may be made in a ribbed or garter stitch band which is sewn on to the fronts of jackets and cardigans. For smaller openings, such as at a neckline or cuff, the buttonholes are usually worked into the body of the fabric as work progresses. There are three principal types of buttonholes.

Very small buttonholes. A tiny buttonhole suitable for a small button at the neck or cuff, especially on baby wear, can be made simply by working 'yarn forward, knit two stitches together' at the point where the hole is required. On the following row the made stitch is worked in the usual way into the pattern. For extra strength, it is advisable to oversew or work buttonhole stitches round the hole.

Horizontal buttonhole. This is worked across the fabric by casting off a few stitches (the exact number will depend on the width of the button you will be using) at the point where the buttonhole is required. On the following row, the same number of stitches are cast on immediately above the cast-off stitches. This forms a small horizontal slit in the fabric.

Occasionally this method will produce a loose stitch at the inner corner. This can be avoided by casting off the required number of stitches (say, four), and then on the following row cast on only three stitches (i.e. one fewer than specified), and work to the end. On the row after this, work twice into the first cast-on stitch thus bringing the number back to the correct total.

Vertical buttonhole. To work a vertical buttonhole, work up to the point where the buttonhole is required, then turn the work, knitting back across the stitches just worked. Continue on this group only for the number of rows required to give depth of buttonhole. Leave these stitches, and join the yarn to the stitches which were left. Work an equal number of rows in pattern on these stitches. Now work across all stitches, and you will have made an upright slit in the fabric.

To prevent stretching, it is advisable to work round both horizontal and vertical buttonholes with matching yarn and using buttonhole or over stitches, especially if you intend to use large buttons.

When stitching buttons on to your garment, always stitch the centre of the button opposite the outside corner of the buttonhole, to prevent pulling.

POCKETS

A pocket may either be made separately, then sewn on to the finished garment; or it may be knitted into position as you work the main body of the garment.

For a separately-made pocket, press the garment well, and press the pocket. Then pin the pocket carefully in position to the right side of the garment, and sew in place neatly round the sides and lower edge.

For a knitted-in pocket, work as follows: first knit a piece of stocking stitch the size of the pocket required (e.g. twenty stitches wide, and five inches deep). Finish with a right-side row. Leave these stitches on a spare needle. This piece of fabric will form the lining, or backing, for the pocket.

Now work the garment section up to the point where the top of the pocket will naturally come. Work to the desired place, and cast off the same number of stitches which are on the pocket (in this case, twenty). Work to the end of the row. On the following row, work up to the cast-off point, and work across the pocket stitches on the spare needle. Continue to the end of the row.

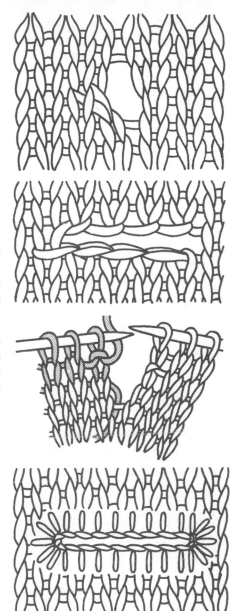

Now continue working in the usual way across all stitches and the backing for the pocket is knitted in, to be sewn down later with a flat seam on the wrong side of work.

When the garment is completed, it is possible either to pick up the cast-off stitches and work a few rows of rib (to form a pocket edge), or to make a separate strip of ribbing and to sew this on horizontally to form an edging.

AFTER-CARE

Knitted clothes will give years of wear if they are treated in a kind and gentle way. It is essential that they are never allowed to become too dirty, and never to let the dirt stay in too long since rubbing spoils the fabric. Even a football sweater, immersed immediately after play, will lose its dirt very quickly.

Nowadays it is possible to put many synthetic yarns, and some woollen ones too, in the washing machine. Where the yarn manufacturer recommends this, you will be perfectly safe in following the instructions given. If you are in any doubt at all, however, it is best to wash by hand in a mild, hand-hot soapy solution. Gently squeeze the garment until the dirt has rolled out, then rinse several times in cool water until the water runs quite clear. Squeeze out as much water as possible but do not wring.

To dry, put the garment flat on a clean, dry towel, pull it gently into shape, and leave to dry flat. If you hang up a knitted fabric, the weight of the water still in the fibres can pull it out of shape.

Similarly, knitted garments should never be kept on a hanger because they may drop in length. Always fold knitteds and keep them in a drawer; if they are being put away for any length of time (perhaps for the winter, or until the start of the next school term), make sure they are clean, fold them and put them in tissue paper or a polythene bag.

ALTERING THE LENGTH

It is possible to lengthen or shorten a sleeve or the body of a garment, provided the lengthening or shortening is done from the hem, and the necessary extra rows, or finishing rows, are worked downwards.

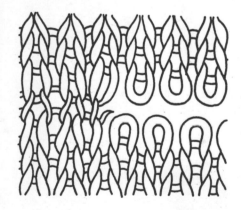

If you want to lengthen a jersey, do it this way: using a crochet hook or knitting needle, pull a thread at the edge of the work. Pull it hard so that it tightens all along the knitted row, then cut it.

If you ease out the knitting and draw it gently apart, you will find that the lower section falls away in a neat piece, leaving a row of loops along the edge of the upper piece. Put these on to a needle and you can then work some more plain knitting, with ribbing to finish, or work a longer piece of ribbing.

To shorten a garment, cut a thread across the work, just above the point at which you wish to shorten the garment, then pick up the row of loops, and either cast off right away, or else work a couple of ribbed rows to finish, then cast off.

USING YARN A SECOND TIME

It is possible to unpick knitting and to use the yarn for a second time, but a certain amount of the yarn's original elasticity will be lost the 'second time round'. So too will some

Simple cross-over top for evening worked in a rayon yarn, with beading on lower, sleeve and front bands.

Above: bedroom bootees in two colours (see page 162).

Top picture: Fair Isle cap (see page 161). Above: pink and blue bathmats (see page 163).

72

of the quantity, so do not expect to get the same size sweater you had before. An adult's garment will produce enough yarn for a child's garment; or a long-sleeved sweater can be turned into a sleeveless waistcoat, or a similar design.

Wash the garment, and when it is completely dry unpick the seams carefully, and then unpick the individual pieces, winding the yarn into skeins (round the back of a chair is the easiest way) as you work. Tie these skeins firmly at each end so they do not unravel and wash them again. When they are dry, wind them into loose balls, and the yarn is ready for its next use.

USING CROCHET FOR EDGINGS

A crochet edging can often give an attractive and neat finish to a knitted garment—lacy borders, for instance, can be added round hem, cuff or neck edges, or an edging in a contrast coloured yarn added to a garment. Sometimes even complete crochet motifs can be incorporated into the main fabric of a knitted garment (see, for instance, the design on page 127). Also, if a cord or drawstring is required for a fastening, this can be more effectively worked in a crochet chain rather than knitted strip.

It is therefore an advantage to be able to work a few basic crochet stitches. The following simple diagrams and instructions show how to do these.

How to begin

Make a slip loop as for knitting (see page 13) but use a crochet hook instead of knitting needle to draw yarn through loop. Pull the short end of yarn and the ball thread in opposite directions to bring the loop close round the hook.

Holding the work

Loop the long thread round the little finger of your left hand, across the palm and behind the forefinger. This should keep the tension of your work even. Catch the knot of the loop on the hook between the thumb and forefinger of left hand (as your work grows you will still continue to steady it by holding in this position). Hold the bar of the hook between thumb and forefinger of the right hand, as you would a pencil, and place the tip of the middle finger on head of hook to guide it.

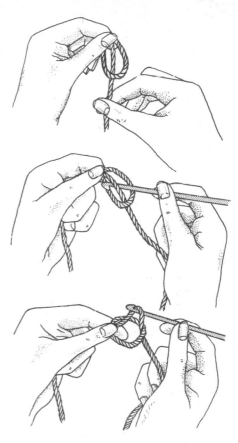

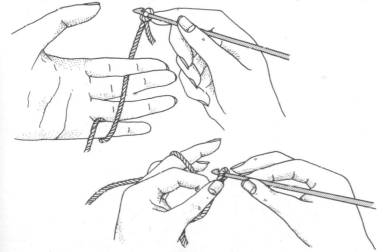

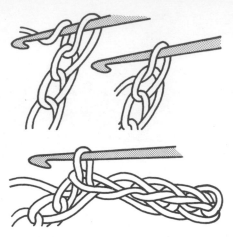

Chain stitch

This is the foundation of all crochet work. With the yarn in position, and the first loop on hook, pass hook under the yarn held between left-hand forefinger and hook, catch yarn with hook. Draw yarn and head of hook through loop already on hook. Each time you pull yarn through loop on hook counts as one chain. Continue until required number of chains are formed.

Slip stitch

Insert the hook into the stitch to the left of the hook (or into a stitch along edge of knitting), catch the long thread and draw it through the stitch and the loop already on the hook. This forms a flat chain, and is sometimes called single crochet.

Double crochet

This stitch is frequently used for edging purposes. Insert the hook into the stitch to the left of the hook (or into a stitch along edge of knitting) and catch yarn with hook. Draw yarn through stitch. You now have two loops on the hook. Put the yarn over the hook and draw it through the two loops. This leaves one loop on the hook.

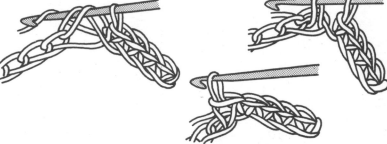

Treble

Pass the hook under yarn which is held in left hand, insert the hook into the stitch to the left of the hook (or into a stitch along edge of knitting) and draw yarn through. You now have three loops on the hook. Put the yarn over the hook again, and pull it through the first two loops on the hook, leaving two loops on the hook. Put the yarn over the hook once more and draw through the last two loops, leaving you with one loop on the hook.

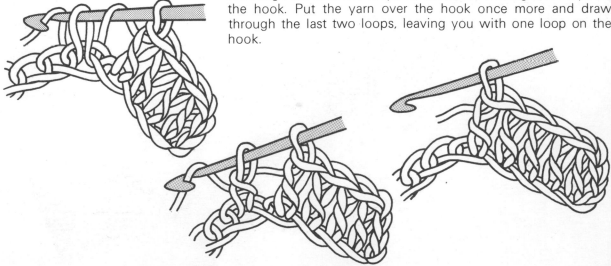

Machine knitting

Knitting by machine is a totally different concept from hand-knitting. Machine knitting, which is growing rapidly in popularity all the time, will produce fabulous garments in next to no time, and for a fraction of the cost of similar ready-made clothes. Chunky pullovers and sweaters can be made in an evening, fine lacy evening dresses in a day. Today's advanced knitting machines will work intricate colour patterns, make lace, even weave—simply at the turn of a dial. Even the older and more basic models will work automatic stocking stitch at up to 8,000 stitches a minute.

Obviously hand-knitting can never achieve results such as this. But for most of us, knitting by hand, as well as being an economic proposition, is a soothing and therapeutic pastime . . . sometimes even the finished garment is almost less important than the pleasure derived from the making, the act of creating by hand a beautiful fabric and pleasing design. On this level, knitting by machine can never hope to compete in terms of personal satisfaction.

However for those who want the speed and convenience of machine knitting, the ease of turning out impressive garments for the whole family in next to no time and at minimal cost, this chapter offers a brief guide.

A moderately-priced knitting machine with 180 needles It will knit a complete row of fancy stitches in ten seconds, a row of two-colour Fair Isle in twenty seconds, a row of stocking stitch in less than two seconds, and a row of weaving in just thirty seconds.

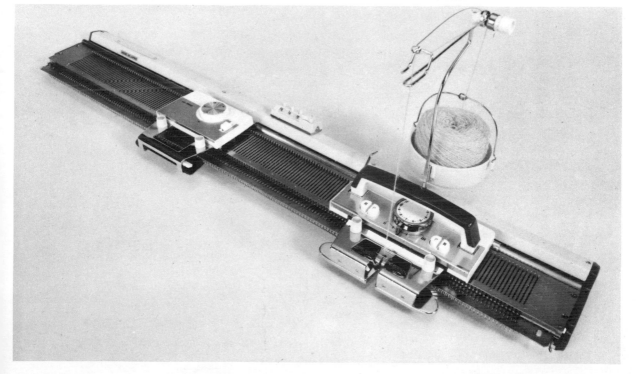

This gaily-striped poncho can be easily knitted on a single-bed machine.

Unfortunately, because different models and makes of machine vary so considerably both in their working methods and their performance, it is impossible to give anything more than the most general of guides. Every machine in any case should come with its own explicit instruction book, which should give full details of how to work that particular model—how to thread up, cast on and cast off, how to work the various pattern permutations available, how to increase, decrease, work buttonholes, and other similar techniques.

If you are seriously thinking of buying a machine for the first time, the first step should be to go to a good showroom where many different models of machines are available for inspection, and a qualified assistant present to advise you. There are many excellent knitting machine manufacturers, each producing a wide range of different machines ranging from relatively inexpensive models which will only work 'plain' patterns, to complex advanced models capable of the most intricate patterning and colour work.

Nevertheless unless you are committed to one particular manufacturer, it is best to go to an independent showroom where different models from different manufacturers can be seen. In this way, you can compare the advantages of one machine against the advantages of the next, and eventually find the model that is going to suit you best, and the type of knitting you want to do.

HOW A MACHINE WORKS

When you knit by hand, you have a needle with a row of stitches, and each stitch is worked off one by one. In machine knitting, you also have a row of stitches, but the difference is that each individual stitch has a needle, or small hook, to itself, and the whole row of stitches is knitted off simultaneously, with one smooth movement. So that to knit a whole row of stitches by machine can take less time than it normally takes to work just one stitch by hand.

The width of the piece of knitting must therefore be governed by the number of needles on the machine—i.e. the maximum number of stitches it is possible to work with. This is an important point to bear in mind when you choose the machine you will buy: if you are only likely to want to make small garments on the machine, then there is no point in going to the expense of a machine with a wide needle bed.

Pattern knitting is produced by arranging the needles in different groupings before you start knitting.

There are two main types of machine available: single-bed and twin-bed machines. The single-bed machines are the simplest and usually least expensive: they have one needle bed, and one set of needles. Normally only stocking stitch can be produced on single-bed machines, although attachments are often available for working ribbing and fancy patterns.

Twin-bed machines have two sets of needles, and therefore give much wider scope both for stitch patterns and bigger pieces of work.

Another important point to check is what type of yarns can be used with the machine. Make sure if you want to work with fine two-ply yarns, the machine of your choice will produce an even, supple fabric from such a yarn. Similarly, if you intend to use a lot of synthetic yarns, or heavyweight chunky wools, check that these can be successfully used on the machine. If possible, get the demonstrator to work a small sample square with each of a number of different yarns, so you may see and feel the resulting fabrics for yourself.

Ask too what tension the machine works to—often this is different from hand-knitting, as there are usually more rows to the inch with a machine than with hand-knitting in an equivalent yarn and stitch. If you can find a machine which works to the same tension as hand-knitting this is more convenient, as it will be easier—once you are an experienced machine knitter—to adapt a hand-knitting pattern to be worked on your machine.

Check too what attachments are available, and how far they will extend the scope of the machine. If you do not want to be bothered with too many attachments, then make sure the machine will automatically deal with such details as cuffs, necklines and waistbands. An automatic yarn carrier and an automatic row counter are also useful gadgets. A detachable carriage face-plate will give you the facility of being able to lift the carriage and rectify errors without disturbing your knitting.

It is also a good idea to check on the quality and construction of the needle bed—the better machines have two separate steel plates laminated together to give extra strength and durability. The carriage guide rail, which is situated on the back of the needle bed, is another important feature, as this controls the smooth trouble-free movement of the carriage. A good guide rail should be of solid steel. An interior rail will give an uneven movement of the carriage, especially with thick yarns, and is likely to create carriage 'wobble' after constant use.

It is as well to look under the carriage and check the solid construction of the carriage itself. Attention to detail in all these features adds up to a solid, well-constructed machine which should give years of reliable service.

HINTS TO HELP

Many of the principles of good hand-knitting apply equally to machine work: it is essential, for instance, that you always

An impressive trouser suit with a motif design in Fair Isle, worked on a modern punch-card machine.

check your tension every time before embarking on a pattern. Machine patterns usually quote the correct tension measurement just as hand patterns do. Work a small sample to check, using the yarn recommended. It is as well however—if you can spare the time—to let the sample rest for about twenty-four hours before measuring the stitches and rows. The fabric is often slightly distorted as it comes off the machine, but if allowed to rest for a while should regain a regular form.

For this same reason, when you have completed making the various parts of a garment, these pieces should be allowed to rest for a while before you stitch them together into their finished form. And, while on the subject of making-up, there are no short cuts available here! The actual knitting may have taken a fraction of the time of hand-knitting, but the making-up must still be done by hand, and the same care and attention to detail are needed—a machine-knitted garment can be spoiled just as easily as a hand-knitted one by careless making-up, and uneven seams.

If it is possible to complete each piece of work at a single sitting so much the better. Leaving work in situ and coming back to it later can produce a slight variation in the tension which may be apparent in the finished garment.

Always keep your machine clean and free from dust and fluff. If you are working with light-coloured yarns then check that the needles are absolutely clean before you cast on. When the machine is not in use, keep it covered preferably with a linen or similar type of cloth. Never cover your machine with a woollen cloth, as fluff from the wool can get into the machine. Also, wool is inclined to attract damp, and could even rust parts of the machine.

THE NEW MACHINES

With the latest modern knitting machines, anything is possible! Machines are available with an ingenious punch-card pattern system: a selection of punch cards is supplied, and each punch card gives a different pattern motif. You simply choose the pattern you want, slot the card into the special 'computer' panel on the machine, turn the dial to the appropriate setting, and slide the carriage back and forth. The machine does the rest: it memorises the pattern and reproduces it continuously.

A punch-card machine which takes all the guesswork out of pattern knitting. You simply slot in a card to the special 'computer' panel on the machine, and the machine then memorises the pattern.

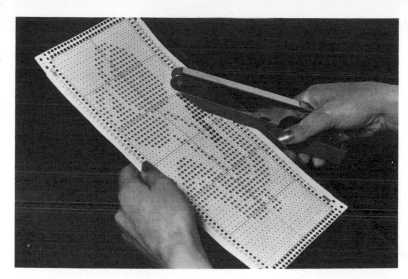

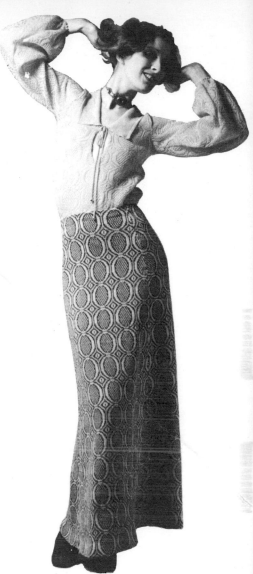

The same punch card pattern can be used for entirely different yarns. The two-piece outfit shown right, for instance, consists of a heavy-weight, two-colour skirt and a delicate lace blouse both worked from the same punch card. The only difference in the working was in the dial setting: Fair Isle for the skirt, lace for the blouse.

You can also make your own punch-card patterns—when you have exhausted the possibilities of those produced by the manufacturers. Sets of blank cards are available. You just draw or trace any design you choose on to a blank card, then punch out the design with a special punching gadget.

Other modern automatic machines are equally simple to operate: with some you merely dial a number for the pattern you want, and the built-in automatic programme pattern system means that the machine will automatically knit all types of fancy stitches, colour patterns, zigzags, jacquard, tuck stitch, and many pattern motifs including monogram letters. Once the dials on the programme panel and the buttons on the carriage are set, then all you have to do is slide the carriage back and forth. It couldn't be easier!

Some machines will produce a woven fabric which can be cut with scissors, and made up into dresses, coats, suits and other garments, just like normal dressmaking fabric.

Other machines will make beautiful sturdy-weight home furnishings—bedspreads, curtains, rugs, and chair covers. And the same machines are capable of taking all yarns from the finest nylon to the thickest blanket or rug wools.

The illustrations on these pages will show you a few of the wonderful patterning effects it is possible to produce with a machine: there are hand-knitting patterns which are impossible to reproduce by machine, but on the other hand there are effects which are possible only on a machine.

In fact, machine knitting becomes a separate craft, with its own standards of design and texture. However, if you are seriously thinking of investing in a knitting machine—and it will be an investment in terms of saving of money, and the increased variety of your family's wardrobe—then the only sensible course is to go to a good showroom and discover exactly what is available.

Above: beautiful fine lace blouse and Fair Isle skirt both worked from the same punch card.

Above, left: it is possible to punch out your own pattern on blank punch cards.

The Patterns

A selection of designs to knit for you, your family and your home, based on the stitches and techniques described in the preceding chapters.

Baby's layette

illustrated in colour on page 90

MATERIALS
For coat, bonnet and leggings: 6 (7, 8) balls (25 gr. each) Mahony's Baby Berella. One pair each Nos. 9 and 11 knitting needles (USA sizes 5 and 2), plus a spare No. 9 needle (USA size 5). Three small buttons. Shirring elastic. ¾ yd. ribbon, 1 in. wide. **For shawl:** 11 balls (25 gr. each) Mahony's Baby Berella. One pair long No. 7 knitting needles (USA size 7).
Note. To make the complete set of garments 16 (17, 18) balls of yarn will be required.

MEASUREMENTS
Coat: all round chest (fastened) 18 (19, 21) in.; length 10¼ (11, 11¾) in.; sleeve seam 5½ (6, 6½) in. **Leggings:** waist to crutch 7 (7½, 8) in. **Bonnet:** all round 10½ (11, 11½) in. **Shawl:** approximately 40 in. square after light pressing.

TENSION
On No. 9 needles 7 sts. to 1 inch over st.st.
On No. 7 needles 5½ sts. to 1 inch over shawl pattern.

ABBREVIATIONS
See page 11.

COAT SLEEVES (make 2 alike)
With No. 11 needles cast on 37 (41, 45) sts. and work 10 (14, 14) rows in k.1, p.1 rib.
Change to No. 9 needles and cont. in patt.:
1st row (right side): k.
2nd row: * k.1, p.1; rep. from * to last st., k.1. Rep. these 2 rows twice more. Inc. 1 st. both ends of the next and every foll. 6th row until there are 49 (53, 57) sts. Cont. straight until sleeve measures 5½ (6, 6½) in. ending on wrong side.

Shape Top
Cast off 3 sts. at beg. of next 2 rows, dec. 1 st. both ends of the next 4 (5, 6) right-side rows then both ends of the next 3 rows. Cast off 5 sts. at beg. of next 2 rows. Cast off rem. 19 (21, 23) sts.

COAT BACK AND FRONTS (worked in one piece to the armholes)
With No. 9 needles cast on 165 (175, 191) sts. and work 7 rows m.st.
Next row: m.st.5, p.77 (82, 90), p.2 tog., p.76 (81, 89), m.st.5.
Next row: m.st.5, k. to last 5 sts., m.st.5.
Cont. in patt. with m.st. borders on 164 (174, 190) sts.
1st row (wrong side): m.st.5, * y.f., k.2 tog.; rep. from * to last 5 sts., m.st.5.
2nd row: as first row.
3rd row: m.st.5, p. to last 5 sts., m.st.5.
4th row: m.st.5, k. to last 5 sts., m.st.5.
5th to 10th rows: rep. 3rd and 4th rows 3 times.
Rep. these 10 rows until work measures 6 (6½, 7) in., ending on right side.
Change to No. 11 needles.
For sizes 1 and 2 only. Next row: m.st. 5, p.4, (p.2 tog., p.2) 8 times, (p.2 tog., p.3) 16 (18) times, (p.2 tog., p.2) 8 times, p.2 tog., p.4, m.st.5: 131 (139) sts.
For size 3 only. Next row: m.st.5, p.4, (p.2 tog., p.3) 34 times, p.2 tog., p.4, m.st.5: 155 sts.
For all sizes. Cont. as follows:
1st row: m.st.5, * p.1, k.1; rep. from * to last 6 sts., p.1, m.st. 5.
2nd row: m.st.5, * k.1, p.1; rep. from * to last 6 sts., k.1, m.st.5.
3rd (buttonhole) row: m.st.3, yarn round needle twice, k.2 tog., rib to last 5 sts., m.st.5.
4th row: as 2nd row, purling into one of the made loops and dropping the other.
5th and 6th rows: rep. first and 2nd rows.
Change to No. 9 needles and cont. in sleeve patt. with m. st. borders as follows:
1st row: m.st.5, k. to last 5 sts., m.st.5.
2nd row: * k.1, p.1; rep. from * to last st., k.1.
These 2 rows form the patt. Rep. them once more.

Divide for Fronts and Back
Next row: m.st.5, k.26 (28, 32), cast off 6, k.57 (61, 69) (including st. on needle), cast off 6, k.26 (28, 32), m.st.5.

** Cont. on the last 31 (33, 37) sts. for left front, dec. 1 st. at armhole edge on the next 5 (5, 7) right-side rows then cont. straight on 26 (28, 30) sts. until armhole measures 2 (2¼, 2½) in. ending at front edge.

Shape Neck

Next row: cast off 7 (8, 9) sts., work to end of row. Now dec. 1 st. at neck edge on the next 3 rows then on the next 2 right-side rows. Work a few rows straight on 14 (15, 16) sts. until armhole measures 3¼ (3½, 3¾) in. ending at armhole edge.

Shape Shoulder

Cast off 7 sts. at beg. of next row. Work 1 row then cast off rem. 7 (8, 9) sts. With wrong side facing rejoin yarn to the 57 (61, 69) sts. for back and dec. 1 st. both ends of the next 5 (5, 7) right-side rows. Cont. straight on 47 (51, 55) sts. until armholes measure 3¼ (3½, 3¾) in. ending on wrong side.
Cast off 7 sts. at beg. of next 2 rows and 7 (8, 9) on foll. 2 rows. Cast off rem. 19 (21, 23) sts.
Now mark left front edge with 2 pins as buttonhole guide, one 2 rows from neck edge and one midway between this pin and buttonhole already made. Rejoin yarn with wrong side facing to rem. 31 (33, 37) sts. and making buttonholes at pin positions, rep. from ** of left front.

Collar

With No. 9 needles cast on 13 (15, 15) sts. and work as follows:
1st to 6th rows: work in m.st.
7th row: m.st. 9 (11, 11), turn.
8th row: sl.1, m.st.8 (10, 10).
Rep. these 8 rows until shorter edge measures about 7½ (8, 8½) in., ending with 6 rows m.st. Cast off in m.st.

BONNET

With No. 11 needles cast on 69 (73, 77) sts. and work 7 rows m.st. Change to No. 9 needles.
Next row: m.st.5, p. to centre st., p. twice in centre st., p. to last 5 sts., m.st.5.
Next row: m.st.5, k. to last 5 sts., m.st.5.
Rep. rows 1 to 10 of coat patt. 3 times, then cont. in st.st. if necessary until work measures 4¼ (4½, 5) in. ending on wrong side and dec. 1 st. in centre on last row.
Work one row m.st. across 69 (73, 77) sts.

Shape Back

1st row: m.st.5 (7, 9), * sl.1, k.2 tog., p.s.s.o., m.st.11; rep. from * 4 times but end last rep. m.st.5 (7, 9).
Work 3 rows m.st.
5th row: m.st.4 (6, 8), * sl.1, k.2 tog., p.s.s.o., m.st.9; rep. from * 4 times, but end last rep. m.st.4 (6, 8).
Work 3 rows m.st.
Cont. dec. as before but on next and every wrong-side row until 19 (13, 17) sts. rem. ending with one row m.st.
For size 1 only. Next row: k.1, (p.2 tog., k.2 tog.) 4 times, p.2 tog.
For all sizes. Break yarn, thread end through rem. sts., draw up and fasten off.

LEGGINGS
Right Leg
With No. 11 needles cast on 71 (75, 83) sts. and work 9 rows k.1, p.1 rib. Change to No. 9 needles and work 1 more row in rib.**

Cont. in patt. with No. 9 needles as follows:

1st row: k.9, turn.

2nd and every wrong-side row: * k.1, p.1; rep. from * to last st., k.1.

3rd row: k.17, turn.

5th row: k.25, turn.

7th row: k.33, turn.

9th row: k.41, turn.

10th row: as 2nd row.

Cont. in sleeve patt. across all sts.

1st row: k.

2nd row: * k.1, p.1; rep. from * to last st., k.1.

These 2 rows form the patt. Rep. them twice more. *** Cont. in patt. inc. 1 st. at longer side on next and every foll. 6th row, until there are 79 (83, 91) sts. Cont. straight until shorter edge measures 7 (7½, 8) in., ending on wrong side.

Shape Leg
**** Cast off 2 sts. at beg. of next 2 rows, dec. 1 st. at both ends of the next and every right-side row until 49 (55, 61) sts. rem. then at both ends of every foll. 4th row until 35 (39, 45) sts. rem. Cont. straight until work measures 7 (7½, 8½) in. from ****
(measured up centre of work) ending on wrong side. Change to No. 11 needles and work 9 rows k.1, p.1 rib, thus ending on right side.

Change to No. 9 needles. *****

Shape Foot
Next row: rib 15 (17, 21), turn, leaving 20 (22, 24) sts. unworked.

Next row: k.11 (11, 13), turn.

Cont. in patt. on these sts. as follows:

1st row: (k.1, p.1) 5 (5, 6) times, k.1.

2nd row: k.

Rep. these 2 rows 8 (9, 10) times more then first row again. Break yarn, rejoin to inner edge of the 20 (22, 24) sts. and rib to end.

Next row: k.20 (22, 24), pick up and k.12 (14, 16) sts. up side of flap and k.11 (11, 13) sts. of flap.

Now using the spare No. 9 needle pick up and k.12 (14, 16) sts. down side of flap and k. rem. 4 (6, 8) sts.

Working all 59 (67, 77) sts. on to one needle again in the first row, work 7 (9, 11) rows in m.st. Cont. as follows, keeping m.st. correct by working k.2 tog. or p.2 tog. as required.

1st row (right side): m.st.4 (6, 8), take 2 tog. twice, m. st. 20 (24, 28), take 2 tog. twice, m.st. 7 (7, 9), take 2 tog. twice, m.st. 16 (18, 20).

2nd and every wrong-side row: m.st. to end.

3rd row: m.st.3 (5, 7), take 2 tog. twice, m.st. 18 (22, 26), take 2 tog. twice, m.st. 5 (5, 7), take 2 tog. twice, m.st. 15 (17, 19).

5th row: m.st.2 (4, 6), take 2 tog. twice, m.st.16 (20, 24),

take 2 tog. twice, m.st.3 (3, 5) take 2 tog. twice, m.st.14 (16, 18).
7th row: m.st.1 (3, 5), take 2 tog. twice, m.st.14 (18, 22), take 2 tog twice, m.st.1 (1, 3), take 2 tog. twice, m.st.13 (15, 17).
8th row: m.st. to end.
Cast off rem. sts.

Left Leg
Work as right leg until ** then k.1 row.

Shape Back
1st row: (k.1, p.1) 4 times, k.1, turn.
2nd and every right-side row: k. to end.
3rd row: (k.1, p.1) 8 times, k.1, turn.
Cont. thus working 8 more sts. into patt. on every wrong-side row until the 9th row: 41 sts. worked in patt.
10th row: k. to end.
Now beg. with a 2nd row work 5 rows in patt. then cont. as for right leg from *** to *****

Shape Foot
Next row: rib 31 (33, 37), turn, leaving 4 (6, 8) sts. unworked.
Next row: k.11 (11, 13), turn.
Work 19 (21, 23) rows in patt. on these sts. as for right foot, then break yarn, rejoin to the inner edge of the 4 (6, 8) sts. and rib to end.
Next row: k.4 (6, 8), pick up and k.12 (14, 16) sts. up side of flap, k.11 (11, 13) sts. of flap then using spare No. 9 needle pick up and k.12 (14, 16) sts. down other side and k. rem. 20 (22, 24) sts.
Complete to match right foot reversing the shaping rows by reading them backwards.

SHAWL
With No. 7 needles cast on 215 sts. and work 7 rows m.st. Cont. in patt. with m.st. borders.
1st and every wrong-side row: m.st.5, p. to last 5 sts., m.st. 5.
2nd row: m.st.5, * k.1, k.2 tog., y.f., k.1, y.f., k.2 tog. t.b.l.; rep. from * to last 6 sts., k.1, m.st.5.
4th row: m.st.5, k.2 tog., * y.f., k 3, y.f., k.3 tog.; rep. from * to last 10 sts., y.f., k.3, y.f., k.2 tog., m.st.5.
6th row: m.st.5, * k.1, y.f., k.2 tog. t.b.l., k.1, k.2 tog., y.f.; rep. from * to last 6 sts., k.1, m.st.5.
8th row: m.st.5, * k.2, y.f., k.3 tog., y.f., k.1; rep. from * to last 6 sts., k.1, m.st. 5.
Rep. these 8 rows until work is approximately 1 inch short of a square, ending with a first patt. row.
Work 7 rows m.st. Cast off in m.st. taking care to match tension of cast-on edge.

TO COMPLETE
Pin out and press very lightly on wrong side with a dry cloth and cool iron.

Coat
Join shoulders. Join sleeve seams and set in sleeves. Tuck about 3 sts. at shorter side of collar inside neck edge and pin in

position. Sew neck edge to wrong side of collar then slipstitch edge of collar in position inside neck. Sew on buttons.

Leggings

Join front and back seams then leg seams. Now join underfoot seams from centre of toe decs. to centre of heel decs. so that leg seam comes towards inside of foot. Thread 4 rows of shirring elastic through wrong side of waist ribbing.

Bonnet

Join back seam as far as beg. of m.st. Sew on ribbons. Press all seams with a dry cloth and cool iron.

Lace-trimmed jacket

...ld Courtier Bri-nylon 3-ply. One pair ...(USA size 3). Twelve small buttons.

TENSION

7 sts. to one inch.

ABBREVIATIONS

See page 11.

TO MAKE

The jacket is worked in one piece to armholes to avoid seams. Cast on 187 sts. and work as follows:
1st row: k.1, * p.1, k.1; rep. from * to end.

Rep. this row once more. These 2 rows form moss st. patt. Cont. in patt.:

1st row: m.st.27, k.1, * y.fwd., sl.1, k.1, p.s.s.o., k.1, k.2 tog., y.fwd., k.1; rep. from * to last 27 sts., m.st. to end.

2nd row: m.st.27, p. to last 27 sts., m.st. to end.

3rd row: m.st.27, k.1, * k.1, y.fwd., sl.1, k.2 tog., p.s.s.o., y.fwd., k.2; rep. from * to last 27 sts., m.st. to end.

4th row: as 2nd row.

These 4 rows complete the patt. Keeping 27 sts. each end in m.st., cont. in patt. on rem. sts. making buttonholes in the 7th and every following 12th row thus: from front edge, m.st.3, y.fwd., take 2 tog., m.st.17, take 2 tog., y.fwd., m.st.3, patt. to last 27 sts., m.st. to end.

Cont. until work measures 4 in., ending with a wrong-side row.

Divide for Armholes

Next row: m.st.27, patt. 23 sts., cast off 8 sts., patt. 71 sts. including st. already on needle, cast off 8 sts., patt. 23 sts. including st. already on needle, m.st.27.

Cont. on the last set of sts. only: still keeping the 27 sts. in m.st. cont. in patt. on rem. sts. dec. 1 st. at armhole edge on the next 8 rows. Cont. without shaping until front measures $6\frac{1}{2}$ in. from lower edge, ending with a right-side row.

Shape Neck

Cast off 19 sts. at beg. of next row, then dec. 1 st. at neck edge on the next 5 rows. Work one row.

Shape Shoulders

Cast off 9 sts. at beg. of next row, work one row, then cast off rem. sts. Return to 71 sts. left for the back, rejoin yarn and cont. in patt., dec. 1 st. each end of the next 8 rows. Cont. without shaping until work measures same as front to shoulder ending with a wrong-side row.

Cast off 9 sts. at beg. of next 4 rows, cast off the rem. sts. Return to sts. for right front, rejoin yarn and cont. to correspond with other front, reversing all shapings and making buttonholes as before.

SLEEVES (make 2 alike)

Cast on 37 sts. and work 2 rows in m.st. as for lower edge of coat. Work one complete patt. as for coat omitting the m.st. borders, then work 2 rows in m.st. Cont. in patt. inc. 1 st. each end of next and every following 6th row until there are 41 sts. on needle, then 1 st. each end of every following 4th row until there are 51 sts. on needle. Cont. without shaping until sleeve measures 5 in., ending with a wrong-side row.

Shape Top

Cast off 4 sts. at beg. of next 2 rows. Dec. 1 st. each end of the next 8 rows.
Cast off the rem. sts.

COLLAR

Cast on 77 sts. and work 2 rows in m.st. then keeping 2 sts. each end in m.st. cont. in patt. on rem. sts. until 3 patts. have been completed. Cast off.

TO COMPLETE

Press gently with a cool iron over a dry cloth. Join shoulder seams, join sleeve seams and set in sleeves. Sew cast-off edge of collar to neck edge so that collar edges meet when the coat is fastened. Cut the lace into five lengths, one for each sleeve edge, one for each front and one for the collar, allowing for the lace to be gathered. Stitch to sleeves, front and collar edge neatly. Sew on buttons to correspond with buttonholes.

Motif-patterned dress

MATERIALS

3 balls (25 gr. each) Wendy 4-ply in main colour, and 2 balls in contrasting colour. One pair No. 10 knitting needles (USA size 3). One crochet hook International Standard Size 3·00. 10 pearl buttons and 2 small buttons for back opening.

MEASUREMENTS

To fit chest size 20 (22) in.; length $13\frac{1}{2}$ ($14\frac{1}{2}$) in.

TENSION

$14\frac{1}{2}$ sts. to 2 in.

ABBREVIATIONS

See page 11; m.1, make a st. by picking up strand between last and next st. and knit into back of it; M., main colour; C., contrasting colour.

SKIRT BACK AND FRONT (make both alike)

Begin at top edge. With M. cast on 66 (69) sts. Work 4 rows in st.st. increasing 1 st. at both ends of every row, then cast on 4 sts. at beg. of next 2 rows: 82 (85) sts.
Place a marker at end of last row.

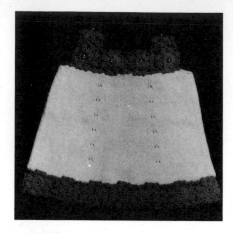

Work 4 rows in st.st.

1st inc. row: k.27 (28), m.1, k.1, m.1, k.26 (27), m.1, k.1, m.1, k.27 (28).

Beg. with p. work 11 rows in st.st.

2nd inc. row- k.28 (29), * m.1, k.1, m.1, k.28 (29); rep. from * once more. Work 11 rows in st.st.

3rd inc. row: k.29 (30), m.1, k.1, m.1, k.30 (31), m.1, k.1, m.1, k.29 (30).

Work 11 rows in st.st.

4th inc. row: k.30 (31), m.1, k.1, m.1, k.32 (33), m.1, k.1, m.1, k.30 (31).

Work 11 rows in st.st.

5th inc. row: k.31 (32), m.1, k.1, m.1, k.34 (35), m.1, k.1, m.1, k.31 (32).

Work 11 rows in st.st.

For 2nd size only. 6th inc. row: k.33, m.1, k.1, m.1, k.37, m.1, k.1, m.1, k.33.

All sizes: 102 (109) sts.

Continue straight until work measures 8 (9) in. from marker. Cast off.

LOWER MOTIF BORDER
First Motif

With C. and crochet hook, make 5 ch. and join into ring.

1st round: 3 ch., (1 h.tr. into ring, 1 ch.) 7 times, s.s. into top of 2nd of 3 ch:

2nd round: s.s. into next sp., 4 ch., 2 d.tr. into same sp. leaving the last loop of each d.tr. on hook, yarn over hook and draw through all 3 loops on hook, 3 ch., (3 d.tr. into next sp. leaving the last loop of each d.tr. on hook, yarn over hook and draw through all 4 loops on hook, 3 ch.) to end, s.s. to top of first gr.

3rd round: (6 ch., 1 d.c. into 4th ch. from hook to form picot, 2 ch., 1 d.c. into next gr., 3 ch., 1 d.c. into same gr., 4 ch., 1 d.c. into next gr., 3 ch., 1 d.c. into same gr.) 4 times, ending last rep. with 1 d.c. into same st. as 6 ch. Fasten off.

Second Motif

Work as for first motif until 2nd round has been completed.

3rd round: 4 ch., 1 d.c. into a corner loop of first motif, 2 ch., 1 d.c. into 4th ch. from hook, 2 ch., 1 d.c. in next gr. of second motif, 3 ch., 1 d.c. in same gr., 2 ch., 1 d.c. in next 4 ch. loop of first motif, 2 ch., 1 d.c. in next gr. of second motif, 3 ch., 1 d.c. in same gr., 4 ch. 1 d.c. in next corner of first motif, 2 ch., 1 d.c. in 4th ch. from hook, 2 ch., 1 d.c. in next gr. of second motif, 3 ch., 1 d.c. in same gr., 4 ch., 1 d.c. in next gr. of second motif, 3 ch., 1 d.c. into same gr., rep. between brackets of 3rd round of first motif twice ending last rep. with 1 d.c. into same st. as 4 ch. Fasten off.

Make a row of 13 (14) motifs, joining as before and joining last motif to first to form a round.

YOKE

Make and join 10 motifs as shown on chart.

TO COMPLETE

Press. Join side seams of skirt. Using crochet hook and M.,

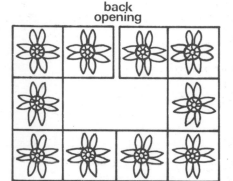

back opening

FRONT YOKE

Matching skating dresses for mother and daughter (instructions start on page 116).

Top picture: four-piece layette for baby (see page 80).
Above: two-colour lacy-patterned dress (see opposite).

work a row of d.c. along each armhole edge. With C. work a
row of d.c. along left back opening edge of yoke, then work a
row of d.c. along right back opening edge, making two ch. loops
for buttonholes.

Place opening of yoke at centre back and sew lower edge of
yoke to top of skirt. Sew longer border to bottom of skirt.
Press seams. Sew a pearl button to centre of each motif of yoke.
Sew 2 buttons to left back opening edge of yoke to correspond
with loops.

Lacy-patterned dress

illustrated in colour opposite

MATERIALS
2 (2) balls (25 gr. each) Mahony's Baby Berella in white (or
main colour wished) and 3 (4) balls in a contrasting colour. One
pair each Nos. 9 and 11 knitting needles (USA sizes 5 and 2). A
fine crochet hook. Six small buttons.

MEASUREMENTS
To fit chest size 19–20 (21–22) in.; length $15\frac{1}{2}$ ($16\frac{1}{2}$) in.

TENSION
7 sts. and 9 rows to 1 in. over st.st. on No. 9 needles.

ABBREVIATIONS
See page 11; k.f.b., k. into front and back of next st.; W., white;
C., contrast.

FRONT AND BACK (make both alike)
With a No. 9 needle and W. cast on 111 (119) sts. Change to
No. 11 needles and work in stripe patt. as follows:
1st row: with W., k.1, * k.f.b., k.1; rep. from * to end of row.

2nd row: with W., k.1, * k.2 tog., k.1; rep. from * to end of row.
3rd row: with C., k.
4th row: with C., p.

These 4 rows form the patt. Rep. them 11 (12) times more then work first and 2nd rows again. Break W., change to No. 9 needles and C. and work 8 rows in st.st.

Next row: k.2, sl.1, k.1, p.s.s.o., k. to last 4 sts., k.2 tog., k.2. Work 5 rows straight. Cont. dec. thus on next and every foll. 6th row until 93 (101) sts. rem. Cont. straight until work measures 11½ (12¼) in. ending with a p. row.

Shape Armholes

Cast off 5 sts. at beg. of next 2 rows, dec. 1 st. both ends of next 3 rows then both ends of next 2 (3) k. rows.

Work 2 rows straight on 73 (79) sts.

Next row: p.1 (4), (p.2 tog., p.1) 23 times, p.2 tog., p.1 (4). Cast off rem. 49 (55) sts. firmly.

YOKE (make 2 pieces alike)

With a No. 9 needle and W. cast on 87 (101) sts. Change to No. 11 needles and work stripe patt. as for lower edge but dec. for corners on 3rd and 4th rows of each rep. as follows:

1st and 2nd rows: with W. work in patt.
3rd row: with C. k.17 (21), k.2 tog. twice, k.45 (51), k.2 tog. twice, k.17 (21).
4th row: with C. p.16 (20), p.2 tog. twice, p.43 (49), p.2 tog. twice, p.16 (20).
5th and 6th rows: with W., work in patt.
7th row: with C. k.15 (19), k.2 tog. twice, k.41 (47), k.2 tog. twice, k.15 (19).
8th row: with C. p.14 (18), p.2 tog. twice, p.39 (45), p.2 tog. twice, p.14 (18).

Cont. dec. thus until 39 (45) sts. rem. after 24 (28) rows.

Next 2 rows: with W., work in patt.

Cast off, not too tightly, working k.2 tog. twice at each corner as before.

POCKETS (make 2 alike)

With a No. 9 needle cast on 23 (25) sts. Change to No. 11 needles and work stripe patt. for about 3 (3¼) in. ending with a 2nd row. Cast off with a No. 9 needle.

TO COMPLETE

Press on wrong side with a dry cloth and warm iron. Sew on pockets to dress front, about 3 (3½) in. apart and 1½ in. above border. Join side seams. Work a row of double crochet in C. round armhole edges. Topstitch yoke pieces to cast-off edges of front and back. Now with right side of back facing, No. 11 needles and W., pick up and k. 15 (17) sts. along shoulder edge (1 st. for each ridge and one between with one extra at cast-on and cast-off corners). Work 2 rows g.st. ** Cast off with wrong side facing. Work front shoulders in a similar way as far as **.

Next row: k.2, y.f., k.2 tog., k.3 (4), y.f., k.2 tog., k.3 (4), y.f., k.2 tog., k.1.

K. 3 more rows g.st.

Cast off.

Sew on buttons. Press seams with a cool iron.

MATERIALS

4 (5, 5) balls (25 gr. each) Wendy Courtelle Crêpe 4-ply in green, and 1 ball in white. One pair each Nos. 9 and 12 knitting needles (USA sizes 5 and 1). One set of four No. 12 needles (USA size 1). Waist length of elastic.

MEASUREMENTS

To fit chest size 20 (22, 24) in.; length of pullover $11\frac{1}{2}$ (13, $14\frac{1}{2}$) in.; length of shorts from front waist to crutch 6 ($6\frac{1}{2}$, 7) in.

TENSION

$6\frac{1}{2}$ sts. and 8 rows to 1 in. on No. 9 needles over patt.

ABBREVIATIONS

See page 11; G., green; W., white.

PULLOVER FRONT

With G. and No. 12 needles cast on 72 (78, 84) sts. and work 12 rows in k.1, p.1 rib, inc. 1 st. at end of final row. Change to No. 9 needles and work in patt. as follows:
1st row: p.1, * k.5, p.1; rep. from * to end.
2nd row: k.1, * p.5, k.1; rep. from * to end.
Rep. these last 2 rows until work measures 8 (9, 10) in. from cast-on edge, ending after a wrong-side row. (*Note.* If necessary, adjust length here.)

Shape Armholes and Front Neck

Cont. in patt. as follows:
1st row: cast off 3, patt. 31 (34, 37), k.2 tog., turn: 33 (36, 39) sts. on needle. Dec. 1 st. at neck edge every right-side row, complete armhole shaping by dec. 1 st. at side edge on next 5 (6, 7) rows and on foll. 2 alt. rows. Then keep side edge straight and cont. to dec. as before at neck edge until 15 (16, 17) sts. rem.
Work straight to complete 3 ($3\frac{1}{2}$, 4) in. from beg. of armhole, ending at side edge.

Shape Shoulder

Cast off 5 sts. at beg. of next and foll. alt. row, and 5 (6, 7) sts. at beg. of next alt. row.
Returning to sts. on needle, join in G. work in patt. to end of row.
Next row: cast off 3, patt. until 2 sts. rem., p.2 tog.
Working dec. at neck edge every wrong-side row, cont. and complete this shoulder to match first, reversing shapings.

PULLOVER BACK

Work as front to beg. of armholes.

Shape Armholes

Cont. in patt., cast off 3 sts. at beg. of next 2 rows; dec. 1 st. at both ends of next 5 (6, 7) rows and of foll. 2 alt. rows. Work straight on rem. 53 (57, 61) sts. until back matches front to beg. of shoulders.

Shape Shoulders

Cast off 5 sts. at beg. of next 4 rows and 5 (6, 7) sts. at beg. of foll. 2 rows. Leave rem. 23 (25, 27) sts. on a stitch holder.

TO COMPLETE PULLOVER
Sew shoulder seams.

Neck Ribbing
With right side facing and using the set of four No. 12 needles, start at left front shoulder and pick up 28 (32, 36) sts. along each side of neck, 1 st. from centre of V, and sts. from holder at back.

Work in rounds as follows:

1st round: with G., (k.1, p.1) 13 (15, 17) times, p.2 tog., k.1, p.2 tog., * p.1, k.1; rep. from * to end.

2nd round: with W., k.

3rd round: with W., rib 25 (29, 33), p.2 tog., k.1, p.2 tog., rib to end.

4th round: with G., k.

5th round: with G., rib 24 (28, 32), p.2 tog., k.1, p.2 tog., rib to end.

Work 2 rounds in W. in a similar way, then 2 rounds in G.

Cast off in rib in G.

Armbands (make both alike)
With right side facing and using a pair of No. 12 needles pick up 56 (64, 72) sts. round each armhole.

With G., work one row in k.1, p.1 rib.

With W., k. 1 row, rib 1 row.

With G., k.1 row, rib 1 row. Cast off in rib.

Sew side seams, joining sides of armbands.

SHORTS FRONT
Right Leg
With G. and No. 12 needles cast on 37 (40, 43) sts. and k. 6 rows.

Change to No. 9 needles.

1st row: p.1, * k.5, p.1; rep. from * until 6 (3, 6) sts. rem., k. to end.

2nd row: p.6 (3, 6), k.1, * p.5, k.1; rep. from * to end.

Rep. these last 2 rows once more.

Leave sts. on a stitch holder.

Left Leg
Cast on and k. 6 rows as for right leg. Change to No. 9 needles.

1st row: k.6 (3, 6), p.1, * k.5, p.1; rep. from * to end. Work 3 more rows as before.

To Join Legs and Work Crutch
Work across sts. for left leg as follows: k.6 (3, 6), p.1, * k.5, p.1; rep. from * to end; cast on 10 sts.; patt. sts. for right leg.

2nd row: patt. 36 (39, 42), k.2 tog., p.8, k.2 tog., patt 36 (39, 42).

3rd row: patt. 36 (39, 42), p.1, k.8, p.1, patt. 36 (39, 42).

4th row: patt. 36 (39, 42), k.2 tog., p.6, k.2 tog., patt. 36 (39, 42).

Cont. to dec. by 2 sts. in a similar way every wrong-side row until you have 74 (80, 86) sts., ending after a right-side row.

Next row: patt. 36 (39, 42), k.2 tog., patt 36 (39, 42).

Now cont. straight in patt. on rem. 73 (79, 85) sts. until work measures 4 (4½, 5) in. from joining of legs, ending after a wrong-

side row. (*Note*. If necessary, adjust length here.)
Dec. 1 st. at both ends of first row, patt. another 8 rows.

Waistband
Change to No. 12 needles and work 1 in. in k.1, p.1 rib.
Cast off in rib.

SHORTS BACK
Work as front until back is one row shorter than front to beg. of
waistband: 71 (77, 83) sts.
Next 2 rows: patt. until 11 (14, 11) sts. rem., turn.
Next 2 rows: patt. until 17 (20, 17) sts. rem., turn.
Next 2 rows: patt. until 23 (26, 23) sts. rem., turn. Patt. to
end of row.
Change to No. 12 needles and work waistband to match front.

TO COMPLETE SHORTS
Do not press. Sew side seams and inner leg seams. If any
pressing is necessary, use a very cool iron and a dry cloth.
Make a crochet casing inside waistband and thread with elastic.

Military-style coat dress

MATERIALS
8 (9, 10) oz. Hayfield Nucrêpe. One pair each Nos. 8 and 10
knitting needles (USA sizes 6 and 3). 10 (11, 11) small brass
buttons. One press stud.

MEASUREMENTS
To fit chest size 18 (20, 22) in.; length 16½ (18½, 20½) in.;
sleeve seam 9 (10, 11) in.

TENSION

$5\frac{1}{2}$ sts. and $7\frac{1}{2}$ rows to 1 in. over st.st. with No. 8 needles.

ABBREVIATIONS

See page 11.

BACK

With No. 8 needles cast on 83 (89, 95) sts. and work 6 (7, 8) rows in moss st. (see page 25).
Change to st.st., dec. 1 st. at each end of the row 1 in. from border then at 1-in. intervals until 65 (67, 69) sts. remain.
Cont. straight until work measures $11\frac{1}{2}$ ($13\frac{1}{4}$, 15) in. ending with a wrong-side row.

Shape Armholes

Cast off 5 sts. at beg. of next 2 rows, then dec. 1 st. at each end of every k. row until 51 (53, 55) sts. remain.
Cont. straight until work measures $16\frac{1}{2}$ ($18\frac{1}{2}$, $20\frac{1}{2}$) in. ending with a wrong-side row.

Shape Shoulders

Cast off 15 (16, 16) sts. at beg. of next 2 rows. Cast off rem. sts.

RIGHT FRONT

With No. 8 needles cast on 39 (42, 46) sts. and work 6 (7, 8) rows in moss st.
Change to st.st., dec. 1 st. at the end of a k. row 1 in. from border then at same edge at 1-in. intervals until 30 (31, 33) sts. remain.
Cont. straight until work measures $11\frac{1}{2}$ ($13\frac{1}{4}$, 15) in., ending with a k. row.

Shape Armholes

Cast off 5 sts. at beg. of next row, then dec. 1 st. at beg. of every p. row until 23 (24, 26) sts. remain.
Cont. straight until work measures $15\frac{1}{2}$ ($17\frac{1}{4}$, $19\frac{1}{4}$) in. ending with a p. row.

Shape Neck

Cast off 4 sts. at beg. of next row, then dec. 1 st. at neck edge on every row until 15 (16, 16) sts. remain. Cont. straight until work measures $16\frac{1}{2}$ ($18\frac{1}{2}$, $20\frac{1}{2}$) in.
Cast off.

LEFT FRONT

Work as Right Front, reversing all shapings by reading k. for p. and p. for k.

SLEEVES (make 2 alike)

With No. 10 needles cast on 36 (38, 40) sts. and work 5 rows in st.st. beg. with a k. row.
6th row (hem ridge): k.
Work another 6 rows in st.st. beg. with a k. row.
Change to No. 8 needles, and cont. in st.st., inc. 1 st. at each end of next and every foll. 8th row until there are 50 (52, 54) sts.
Work straight until sleeve measures 9 (10, 11) in. from hem ridge, ending with a p. row.

Shape Top

Cast off 5 sts. at beg. of next 2 rows, then dec. 1 st. at beg. of every row until 28 (30, 32) sts. remain.
Work straight until sleeve measures 11 (12½, 13¾) in. from hem ridge, then dec. 1 st. at beg. of every row until 15 (16, 16) sts. remain. Cast off.

LEFT FRONT BORDER

With No. 10 needles cast on 9 sts. and work in moss st. until strip is long enough to reach from cast-on edge of Left Front to beg. of neck shaping. Leave sts. on safety pin.

RIGHT FRONT BORDER

With No. 10 needles cast on 9 sts. and work in moss st. Work ½ in. straight, ending with a wrong-side row.
Next (buttonhole) row: patt. 4, m.1, work 2 tog., patt. to end. Now cont. in moss st. making buttonholes at 3⅛ (2⅞, 3¼) in. intervals until 5 (6, 6) have been worked in all. Cont. straight until strip is same length as Left Front Border, then leave sts. on safety pin.

SHOULDER TABS (make 2 alike)

With No. 10 needles cast on 6 sts. and work in moss st. Work 1¼ (2, 2¼) in. then cast off 1 st. at beg. of every row until all sts. have been worked off. Fasten off.

SLEEVE TABS (make 2 alike)

Work as Shoulder Tabs, but make strips 2½ (2¾, 3) in. long before beg. to dec.

TO COMPLETE

Join shoulder seams.

Neckband

With right side facing and No. 10 needles, patt. across 9 sts. of right front border, then pick up and k.11 (12, 13) sts. round front neck, pick up and k.21 (23, 23) sts. round back neck, pick up and k.11 (12, 13) sts. down left front neck and patt. across 9 sts. of left front border: 61 (65, 67) sts. Work in moss st. on these sts. for 1 in., working a final buttonhole at the correct interval from the last.
Cast off loosely.

To Make Up

Join borders to fronts and join side seams. Set in sleeves. Turn under hems of sleeves and catch down lightly. Sew on sleeve tabs (see photograph on page 95). Join sleeve seams. Sew on shoulder tabs (see photograph). Sew buttons to left front border, shoulder and sleeve tabs. Sew press stud to top of neck. Press.

Dress with roll collar

MATERIALS
9 (10, 11) balls (25 gr. each) Wendy Courtelle Crêpe 4-ply. One pair each Nos. 10 and 12 knitting needles (USA sizes 3 and 1).

MEASUREMENTS
To fit chest size 22 (24, 26) in.; length 15 (17, 20) in.; sleeve seam 8 (10, 11½) in.

TENSION
7½ sts. and 10 rows to 1 in. over bodice patt. on No. 10 needles.

ABBREVIATIONS
See page 11.

FRONT
With No. 10 needles cast on 133 (145, 159) sts.
1st row (right side): p.2 (4, 3), * k.1, p.7; rep. from * until 3 (5, 4) sts. rem., k.1, p.2 (4, 3).
2nd row: k.2 (4, 3), * y.fwd., sl.1 purlwise, y.b., k.7; rep. from * until 3 (5, 4) sts. rem., y.fwd., sl.1 purlwise, y.b., k.2 (4, 3).
Rep. these 2 rows until work measures 4 (5, 6½) in. from cast-on edge, ending after a right-side row.
Next row: k.2 (4, 3), * y.fwd., sl.1 purlwise, y.b., k.2 tog., k.3, k.2 tog.; rep. from * until 3 (5, 4) sts. rem., y.fwd., sl.1 purlwise, y.b., k.2 (4, 3): 101 (111, 121) sts.
This completes skirt section.

Bodice
Next row: k.
Next row: k.1, * p.1, k.1; rep. from * to end.
These last 2 rows form bodice patt. Cont. in patt., keeping patt. correct and dec. 1 st. at both ends of 3rd row and of every foll. 8th row until you have 89 (97, 105) sts.
Work straight until work measures 10½ (12, 14½) in. from cast-on edge, ending after a wrong-side row. (If necessary, adjust length here.)

Shape Armhole and Neck
Next row: cast off 3, patt. 31 (34, 37); turn: 32 (35, 38) sts. on needle.
Cont. in patt., dec. 1 st. at neck edge on next and every foll. 6th row. At the same time complete armhole shaping by dec. 1 st. at side edge on next 6 (7, 8) rows and on foll. 2 alt. rows. Then keep side edge straight and cont. to dec. as before at neck edge until 18 (20, 22) sts. rem. Work straight to complete 4 (4½, 5) in. from beg. of armhole, ending at side edge.

Shape Shoulder
Cast off 6 (6, 7) sts. at beg. of next and foll. alt. row, and 6 (8, 8) sts. at beg. of next alt. row. Returning to sts. still on needle, slip first 19 (21, 23) sts. on to a spare needle and complete second shoulder to match first, reversing shapings.

BACK
Work as for Front to beg. of armholes.

Shape Armholes
Cast off 3 sts. at beg. of next 2 rows, dec. 1 st. at both ends of next 6 (7, 8) rows and of foll. 2 alt. rows. Work straight in patt. on rem. 67 (73, 79) sts. until Back matches Front to beg. of shoulders.

Shape Shoulders
Cast off 6 (6, 7) sts. at beg of next 4 rows and 6 (8, 8) sts. at beg. of foll. 2 rows.
Cast off firmly the rem. 31 (33, 35) sts.

SLEEVES (make 2 alike)
With No. 12 needles cast on 40 (44, 48) sts. and work 2 in. in k.1, p.1 rib. inc. 1 st. at end of final row. Change to No. 10 needles and cont. in patt. as given for bodice, inc. 1 st. at both ends of 3rd and every foll. 5th row until you have 57 (65, 71) sts.
Work straight until sleeve measures 8½ (10, 11½) in. (or length required) from cast-on edge, ending after a wrong-side row. Cast off 3 sts. at beg. of next 2 rows, 1 st. at beg. of next 6 rows and 2 sts. at beg. of foll. 14 (16, 18) rows. Cast off.

TO COMPLETE
Do not press. Sew side and shoulder seams.
Set in sleeves and sew sleeve seams.

Roll Collar
With No. 10 needles pick up the 19 (21, 23) sts. from spare

needle so that the first row worked will be a right-side row. Work in k.1, p.1 rib, inc. 1 st. at end of 3rd and of every foll. 4th row until work will fit comfortably as far as shoulder seam, ending after an inc. row. Rib one row.

To Shape Collar
** **Next row:** rib 15 (16, 17); turn, rib to end. Rib 4 rows on all sts. Rep. from ** until collar will fit comfortably across back of neck as far as left shoulder seam, ending after the 2 short shaping rows. Then cont. in rib on all sts., dec. 1 st. at end of next and of every foll. 4th row until 19 (21, 23) sts. rem. Rib 2 rows. Cast off.

To Make Up
Catch the cast-off edge of collar in position behind first side. Sew collar in position. Press very lightly, dry, with iron set at its lowest point.

Three-colour dress

illustrated in colour on page 53

MATERIALS
4 (5, 5, 6) balls (25 gr. each) Wendy Courtelle Crêpe 4-ply in main shade and 1 (1, 2, 2) balls in each of 2 contrasting shades. One pair each Nos. 12 and 10 knitting needles (USA sizes 1 and 3).

MEASUREMENTS
To fit chest size 22 (24, 26, 28) in.; length 15 (17, 20, 23) in. (adjustable); length of sleeve seam 8½ (10, 11½, 13) in. (adjustable).

TENSION
7 sts. and 10 rows to 1 in. over st.st. with No. 10 needles.

ABBREVIATIONS
See page 11; sl.1 p., slip 1 purlwise; M., main shade; A., first contrasting shade; B., 2nd contrasting shade.

FRONT
With No. 12 needles and M. cast on 91 (99, 109, 117) sts. and work 7 rows in st.st. beg. with a k. row.
8th row (hemline): k.
Change to No. 10 needles.
Beg. with a k. row, cont. straight in st.st. until work measures 3½ (4½, 1½, 3) in. from hemline, ending with a p. row, and dec. 1 st. at each end of final row (if necessary, adjust length here). Now cont. in st.st. in foll. colour patt.
1st row: k.: 1 M., * 1 A., 1 M.; rep. from * to end.
2nd row: with A., p.
3rd row: with A., k.
4th row: with A. p.2 (2, 1, 1), * p. next st. winding yarn twice round needle, p. 3; rep. from * to last 3 (3, 2, 2) sts., p. next st. winding yarn twice round needle, p. 2 (2, 1, 1).
5th row: with B. k.2 (2, 1, 1), * keeping y.b. sl.1 p., k.3; rep. from * to last 3 (3, 2, 2) sts., keeping y.b. sl.1 p., k.2 (2, 1, 1).
6th row: with B. k.2 (2, 1, 1), * y.f., sl.1 p., y.b., k.3; rep. from * to last 3 (3, 2, 2) sts., y.f., sl.1 p., y.b., k.2 (2, 1, 1).

Rep. last 2 rows once.

With A. k. 1 row, p. 1 row, k. 1 row.

12th row: with A. p.3 (3, 2, 2), * p.1, p. next st. winding yarn twice round needle, p.2; rep. from * to last 2 (2, 1, 1) sts., p.2 (2, 1, 1).

13th row: with B. k.3 (3, 2, 2), * k.1, keeping y.b. sl.1 p., k.2; rep. from * to last 2 (2, 1, 1) sts., k.2 (2, 1, 1).

14th row: with B. k.3 (3, 2, 2), * k.1, y.f., sl.1 p., y.b., k.2; rep. from * to last 2 (2, 1, 1) sts., k.2 (2, 1, 1).

Rep. last 2 rows once.

With A., k. 1 row, p. 1 row, k. 1 row.

20th row: p.: with M. work 2 tog., * 1 M., 1 A.; rep. from * to last 3 sts., 1 M., with M. work 2 tog.

With M. and beg. with a k. row, work 22 (24, 28, 32) rows in st.st., dec. 1 st. at each end of final row: 85 (93, 103, 111) sts.

Work the 20-row colour patt. once more, dec. as before at each end of 20th row.

Beg. with a k. row, work 10 (12, 28, 32) rows with M. in st.st.

For sizes 26 and 28 only. Dec. 1 st. at each end of final row. Work the 20-row colour patt. again, dec. as before at each end of 20th row. Beg. with a k. row, work 14 (18) rows with M. in st.st.

For all sizes. 83 (91, 97, 105) sts.

Shape Armholes

Cont. with M. in st.st., cast off 4 sts. at beg. of next 2 rows. Dec. 1 st. at each end of next 5 (6, 7, 8) rows and of foll. 2 alt. rows. Where necessary p. 1 row to complete 12 (12, 14, 14) rows from beg. of armholes: 61 (67, 71, 77) sts.

Work first 3 rows of colour patt.

4th row: with A. p.2 (1, 1, 2), * p. next st. winding yarn twice round needle, p.3; rep. from * to last 3 (2, 2, 3) sts., p. next st. winding yarn twice round needle, p.2 (1, 1, 2).

Without dec. on 20th row, complete colour patt. on sts. now set.

Cont. with M. in st.st. ** Work 2 (2, 6, 12) rows straight.

Shape Neck

Next row: k.21 (23, 25, 27); turn.

Work another 5 (9, 9, 9) rows on these sts. dec. 1 st. at neck edge on next and foll. alt. rows: 18 (18, 20, 22) sts.

Shape Shoulder

For size 22 only. Dec. 1 st. at neck edge on next 2 wrong-side rows.

For all sizes. Cast off 5 (6, 6, 7) sts. at beg. of next and foll. alt. row, and 6 (6, 8, 8) sts. at beg. of next alt. row.

Return to sts. still on needle, slip first 19 (21, 21, 23) sts. on to a st. holder then complete 2nd side of neck to match first, reversing shapings.

BACK

Work as Front to **. Work straight until Back matches Front to beg. of shoulder shaping.

Shape Shoulders

Cast off 5 (6, 6, 7) sts. at beg. of next 4 rows and 6 (6, 8, 8) sts.

at beg. of foll. 2 rows. Leave rem. 29 (31, 31, 33) sts. on st. holder.

SLEEVES (make 2 alike)

With No. 12 needles and M. cast on 38 (40, 42, 44) sts. and work 2 in. in k.1, p.1 rib.

Change to No. 10 needles and, beg. with a k. row, cont. in M. in st.st., inc. 1 st. at each end of 3rd and of every foll. 5th row until there are 54 (58, 62, 66) sts.

Work straight until Sleeve measures $8\frac{1}{2}$ (10, $11\frac{1}{2}$, 13) in. (or required length) from cast-on edge, ending with a p. row.

Shape Top

Cast off 4 sts. at beg. of next 2 rows, 1 st. at beg. of next 6 rows and 2 sts. at beg. of foll. 10 (12, 14, 16) rows. Cast off.

TO COMPLETE

Sew right shoulder seam.

Polo Neck

With right side facing and No. 12 needles, beg. at left side of front and pick up 11 (13, 13, 15) sts. down side of neck, pick up sts. from holder, pick up 11 (13, 13, 15) sts. up other side of front neck, then sts. from back st. holder: 70 (78, 78, 86) sts. With M. work 1 in. in k.1, p.1 rib. Change to No. 10 needles and work a further $2\frac{1}{2}$ in. in rib. Cast off loosely in rib.

To Make Up

Do not press. Sew left shoulder seam, joining sides of neck ribbing as well. Sew side seams. Set in Sleeves and sew sleeve seams. Turn up hem and catch lightly on wrong side. Press very lightly on wrong side with iron at lowest setting.

Cotton jumper -in four sizes

illustrated in colour on page 35

MATERIALS

6 (7, 8, 9) balls (25 gr. each) Twilley's Lysbet. One pair each Nos. 12 and 14 knitting needles (USA sizes 1 and 0). One medium button.

MEASUREMENTS

To fit chest size 24 (26, 28, 30) in.; length 16 (17, 18, 19) in.

TENSION

8 sts. and 11 rows to 1 inch.

ABBREVIATIONS

See page 11.

BACK

** With No. 14 needles cast on 92 (100, 108, 116) sts. Work in k.2, p.2 rib for 2 in. Change to No. 12 needles and work as follows:

1st row: sl.1, k.6, * y.f., k.2 tog., k.2, p.1, k.3; rep. from * to last 5 sts., y.f., k.2 tog., k.3.

2nd row: sl.1, * p.7, k.1; rep. from * to last 3 sts., p.3.

3rd row: sl.1, k.4, * k.2 tog., y.f., k.1, y.f., sl.1, k.1, p.s.s.o., k.1, p.1, k.1; rep. from * to last 7 sts., k.2 tog., y.f., k.1, y.f., sl.1, k.1, p.s.s.o., k.2.

4th row: as 2nd row.

5th row: sl. 1, k.3, * k.2 tog., y.f., k.3, y.f., sl.1, k.1, p.s.s.o., p.1; rep. from * to end.

6th row: as 2nd row.

7th row: sl.1, k.6, * p.1, k.3, y.f., k.2 tog., k.2; rep. from * to last 5 sts., p.1, k.4.

8th row: sl.1, p.3, * k.1, p.7; rep. from * to end.

9th row: sl.1, k.3, * y.f., sl.1, k.1, p.s.s.o., k.1, p.1, k.1, k.2 tog., y.f., k.1; rep. from * to end.

10th row: as 8th row.

11th row: sl.1, k.4, * y.f., sl.1, k.1, p.s.s.o., p.1, k.2 tog., y.f., k.3; rep. from * to last 7 sts., y.f., sl.1, k.1, p.s.s.o., p.1, k.2 tog., y.f., k.2.

12th row: as 8th row.

These 12 rows form main patt. and are repeated to Yoke. Cont. straight until work measures 10½ (11, 11½, 12) in. ending with a 6th or 12th patt. row. **

Shape Armholes

Cast off 4 sts. at beg. of next 4 rows. then dec. 1 st. each end of next row and 3 (5, 5, 5) foll. alt. rows. Cont. on 68 (72, 80, 88) sts. until armhole measures 3½ (3¾, 4, 4¼) in. increasing 1 st. at end of last row and ending with a 6th or 12th patt. row.

Yoke

Next row: k.1, * p.1, k.1; rep. from * to end.
Rep. last row moss stitch from now on. Cont. until armholes measure 5 (5½, 6, 6½) in.

Shape Shoulders

Cast off 6 sts. at beg. of next 4 (4, 6, 6) rows and 6 (7, 3, 6) sts. at beg. of 2 foll. rows. Cast off rem. 33 (35, 39, 41) sts. for neck loosely.

FRONT

With No. 14 needles cast on 100 (108, 116, 124) sts. Work as back from ** to ** but with 8 sts. more throughout.

Shape Armholes

Cast off 4 sts. at beg. of next 4 rows, then dec. 1 st. at each end of next row and 7 (9, 9, 9) foll. alt. rows. Cont. on 68 (72, 80, 88) sts. until armholes measure 2 (2½, 3, 3½) in. ending with a 6th or 12th patt. row and increasing 1 st. at end of last row.

Yoke

Next row: k.1, * p.1, k.1; rep. from * to end.
Cont. in m.st. and work 1 row.
3rd row: patt. 30 (32, 36, 40) sts., turn, leave rem. sts. on a holder and finish this side first.
Next row: cast on 9 sts., patt. to end.
*** Cont. straight until armhole measures 3½ (4, 4½, 5) in. ending at neck edge.

Shape Neck

Cast off 12 sts. at beg. of next row, then dec. 1 st. at end of next row and cast off 2 sts. at beg. of foll. row. Rep. last 2 rows then dec. 1 st. at neck edge on next 1 (2, 4, 5) rows. Cont. on 20 (21, 23, 26) sts. until armhole measures same as back to beg. of shoulder, ending at armhole edge.

Shape Shoulder
Cast off 6 sts. at beg. of next row, and then cast off 6 sts. at beg. of 1 (1, 2, 2) foll. alt. rows.
Sizes 28 and 30 only. Work one row.
All sizes. Cast off rem. sts.
Mark position for button 4 rows below cast-off sts. for neck.

Right Side
Join yarn to inside edge of rem. sts. Work in m.st. to end. Work as for left side from *** to end, but working a buttonhole to correspond with marker, as follows:
1st buttonhole row: patt. 3, cast off 3, patt. to end.
2nd buttonhole row: patt. to last 3 sts., cast on 3 sts., patt. 3.

SLEEVES (make 2 alike)
With No. 14 needles cast on 76 (84, 92, 100) sts. Work in k.2, p.2 rib for 1 ($1\frac{1}{4}$, $1\frac{1}{2}$, $1\frac{3}{4}$) in.
P. 1 row.
Change to No. 12 needles and work 12 rows in main patt. decreasing 1 st. at end of last row.
Work in m.st. from now on, increasing 1 st. each end of 3rd row and 1 (1, 2, 2) foll. 4th rows, then on foll. alt. rows. Work 1 row on 83 (91, 101, 109) sts.

Shape Top
Cast off 4 sts. at beg. of next 4 rows and dec. 1 st. each end of 9 foll. rows, then on foll. alt. rows until 29 (31, 35, 37) sts. rem. Cast off.

COLLAR
With No. 12 needles cast on 33 (35, 39, 41) sts. loosely. Work in m.st. throughout. Work 2 rows.
Cast on 4 (5, 6, 7) sts. at beg. of next 2 rows and 6 sts. at beg. of 8 foll. rows. Work $1\frac{1}{2}$ in. straight. Cast off in m.st.

TO COMPLETE
Avoiding all ribbing, press all pieces on wrong side, under a damp cloth. Back-stitch shoulder seams. Sew cast-on edge of collar to neck, leaving 4 sts. at each front edge free. Work 1 row d.c. along each side of front opening and neck edge to collar. Turn in this edging and slip stitch. Catch down under-wrap. Sew side and sleeve seams and set in sleeves. Work buttonhole in buttonhole stitch. Sew on button. Press all seams and turnings.

MATERIALS

8 (9, 10) balls (50 gr. each) Mahony's Blarney Bainin (USA Blarneyspun) for version with neck border; 8 (9, 11) balls for version with roll collar. One pair each Nos. 7 and 9 knitting needles (USA sizes 7 and 5). Two cable needles. For version with roll collar only: one pair No. 10 knitting needles (USA size 3).

MEASUREMENTS

To fit chest size 24–25 (26–28, 29–30) in.; length 17 (19, 21) in.; sleeve seam 11 (13, 15) in.

TENSION

5 sts. to 1 inch over d.m.st.

ABBREVIATIONS

See page 11; d.m.st., double moss st.; c.n., cable needle; k.b.1 or p.b.1, knit or purl into back of next st.; cable 5, sl. next 2 sts. on c.n. and leave at front, sl. next st. on to 2nd c.n. and leave at back, k. next 2 sts. then p.1 from back c.n. and k.2 from front c.n.; C.3 R., (cable 3 to the right) sl. next st. on c.n. and leave at back, k.2 then p.1 from c.n.; C.3 L., (cable 3 to the left) sl. next 2 sts. on c.n. and leave at front, p.1 then k.2 from c.n.; 3 into 1, (k.1, p.1, k.1) all into next st.; tw.2f., sl. next st. on c.n. at front, p.1 then k.b.1 from c.n.; tw.2b., sl. next st. on c.n. at back, k.b.1 then p.1 from c.n.; inc. in loop, pick up thread between sts. and p. into the back of it.

THE PATTERNS

Panel One: Double moss stitch

Worked on 7 (9, 11) sts. (for sides of front and back).
1st row: (k.1, p.1) 3 (4, 5) times, k.1.
2nd row: (p.1, k.1) 3 (4, 5) times, p.1.
3rd row: as 2nd row.
4th row: as first row.
Rep. these 4 rows.

Panel Two: V-pattern

Worked on 17 sts.
1st row: p.6, cable 5, p.6.
2nd row: k.6, p.2, k.1, p.2, k.6.
3rd row: p.5, C.3 R., k.1, C.3 L., p.5.
4th row: k.5, p.2, k.1, p.1, k.1, p.2, k.5.
5th row: p.4, C.3 R., k.1, p.1, k.1, C.3 L., p.4.
6th row: k.4, p.2, (k.1, p.1) twice, k.1, p.2, k.4.
(Centre sts. of V will now be referred to as d.m.st.)
7th row: p.3, C.3 R., d.m.st.5, C.3 L., p.3.
8th row: k.3, p.2, d.m.st.7, p.2, k.3.
9th row: p.2, C.3 R., d.m.st.7, C.3 L., p.2.
10th row: k.2, p.2, d.m.st.9, p.2, k.2.
11th row: p.1, C.3 R., d.m.st.9, C.3 L., p.1.
12th row: k.1, p.2, d.m.st.11, p.2, k.1.
Rep. these 12 rows.

Panel Three: Long-ribbed cable

Worked on 8 sts.
1st row: k.b.1, p.1, k.b.1, p.2, k.b.1, p.1, k.b.1.

Children's Aran sweaters

illustrated in colour on page 107

2nd row: p.b.1, k.1, p.b.1, k.2, p.b.1, k.1, p.b.1.
3rd to 6th rows: rep. first and 2nd rows twice.
7th row: k.b.1, p.1, tw.2f., tw.2b., p.1, k.b.1.
8th row: p.b.1, k.2, p.b.2, k.2, p.b.1.
9th row: k.b.1, p.2, sl. next st. on c.n. at front, k.b.1 then k.b.1 from c.n., p.2, k.b.1.
10th row: as 8th row.
11th row: k.b.1, p.1, tw.2b., tw.2f., p.1, k.b.1.
12th row: as 2nd row.
Rep. these 12 rows.

Panel Four: Bramble stitch

Worked on 11 (15, 19) sts.
1st row: p.11.
2nd row: k.1, (3 into 1, p.3 tog.) 2 (3, 4) times, 3 into 1, k.1.
3rd row: p. 13.
4th row: k.1, (p.3 tog., 3 into 1) 2 (3, 4) times, p.3 tog., k.1.
Rep. these 4 rows, remembering when counting sts. to allow for the 2 extra sts. made in 2nd row and lost in 4th row.

BACK

With No. 9 needles cast on 67 (75, 83) sts. and work in twisted rib as follows:
1st row: (p.1, k.b.1) to last st., p.1.
2nd row: k.1, (p.b.1, k.1) to end of row.
Rep. these 2 rows 3 (5, 6) times more then rep. first row again.
Change to No. 7 needles.
Inc. row: p.5 (6, 6), * inc. in loop, p.8 (9, 10); rep. from * ending last rep. p.6 (7, 7).
Cont. in patt. on 75 (83, 91) sts. working first row of each panel as follows:
1st row: Panel One across 7 (9, 11) sts., Panel Two across 17 sts., Panel Three across 8 sts., Panel Four across 11 (15, 19) sts., Panel Three across 8 sts., Panel Two across 17 sts., Panel One across 7 (9, 11) sts.
Cont. in patts. as set until work measures 11 (12½, 14) in. ending on wrong side.

Shape Armholes

Dec. 1 st. both ends of the next 7 (9, 11) rows then cont. straight on 61 (65, 69) sts. until straight edges of armholes measure 5 (5½, 6) in. ending on wrong side.

Shape Neck and Shoulders

Next row: patt. 21 (22, 23), turn, leaving rem. sts. on spare needle. Cont. on the first set of sts. as follows: * dec. 1 st. at neck edge on next 3 rows *and at the same time* cast off at beg. of armhole edge rows 6 sts. twice then rem. 6 (7, 8) sts.
Now sl. first 19 (21, 23) sts. from spare needle on to a holder for neck (remembering that there will be 2 sts. extra if a 2nd row of bramble st. has just been worked).
Rejoin wool at neck edge and patt. to end, then rep. from * of first side.

FRONT

Work as for back until straight edges of armhole measure 2¾ (3¼, 3¾) in. ending on wrong side.

Matching Aran sweaters with alternative necklines (instructions start on page 105).

Top picture: smart two-colour waistcoat in cotton (see page 110).
Above: teenage trouser suit (see page 112).

Shape Neck

Next row: patt. 24 (25, 26), turn, leaving rem. sts. on spare needle. Cont. on the first set of sts. dec. 1 st. at neck edge on the next 2 rows then on the next 4 right-side rows. Cont. straight on 18 (19, 20) sts. until armhole matches back ending at armhole edge.

Shape Shoulder

Cast off at beg. of armhole edge rows 6 sts. twice then rem. 6 (7, 8) sts. Now sl. first 13 (15, 17) sts. from spare needle on to holder for neck, rejoin wool at neck edge and patt. to end then complete to match first side.

SLEEVES (make 2 alike)

With No. 9 needles cast on 35 (37, 39) sts. and work 13 (15, 17) rows in twisted rib as for welt. Change to No. 7 needles.
Inc. row: * p.12 (8, 6), inc. in loop; rep. from * 1 (3, 5) times more, p.11 (5, 3).
Cont. in patt. on 37 (41, 45) sts. with centre bramble st. panel, long-ribbed cable each side and 5 d.m.st. at side edges as follows:
1st row: (k.1, p.1) twice, k.1, Panel Three across 8 sts., Panel Four across 11 (15, 19) sts., Panel Three across 8 sts., (k.1, p.1) twice, k.1.
Cont. in patts. as set, inc. 1 st. both ends of the 3rd and every foll. 8th row working inc. sts. into d.m.st. until there are 51 (57, 63) sts. Cont. straight until sleeve measures 11 (13, 15) in. or finished length required, then work a further $1\frac{1}{2}$ (2, $2\frac{1}{2}$) in. straight (which will be sewn to armhole slope) ending on wrong side.

Shape Top

1st row: cast off 3, patt. to last 2 sts., take 2 tog.
2nd to 6th rows: rep. first row 5 times.
7th and 8th rows: cast off 3 (4, 5), patt. to last 2 sts., take 2 tog. Cast off rem. 19 (23, 27) sts. firmly.

TO COMPLETE

Join left shoulder seam.

Neck Border

With right side facing, and No. 9 needles, pick up and k.5 sts. down back neck, k. sts. from holder but dec. bramble panel to 10 (14, 18) sts., pick up and k. 5 sts. up other side, 18 down front neck, then k. sts. from holder but dec. twice if last row worked was a 2nd patt. row, pick up and k. 18 sts. up other side: 77 (81, 85) sts.
Beg. with a 2nd row of rib, work 13 (15, 17) rows in twisted rib. *
Cast off loosely in rib.

Roll Collar

With No. 10 needles, work as for neck border to * but beg. with a first row of rib, then cont. until collar measures $2\frac{1}{4}$ ($2\frac{1}{2}$, 3) in. Change to No. 9 needles and cont. until collar measures $4\frac{1}{4}$ ($4\frac{3}{4}$, $5\frac{1}{4}$) in.
Cast off in rib with a No. 7 needle.

To Make Up

Press on wrong side with a damp cloth and hot iron. Join shoulder seams including neck border, but join collar seam on reverse side to turn back. Join side seams. Join sleeve seams leaving last 1½ (2, 2½) in. open then set in sleeves placing the open part to the armhole slope. Turn neck border in half to wrong side and slipstitch. Press seams.

Two-colour waistcoat

illustrated in colour on page 108

MATERIALS

2 (2, 2, 3) balls (2 oz. each) Twilleys Stalite in pink, and 2 (3, 3, 3) balls in orange. One pair each Nos. 9 and 10 knitting needles (USA sizes 5 and 3). Four medium buttons.

MEASUREMENTS

To fit bust/chest size 24 (26, 28, 30) in.; length 19 (21, 23, 25) in.

TENSION

6¼ sts. and 11 rows to 1 in. over ridge patt. on No. 10 needles; 6¼ sts. and 7 rows to 1 in. over colour patt. on No. 9 needles.

ABBREVIATIONS

See page 11; P., pink; O., orange.

TO MAKE

Note. Waistcoat is worked in one piece to start of armhole shaping.

With No. 10 needles and P., cast on 168 (180, 192, 204) sts. K. 11 rows.

Change to No. 9 Needles, join in O., and work in colour patt. as follows:

1st row: in O., k., winding yarn twice round needle each st.
2nd row: in O., * sl. next 3 sts. on to right-hand needle, dropping extra loops, sl. sts. back on to left-hand needle and counting all 3 sts. as one, work p.1, k.1, p.1 into these sts.; rep. from * to end.
3rd and 4th rows: in P., k.

These 4 rows form the colour patt. Work straight until work measures 3½ (4, 4, 4½) in. from beg., ending with a 2nd patt. row.
1st dec. row: k.18 (19, 20, 21), (k.2 tog., k.24 (26, 28, 30) sts.) 5 times, k.2 tog., k. to end: 162 (174, 186, 198) sts. Work 23 (23, 27, 31) rows straight in patt.
2nd dec. row: k.17 (18, 19, 20), (k.2 tog., k.23 (25, 27, 29) sts.) 5 times, k.2 tog., k. to end: 156 (168, 180, 192) sts. Work 19 (23, 27, 27) rows straight.
3rd dec. row: k.17 (18, 19, 20), (k.2 tog., k.22 (24, 26, 28) sts.) 5 times, k.2 tog., k. to end: 150 (162, 174, 186) sts. Work straight until work measures 12½ (14, 15, 16½) in. from beg. ending with a 2nd patt. row.

Shape Front Slopes

Dec. 1 st. at each end of next and every foll. 4th row until 144 (156, 166, 178) sts. remain. Work 3 rows straight, thus ending with right side facing.

Right Front

Next row: k.2 tog., k. 28 (28, 30, 33) sts., turn.
Next row: in patt.
Work on this group of sts. only for right front as follows: dec. 1 st. at armhole edge on next and every alt. row, at the same time cont. to dec. at front edge on every 4th row from previous dec. until 16 (16, 18, 21) sts. remain.
Keep armhole edge straight and dec. at neck edge only as before until 12 (12, 12, 15) sts. remain.
Work a few rows straight until work measures 19 (21, 23, 25) in. from beg., ending at armhole edge.

Shape Shoulder

Cast off 6 (6, 6, 7) sts. at beg. of next row.
Work one row. Cast off.

Back

With right side facing rejoin yarn to rem. sts., cast off 9 (12, 12, 12) sts., k.66 (66, 72, 78) sts. (including st. already on needle), turn. Work on this group of sts. only for back as follows:
Dec. 1 st. at each end of next and every foll. alt. row until 48 (48, 54, 60) sts. remain. Work straight until back measures same as right front to shoulder shaping.

Shape Shoulders

Cast off 6 (6, 6, 7) sts. at beg. of next 2 rows, 6 (6, 6, 8) sts. at beg. of next 2 rows.
Cast off.

Left Front

With right side facing rejoin yarn to rem. sts., cast off 9 (12, 12, 12) sts., k. to last 2 sts., k.2 tog.
Next row: in patt.
Complete to match right front, reversing all shapings.

TO COMPLETE

Press on wrong side with a warm iron and damp cloth.

Armhole Border

With right side facing, No. 10 needles and P., pick up and k. 80 (89, 95, 101) sts. round each armhole.
K.2 rows. Cast off.

Neck Border

Join shoulder seams. With right side facing, No. 10 needles and P., pick up and k.74 (83, 89, 98) sts. up right front edge to start of front slope, 39 (42, 48, 51) sts. to shoulder, 12 (12, 18, 18) sts. to centre of back neck: 125 (137, 155, 167) sts.
Next row: k.52 (55, 67, 70) sts., (cast off 3, k.10 (11, 12, 13) sts. including st. on needle) 3 times, cast off 3, k. to end.
Next row: k., casting on 3 over the cast-off sts. of previous row.
Omitting buttonholes complete left border to match.

To Make Up

Press shoulder seams. Sew on buttons to correspond with buttonholes.

Teenage trouser suit

illustrated in colour on page 108

MATERIALS

23 (25, 27) balls (50 gr. each) Mahony's Blarney Bainin (USA Blarneyspun). One pair each Nos. 7, 8, 9 and 10 knitting needles (USA sizes 7, 6, 5 and 3). One crochet hook International Standard Size 3.00. Seven medium buttons. Waist length of elastic.

MEASUREMENTS

Jacket: to fit bust size 29–30 (31–32, 33–34) in.; length $17\frac{1}{4}$ (18, $18\frac{1}{2}$) in.; sleeve seam 15 ($15\frac{1}{2}$, $16\frac{1}{2}$) in. **Trousers:** to fit hip size 31–32 (33–34, 35–36) in.; inside leg seam 25 (26, 27) in.

TENSION

5 sts. to 1 in. over side panel patt.

ABBREVIATIONS

See page   ; c.n., cable needle; C.3 L., (cable 3 to the left) sl. next 2 sts. on c.n. and leave at front, p.1 then k.2 from c.n.; C.3 R., (cable 3 to the right) sl. next st. on c.n. and leave at back, k.2 then p.1 from c.n.; C.4 F., (cable 4 front) sl. next 2 sts. on c.n. at front, k.2 then k.2 from c.n.; C.4 B., (cable 4 back) as C.4 F. but leave the 2 sts. at back; C.6, (cable 6) sl. next 2 sts. on c.n. at front, k. next 2 sts., pass c.n. to back of work, k. next 2 sts., then 2 sts. from c.n.; inc. in loop, pick up thread between needles and k. into back of it.

JACKET BACK

With No. 10 needles cast on 75 (81, 87) sts. and work 21 rows in k.1, p.1 rib. Change to No. 7 needles.

Inc. row: k.4 (3, 1), (inc. in loop, k.4) 17 (19, 21) times, inc. in loop, k.3 (2, 2). Cont. in patt. on 93 (101, 109) sts.

1st row (wrong side): p.4 (6, 10), k.1, * p.3, k.1, p.2, (k.4, p.4) twice, k.4, p.2, k.1, p.3, * k.1 (2, 2), p.6, k.1 (2, 2), p.3, k.1 (2, 2), p.6, k.1 (2, 2); rep. from * to *, k.1, p.4 (6, 10).

2nd row: (p.1, k.1) 2 (3, 5) times, p.1, * sl.1, k.2, p.s.s.o., p.1, (C.3 L., p.2, C.3 R.) 3 times, p.1, sl.1, k.2, p.s.s.o., * p.1 (2, 2), k.6, p.1 (2, 2), sl.1, k.2, p.s.s.o., p.1 (2, 2), k.6, p.1 (2, 2); rep. from * to *, p.1, (k.1, p.1) 2 (3, 5) times.

These 2 rows form the patt. of the side panels which will be called patt. 5 (7, 11).

3rd row: patt. 5 (7, 11), * p.1, y.r.n., p.1, (k.2, p.2) 6 times, k.2, p.1, y.r.n., p.1, * k.1 (2, 2), p.6, k.1 (2, 2), p.1, y.r.n., p.1, k.1 (2, 2), p.6, k.1 (2, 2); rep. from * to *, patt. 5 (7, 11).

4th row: patt. 5 (7, 11), * k.3, (p.2, C.3 L., C.3 R.) 3 times, p.2, k.3, * p.1 (2, 2), C.6, p.1 (2, 2), k.3, p.1 (2, 2), C.6, p.1 (2, 2); rep. from * to *, patt. 5 (7, 11).

5th row: patt. 5 (7, 11), * p.3, k.3, (p.4, k.4) twice, p.4, k.3, p.3, * k.1 (2, 2), p.6, k.1 (2, 2), p.3, k.1 (2, 2), p.6, k.1 (2, 2); rep. from * to *, patt. 5 (7, 11).

6th row: patt. 5 (7, 11), * sl.1, k.2, p.s.s.o., p.3, (C.4 F., p.4) twice, C.4 F., p.3, sl.1, k.2, p.s.s.o., * p.1 (2, 2), k.6, p.1 (2, 2), sl.1, k.2, p.s.s.o., p.1 (2, 2), k.6, p.1 (2, 2); rep. from * to *, patt. 5 (7, 11).

7th row: patt. 5 (7, 11), * p.1, y.r.n., p.1, k.3, (p.4, k.4) twice, p.4, k.3, p.1, y.r.n., p.1, * k.1 (2, 2), p.6, k.1 (2, 2), p.1, y.r.n., p.1, k.1 (2, 2), p.6, k.1 (2, 2); rep. from * to *, patt. 5 (7, 11).

8th row: patt. 5 (7, 11), * k.3, (p.2, C.3 R., C.3 L.) 3 times, p.2, k.3, * p.1 (2, 2), k.6, p.1 (2, 2), k.3, p.1 (2, 2), k.6, p.1 (2, 2); rep. from * to *, patt. 5 (7, 11).

9th row: patt. 5 (7, 11), * p.3, (k.2, p.2) 6 times, k.2, p.3, * k.1 (2, 2), p.6, k.1 (2, 2), p.3, k.1 (2, 2), p.6, k.1 (2, 2); rep. from * to *, patt. 5 (7, 11).

10th row: patt. 5 (7, 11), * sl.1, k.2, p.s.s.o., p.1, (C.3 R., p.2, C.3 L.) 3 times, p.1, sl.1, k.2, p.s.s.o., * p.1 (2, 2), C.6, p.1 (2, 2), sl.1, k.2, p.s.s.o., p.1 (2,2), C.6, p.1 (2, 2); rep. from * to *, patt. 5 (7, 11).

11th row: patt. 5 (7, 11), * p.1, y.r.n., p.1, k.1, p.2, (k.4, p.4) twice, k.4, p.2, k.1, p.1, y.r.n., p.1, * k.1 (2, 2), p.6, k.1 (2,2), p.1, y.r.n., p.1, k.1 (2, 2), p.6, k.1 (2, 2); rep. from * to *, patt. 5 (7, 11).

12th row: patt. 5 (7, 11), * k.3, p.1, k.2, (p.4, C.4 B.) twice, p.4, k.2, p.1, k.3, * p.1 (2, 2), k.6, p.1 (2, 2), k.3, p.1 (2, 2), k.6, p.1 (2, 2); rep. from * to *, patt. 5 (7, 11).

These 12 rows form the patt.

Rep. them until work measures 10½ (11, 11) in. ending on wrong side. **

Shape Armholes

Cast off 3 (4, 5) sts. at beg. of next 2 rows, dec. 1 st. both ends of the next 5 (6, 9) right-side rows. Cont. straight on 77 (81, 81) sts. until armholes measure 4½ (4¾, 5¼) in. ending on right side ***. Change to No. 10 needles and patt.

1st row (wrong side): p.

2nd row: * p.1, k.1; rep. from * to last st., p.1.

Rep. these 2 rows until armholes measure 6¾ (7, 7½) in. ending on wrong side.

Shape Shoulders

Cast off 5 (6, 6) sts. at beg. of next 2 rows and 7 sts. on foll. 6 rows. Cast off rem. 25 (27, 27) sts.

JACKET LEFT FRONT

With No. 10 needles cast on 39 (41, 45) sts. and work 21 rows in k.1, p.1 rib.

Change to No. 7 needles.

Inc. row: k.7 (3, 5), (inc. in loop, k.5) 5 (7, 7) times, inc. in loop, k.7 (3, 5). Cont. in patt. on 45 (49, 53) sts. as for right half of Back with centre mock cable omitted as follows:

1st row: k.1 (2, 2), p.6, k.1 (2, 2); rep. from * to * of first patt. row of Back, k.1, p.4 (6, 10).

2nd row: (p.1, k.1) 2 (3, 5) times, p.1; rep. from * to * of 2nd patt. row, p.1 (2, 2), k.6, p.1 (2, 2).

Cont. in patt. as set until work matches back to **

Shape Armhole

Cast off 3 (4, 5) sts. at beg. of next row, dec. 1 st. at same edge on next 5 (6, 9) right-side rows. Cont. straight on 37 (39, 39) sts. until work matches back to ***. Change to No. 10 needles and work 3 rows in yoke patt. as for back .

Shape Neck

Next row: patt. to last 5 (6, 6) sts., cast off these sts. Break yarn, rejoin at needle point and dec. 1 st. at neck edge on the next 6 rows then cont. straight on 26 (27, 27) sts. until armhole matches back ending at armhole edge.

Shape Shoulder

Cast off at beg. of armhole edge rows 5 (6, 6) sts. once and 7 sts. 3 times.

JACKET RIGHT FRONT

Work the ribbing and inc. row as for left front then reverse patt. as follows:

1st row: p.4 (6, 10), k.1; rep. from * to * of first patt. row, k.1 (2, 2), p.6, k.1 (2, 2).

2nd row: p.1 (2, 2), k.6, p.1 (2, 2); rep. from * to * of 2nd patt. row, p.1, (k.1, p.1) 2 (3, 5) times.

Cont. to match left front, working one extra row at ** before shaping armhole, until the 3 rows of yoke patt. have been worked.

Shape Neck

Next row: cast off 5 (6, 6), patt. to end. Now without breaking yarn, complete as for left front.

JACKET SLEEVES (make 2 alike)

With No. 10 needles cast on 41 (43, 45) sts. and work 21 rows in k.1, p.1 rib. Change to No. 7 needles.

Inc. row: k.13 (11, 9), inc. in loop, (k.3, inc. in loop) 5 (7, 9) times, k.13 (11, 9).

Cont. on 47 (51, 55) sts. with centre 25 (29, 29) sts. in mock cables and 6-stitch cables as for centre of back and side sts. in panel patt. as follows:

1st row: p. 10 (10, 12), k.1, * p.3, k.1 (2, 2), p.6, k.1 (2, 2); rep. from * once, p.3, k.1, p.10 (10, 12).

2nd row: (p.1, k.1) 5 (5, 6) times, p.1, * sl.1, k.2, p.s.s.o., p.1 (2, 2), k.6, p.1 (2, 2); rep. from * once, sl.1, k.2, p.s.s.o., p.1, (k.1, p.1) 5 (5, 6) times.

Cont. in patt. as set, but inc. 1 st. both ends of the next and every foll. 10th (10th, 9th) row until there are 63 (67, 73) sts. working inc. sts. into side panel patt. Cont. straight until sleeve measures 15 (15½, 16½) in. ending on wrong side.

Shape Top

Cast off 3 (4, 5) sts. at beg. of next 2 rows, dec. 1 st. both ends of every right-side row until 37 sts. rem. for all sizes ending with a dec. row, then both ends of the next 5 rows. Cast off 3 sts. at beg. of next 2 rows then cast off rem. sts. but work k.2 tog. twice across the centre 4 sts. of each 6-stitch cable while casting off.

FRONT BORDERS AND COLLAR

With No. 10 needles cast on 8 sts. for left front border and work in p.1, k.1 rib (every row p.1, k.1 to end but regard first row as right side) until border fits front edge to neck ending on wrong side. Break yarn and leave sts. on a stitch holder. Mark this border with pins as buttonhole guide on 4th, 14th and 24th rows from cast-on edge then four more evenly-spaced to leave 9 rows at top. Now work buttonhole border to correspond with plain border but work every row k.1, p.1 to end, making buttonholes at pin positions as follows:

Buttonhole row (wrong side): k.1, p.1, k.2 tog., y.r.n., p.2 tog., k.1, p.1.

Next row: k.1, p.1, k.1, (p.1, k.1) into made st., p.1, k.1, p.1. When 9 rows have been worked after last buttonhole thus ending on wrong side, do not break yarn but cont. for collar as follows:

Rib 8, then on to same needle cast on 75 (79, 79) sts. and rib 8 from stitch holder.

Next row: * p.1, k.1; rep. from * to last st., p.1.

Next row: * k.1, p.1; rep. from * to last st., k.1.

Work 4 more rows in rib.

Next row: rib 17 (19, 19), * (k.1, p.1, k.1) all into next st., rib 7; rep. from * 6 times more, (k.1, p.1, k.1) into next st., rib 17 (19, 19). Cont. in rib until collar measures 1½ (2, 2) in. then change to No. 9 needles for 1 in. then to No. 8 needles for 1 in. Cast off in rib.

TROUSERS RIGHT LEG

With No. 10 needles cast on 94 (100, 104) sts. and work 4 rows k.1, p.1 rib. Change to No. 7 needles and k.1 row then cont. in patt. with central cable, panels each side as from * to * and side edges as for side edges of jacket as follows:

1st row (wrong side): p.10 (12, 14), k.1; rep. from * to * of first patt. row of back, k.1 (2, 2), p.6, k.1 (2, 2); rep. from * to * again, k.1, p.10 (12, 14).

2nd row: (p.1, k.1) 5 (6, 7) times, p.1; rep. from * to * of 2nd patt. row, p.1 (2, 2), k.6, p.1 (2, 2), rep. from * to * again, p.1, (k.1, p.1) 5 (6, 7) times.

Cont. in patt. as set (working C.6 on centre cable in 4th row) until work measures 3½ (4, 4½) in. ending on wrong side. Dec. 1 st. both ends of the next and every foll. 24th (16th, 16th) row until 88 (92, 96) sts. rem. Cont. straight until work measures 13 (14, 14½) in. ending on wrong side (adjust length here if required). Inc. 1 st. both ends of the next and every foll. 8th row until there are 98 (102, 106) sts., both ends of foll. 6th row until there are 110 (114, 118) sts. then both ends of every foll. 4th row until there are 116 (120, 126) sts. Work a few rows straight until work measures 25 (26, 27) in. or length required, ending on wrong side. ***

Shape for Crotch and Seat

Cast off 3 sts. at beg. of next 2 rows and 2 sts. on foll. 2 rows then dec. 1 st. both ends of the next 4 right-side rows then both ends of every foll. 4th row 8 (8, 9) times. Work 5 rows straight on 82 (86, 90) sts. then dec. both ends of the next and every foll. 6th row 3 times. Work a few rows straight on 76 (80, 84) sts. until work measures 9 (9½, 10) in. from *** ending on right side ****

Shape Waist Edge

Next row: patt. 35 (37, 39), turn, leave rem. 41 (43, 45) sts. on stitch holder. Now cast off at beg. of right-side rows 8 sts. 3 times then rem. 11 (13, 15) sts.

With right side facing, and No. 10 needles, k. across sts. on stitch holder working k.2 tog. 3 times across the 6 cable sts. then on to same needle pick up and k.1 st. for each cast-off st.

Work 8 rows k.1, p.1 rib. Cast off in rib.

LEFT LEG
Work as for right leg until****

Shape Waist Edge
Next row: sl. first 41 (43, 45) sts. on stitch holder.
Break yarn, rejoin at needle point to rem. 35 (37, 39) sts. and cast off at beg. of wrong-side rows 8 sts. 3 times then rem. 11 (13, 15) sts. Now with right side facing, and No. 10 needles, pick up and k.1 st. for each cast-off st. and on to same needle k. across sts. on stitch holder working k.2 tog. 3 times across the 6 cable sts. Work 8 rows k.1, p.1 rib. Cast off in rib.

TO COMPLETE
Pin out and press pieces on wrong side with a damp cloth and hot iron, avoiding ribbing.

Jacket
Join side and shoulder seams. Join sleeve seams and set in sleeves. Sew borders to front edges and cast-on edge of collar to neck edge. Sew on buttons.

Trousers
Join front and back seams then leg seams. Make a crochet casing on wrong side of waist ribbing and thread elastic through. Press seams.

Mother and daughter skating dresses

illustrated in colour on page 89

MATERIALS
13 (24) oz. Emu Scotch double knitting. One pair each Nos. 8, 9 and 10 knitting needles (USA sizes 6, 5 and 3). One cable needle.

MEASUREMENTS
To fit chest size 24 (32) in.; length 21 (30) in; length of sleeve seam 12½ (17) in.

TENSION
6 sts. to 1 in. with No. 8 needles.

ABBREVIATIONS
See page 11; m.1, make 1: pick up loop lying between last and next sts. and p. it t.b.l.

LEFT BACK
With No. 10 needles cast on 52 (78) sts. Work 4 rows in k.1, p.1 rib.
Change to No. 8 needles and st.st. (1 row k., 1 row p.) Dec. 1 st. at each end of every 3rd row until 14 (22) sts. remain. Cont. straight until work measures 8 (12½) in.
Now inc. 1 st. at each end of the 11th (15th) row and every foll. 10th row until there are 22 (32) sts.
Cont. straight until work measures 14 (21½) in., ending with a k. row.

Shape Armhole and Neck

Cast off 3 (4) sts. at the beg. of next row, 2 sts. on next 1 (2) alt. rows and 1 st. on next 3 (4) alt. rows, then dec. 1 st. at each end of every foll. 10th row until 10 (14) sts. remain.
Cont. straight until armhole measures 5 (7) in., ending with a k. row.

Shape Shoulder

Cast off 5 (7) sts. at beg. of next and foll. alt. row.

RIGHT BACK

Work as Left Back but end with p. rows before shaping armhole and shoulder.

CENTRE BACK

With No. 10 needles cast on 62 (90) sts. and work 4 rows in k.1, p.1 rib. Change to No. 8 needles and cont. in st.st. dec. 1 st. at each end of every foll. 3rd row until 26 (36) sts. remain.
Cont. straight until work measures 8 (12½) in., then inc. 1 st. at each end of every foll. 6th (7th) row until there are 50 (70) sts.
Cont. straight until work measures same as Right and Left Backs to shoulder, ending with a wrong-side row.

Shape Shoulders

Cast off 6 (8) sts. at the beg. of the next 2 rows and 5 (8) sts. at the beg. of the next 2 rows.
Leave rem. sts. on a st. holder.

LEFT FRONT

Work as Right Back.

RIGHT FRONT

Work as Left Back.

CENTRE FRONT

With No. 10 needles cast on 69 (99) sts. and work 4 rows in k.1, p.1 rib. Change to No. 8 needles.
1st row: k.15 (23), p.3, k.6, p.5, (k.4, p.3) 1 (3) times, k.4, p.5, k.6, p 3, k. to end.
2nd row: p.15 (23), k.3, p.6, k.5, (p.4, k.3) 1 (3) times, p.4, k.5, p.6, k.3, p. to end.
3rd row: k.2 tog., k.13 (21), p.3, k.6, p.5, (k.4, p.3) 1 (3) times, k.4, p.5, k.6, p.3, k. to last 2 sts., k.2 tog.
4th row: p.14 (22), k.3, p.6, k.5, (p.4, k.3) 1 (3) times, p.4, k.5, p.6, k.3, p. to end.
5th row: k.14 (22), p.3, sl. next 3 sts. on to cable needle and leave at front of work, k.3, then k.3 from cable needle, p.5, (k.4, p.3) 1 (3) times, k.4, p.5, sl. next 3 sts. on to cable needle and leave at back of work, k.3, then k.3 from cable needle, p.3, k. to end.
6th row: keeping continuity of patt. dec. 1 st. at each end of row.
Cont. to dec. 1 st. at each end of every foll. 3rd row and *at the same time* work cable row on every 6th row, until 43 (57) sts. remain, ending with a wrong-side row.
Next row: k.2, p.3, k.6 or cable 6, p.2 tog., p.1, p.2 tog., (k.4, p.3) 1 (3) times, k.4, p.2 tog., p.1, p.2 tog., k.6 or cable 6,

p.3, k.2.

Next row: patt. to end.

Next row: k.2, p.3, k.6 or cable 6, p.3, (k.4, p.2 tog., p.1) 1 (3) times, k.4, p.3, k.6 or cable 6, p.3, k.2. Keeping continuity of patt., cont. straight until work measures 8 (12½) in., then inc. 1 st. at each end of the next and every foll. 7th row and *at the same time* after ¾ (1) in. has been worked end with a wrong-side row.

Next row: k.4, p.3, k.6 or cable 6, p.2, m.1, p.1, (k.4, p.1, m.1, p.1) 1 (3) times, k.4, p.2, m.1, p.1, k.6 or cable 6, p.3, k. to end. Work a further ¾ (1) in.

Next row: k.5, p.3, k.6 or cable 6, p.2, m.1, p.2, (k.4, p.3) 1 (3) times, k.4, p.2, m.1, p.2, k.6 or cable 6, p.3, k. to end. Still inc. at side edges until there are 51 (71) sts. Cont. straight until work measures 17½ (26½) in.

Shape Neck

Next row: patt. 21 (30) sts.; turn and leave rem. sts. on a st. holder.

Cast off at neck edge 2 (3) sts. on next row, 2 sts. on next 3 (4) alt. rows and 1 st. on next 2 (3) alt. rows. When work measures the same as Back to shoulder, ending at side edge, cast off 5 (8) sts. on next row and 6 (8) sts. on foll. alt. row. Slip centre 9 (11) sts. on to a safety pin. Join yarn to rem. sts. and work to match the first side of neck.

SLEEVES (make 2 alike)

With No. 10 needles, cast on 38 (48) sts. Work 2 (2½) in. in k.1, p.1 rib. Change to No. 8 needles and cont. in st.st., inc. 1 st. at each end of the 5th and every foll. 6th row until there are 64 (80) sts. Cont. straight until Sleeve measures 12½ (17) in., ending with a wrong-side row.

Shape Top

Cast off 3 (5) sts. at the beg. of the next 2 rows and 2 sts. at the beg. of the next 4 rows, then dec. 1 st. at the beg. of every row until 30 (32) sts. remain. Cast off 2 sts. at beg. of next 2 rows, 3 sts. on next 2 rows and 4 sts. on the next 2 rows. Cast off rem. sts.

TO COMPLETE

Using back st., join left shoulder seam.

Collar

With No. 10 needles, k. across sts. on st. holder at back neck, pick up and k. t.b.l. the loop between every 5th and 6th (7th and 8th) sts., pick up and k. 18 (24) sts. down side of front neck, k. across centre front sts., inc. between every 3rd st., pick up and k. 18 (24) sts. up other side of front neck. Work 2½ (3) in. in k.1, p.1 rib. Change to No. 9 needles and work a further ¾ (1) in. With No. 8 needles cast off in rib.

To Make Up

Press work on wrong side, avoiding the cables. Join Centre Back to Left and Right Backs and Centre Front to Left and Right Fronts. Join the right shoulder seam. Set in Sleeves. Join side and sleeve seams. Join collar with a flat seam. Press seams.

Sleeveless pullover

MATERIALS
9 (10, 10) balls (25 gr. each) Twilleys Cortina. One pair each Nos. 9 and 11 knitting needles (USA sizes 5 and 2), and a set of four No. 12 needles (USA size 1) with points at both ends.

MEASUREMENTS
To fit bust size 34 (36, 38) in.

TENSION
8 sts. and 8 rows to 1 in. without stretching (6 sts. to 1 in. when stretched).

ABBREVIATIONS
See page 11.

FRONT
With No. 11 needles cast on 112 sts. and work 2½ in. in k.1, p.1 rib, on the last row dec. 1 st. at the end.
Change to No. 9 needles and work in patt. as follows:
1st row: p.1, * k.1, p.2, 2 sts. crossed to the right (k. into the 2nd st. and then into the first st.), 2 sts. crossed to the left (put the needle at the back of the sts. and k. into the back of 2nd st., then into the first st.), p.2; rep. from * to last 2 sts., k.1, p.1.
2nd row: k. the k. sts. and p. the p. sts.
3rd row: p 1, * k.1, p.2, 2 sts. crossed to the left, 2 sts. crossed to the right, p.2; rep. from * to last 2 sts., k.1, p.1.
4th row: as 2nd row.
These 4 rows form the patt. and are rep. throughout. When work measures 6 (6, 4) in., inc. 1 st. at the beg. and end of each foll. 10th (10th, 8th) row 2 (4, 6) times. Cont. in patt. until work measures 14½ (15, 15) in., ending with a wrong-side row.

Shape Top

Cast off 6 sts., rib 50 (52, 54) sts. (51 (53, 55) sts. on needle). cast off next (centre) st., rib to end and finish this side first.
Cast off 6 sts., rib to last 2 sts., k.2 tog.; turn. K.2 tog., rib to last 2 sts., k.2 tog.
Rep. the last row 3 times, then k.2 tog. at beg. of every row at side edge, and k.2 tog. at the beg. and end of every row at neck edge until 27 sts. remain, then keep neck edge straight, but continue to dec. at the side edges until 3 sts. remain. Cast off. Work the other side in a similar way.

BACK

Work as the Front.

TO COMPLETE

Do not press. With right side of work facing and set of No. 12 needles pick up 60 (62, 64) sts. along one side of neck, pick up the centre st., then using another No. 12 needle pick up 60 (62, 64) sts. along the other side of neck; work back in k.1, p.1 rib; on the next row dec. on each side of the centre st. as follows: work to 3 sts. before centre st., then sl.1, k.2 tog., p.s.s.o.; work centre st.; k.3 tog. Work 5 rows in all, working another dec. each side of centre st. as before on 4th row only. Cast off in rib on the 6th row. Work the back in the same way. With No. 12 needles pick up 140 (144, 148) sts. evenly along the side edges of the front and back and work 5 rows in k.1, p.1 rib. Cast off in rib on the 6th row. Work the other side to match. Join side seam. Join shoulder seams. Press seams lightly.

Cotton blouse

MATERIALS

12 (13, 14, 14, 15) oz. Twilleys Crysette. One pair each Nos. 10 and 12 knitting needles (USA sizes 3 and 1).

MEASUREMENTS

To fit bust sizes 32 (34, 36, 38, 40) in.; length 21 (22, 22, 23, 23) in.

TENSION

7 sts. and 9 rows to 1 in.

ABBREVIATIONS

See page 11.

BACK

With No. 12 needles cast on 118 (126, 132, 140, 146) sts. Work 6 rows in k.1, p.1 rib.
Change to No. 10 needles and work in patt. as follows:
1st row (right side): k.
2nd row: p.
3rd and 4th rows: * p.1, k.1; rep. from * to end.
5th row: k.
6th row: p.
7th and 8th rows: * k.1, p.1; rep. from * to end.
These 8 rows form rib patt. Cont. in patt. until work measures 14 (14½, 14½, 15½, 15½) in.

Armhole Shaping

Cast off 6 (7, 7, 8, 8) sts. at beg. of next 2 rows, then dec. 1 st. each end of next 10 rows: 86 (92, 98, 104, 110) sts.
Cont. in patt. until work measures 21 (22, 22, 23, 23) in., ending with a p. row.

Shoulder Shaping

Cast off 5 (6, 7, 8, 9) sts. at beg. of next 6 rows: 56 (56, 56, 56, 56) sts. **
Work 4 rows straight in rib as on last row. Cast off ribwise.

FRONT

Work as for Back to **. Cast off ribwise.

TO COMPLETE

Join shoulder seams then join sides of 4 rows at top of back to the cast-off edge of front.

Armbands (make both alike)

With No. 12 needles pick up and k. 116 (124, 126, 134, 136) sts. evenly round armhole edge.
Work 4 rows in k.1, p.1 rib.
Cast off ribwise.

To Make Up

Press lightly. Join side seams. Press seams.

Lace-up jumper

MATERIALS

13 (14, 15) oz. Lister Lavenda Crisp Crêpe 4-ply. One pair each Nos. 12 and 13 knitting needles (USA sizes 1 and 0). One crochet hook International Standard Size 3·00.

MEASUREMENTS

To fit bust size 34 (36, 38) in.; length 24 (24$\frac{1}{4}$, 24$\frac{1}{2}$) in.; sleeve seam 4$\frac{1}{2}$ (5, 5$\frac{1}{2}$) in.

TENSION

8 sts. and 11 rows to 1 in. over st.st. on No. 12 needles.

ABBREVIATIONS

See page 11; k.f.b., knit into the front and back of next st.; y.r.2, wind yarn twice round right-hand needle.

FRONT

** With No. 13 needles cast on 132 (139, 146) sts. and work 14 rows in g.st.

Inc. row (wrong side): k.4 (3, 2), * k.f.b., k.7; rep. from * to end: 148 (156, 164) sts.

Change to No. 12 needles and beg. with a k. row work in st.st. but dec. 1 st. at both ends of every following 10th row until 136 (144, 152) sts. remain.

Continue without shaping until work measures 9 in. from beg.

Inc. 1 st. at both ends of next row and every following 20th row until there are 144 (152, 160) sts., then continue without shaping until work measures 17 in. from beg., ending with a p. row. **

Armhole Shaping and Front Opening
Cast off 5 (6, 7) sts. at beg. of next 4 rows.
5th row: cast off 5, k. until you have 57 (59, 61) sts. on right-hand needle, turn and continue on these sts. for left front, leaving remaining 62 (64, 66) sts. of right front on a spare needle.
6th row: k.6, p. to end.
7th row: cast off 5, k. to end.
8th row: as 6th row: 52 (54, 56) sts.
Continue without shaping keeping the 6 sts. next to opening in g.st. and work 8 rows, then start making eyelet holes in this border as follows.
17th row: k. to last 5 sts., k.2 tog., y.r.2, k.2 tog. t.b.l., k.1.
18th row: k.2, drop one loop to make a long st. and work k.1, p.1 into this st., k.2, p. to end.
Work 10 rows in st.st. with g.st. border. Rep. last 12 rows twice more. Rep. 17th and 18th rows again, then work 4 rows, thus ending at side. .

Neck and Shoulder Shaping
59th row: k.46 (48, 50): turn and sl. the 6 sts. of g.st. border on to a safety pin or st. holder.
60th row: cast off 4, p. to end
*** Working in st.st. cast off at neck edge 2 sts. on next 3 alternate rows and 1 st. at same edge on next 6 (7, 8) alternate rows: 30 (31, 32) sts. remain and you have ended at side edge. Keeping neck edge straight cast off for shoulder 10 sts. at beg. of next row and next alternate row. Work one row. Cast off remaining 10 (11, 12) sts. *** With right side facing rejoin wool to inner edge of right front sts., k. to end.
6th row: cast off 5, p. to last 6 sts., k.6.
7th row: k.
8th row: as 6th row.
This completes armhole shaping. Continue to keep g.st. border next to opening and work 8 rows straight.
17th row: k.1, k.2 tog., y.r.2, k.2 tog. t.b.l., k. to end.
On next row complete eyelet as for right front. Work 10 rows straight. Rep. last 12 rows twice more. Make another eyelet on next 2 rows, then work 4 rows, thus ending at the opening.

Neck and Shoulder Shaping
59th row: k.6 and slip off these sts. on to a safety pin or st. holder, continue along row, cast off 4, k. to end. Complete as for left front from *** to *** working shapings at opposite edges.

BACK
Work as for Front from ** to **

Armhole Shaping
Cast off 5 (6, 7) sts. at beg. of next 4 rows and 5 sts. at beg. of next 4 rows: 104 (108, 112) sts. Cont. without shaping until work measures same as Front to start of shoulder.

Shoulder Shaping

Cast off 10 sts. at beg. of next 4 rows and 10 (11, 12) sts. at beg. of next 2 rows. Cast off remaining 44 (46, 48) sts.

SLEEVES (make 2 alike)

With No. 13 needles cast on 79 (83, 87) sts. and work 6 rows in g.st.

Inc. row (wrong side): k.7 (9, 11), * k.f.b., k.7; rep. from * to last 8 (10, 12) sts., k.f.b., k.7 (9, 11): 88 (92, 96) sts.

Change to No. 12 needles and start centre opening.

1st row: k.44 (46, 48) sts., leave yarn hanging, join another ball and with this k. remaining 44 (46, 48) sts.

2nd row: using second ball p.38 (40, 42), k.6, leave this ball hanging and using first ball k.6, p.38 (40, 42).

Continue using separate balls for the two halves keeping 6 sts. each side of opening in g.st.; do not twist yarns when you cross over as the halves must be kept separate. Work 4 more rows in this way, then start shaping.

**** Inc. 1 st. at both ends of next row; work 5 rows straight.

13th row: inc. in first st., k. until 5 sts. before the opening, k.2 tog., y.r.2, k.2 tog. t.b.l., k.1, leave this ball and with second ball, k.1, k.2 tog., y.r.2, k.2 tog. t.b.l., k. to last st., inc. in this st.

On next row complete the 2 eyelet holes as on front. Work 4 rows straight.****

Rep. from **** to **** once. Now inc. at both ends of next row, work 5 rows straight, rep. 13th row again, then complete eyelet holes on next row: 100 (104, 108) sts.

This completes side incs. Continue working eyelet holes in the g.st. borders until you have 6 (7, 8) pairs in all, always working 10 rows between. At same time work 4 (8, 12) rows straight, then place marker loops of contrast wool at each end of last row to indicate end of sleeve seam. Work 28 (34, 40) rows straight. Cast off 6 sts. at beg. of next 10 rows: 40 (44, 48) sts.

Next row: cast off 6, k. to end of this section, then using same ball of wool k. the 20 (22, 24) sts. of second half so that the two halves are joined.

Next row: cast off 6, p. until there are 8 (10, 12) sts. on right-hand needle, k.12, p. to end. Cast off remaining 28 (32, 36) sts.

NECK BORDER

First join shoulder seams. Slip off the 6 sts. of right front border on to a No.12 needle with point at inner edge then on to same needle, with right side facing, pick up and k.27 (29, 31) sts. along right front neck, 40 (42, 44) sts. across back neck and 27 (29, 31) sts. down left front neck then k. the 6 sts. of border: 106 (112, 118) sts. Work 5 rows in g.st. across all sts. Make an eyelet hole at each front edge on next 2 rows. Change to No. 13 needles and work 6 more rows in g.st. Cast off.

TO COMPLETE

Press shoulder seams and all st.st. sections lightly on wrong side with warm iron and damp cloth. Sew in sleeves joining straight rows above markers to armhole casting-off. Press seams. Remove markers. Join side and sleeve seams and press. Make a crochet chain 36 in. long and lace this through holes in front to tie at neck. Make two crochet chains each 40 (44, 48) in. long and lace these through holes in each sleeve.

Creamy sweaters, worked in traditional Aran stitches, are in five sizes and have a choice of ribbed neck border or polo neckline (instructions start on page 149).

Red, white and blue dress in simple stocking stitch (see page 139).

Vertical stripes make a slimming line for this tunic sweater (see page 133).

Sweater with crochet medallions

instructions for polo-neck sweater start on page 130

MATERIALS
12 (13, 14) balls (25 gr. each) Wendy Invitation Crochet Cotton. One pair each Nos. 11 and 13 knitting needles (USA sizes 2 and 0). One crochet hook International Standard Size 3·00.

MEASUREMENTS
To fit bust size 34 (36, 38) in.; length 22 (22½, 23) in.; sleeve seam 3 (3, 3½) in.

TENSION
7 sts. and 9 rows to 1 in. over st.st. on No. 11 needles.

ABBREVIATIONS
See page 11.

BACK
With No. 11 needles cast on 119 (125, 131) sts. and work as follows:
1st row: (p.2, k.1) 39 (41, 43) times, p.2.
2nd row: (k.2, p.1) 39 (41, 43) times, k.2.
These 2 rows form the patt. Cont. in patt. until work measures 3 in. from beg. Change to No. 13 needles and take 2 tog. at both

ends of next and every foll. 6th row 4 times in all: 111 (117, 123) sts.

Cont. in patt. until work measures 6½ in. from beg. Change back to No. 11 needles and inc. at both ends of next and every foll. 6th row 7 times in all: 125 (131, 137) sts.

Cont. in patt. without further shaping until work measures 14¾ in. from beg.

Shape Armholes

Cast off 6 (7, 7) at beg. of next 2 rows, then take 2 tog. at both ends of next 9 (11, 11) right-side rows: 95 (95, 101) sts.

Cont. until work measures 18 (18½, 19) in. from beg.

Shape Neck

Next row (right side): (p.2, k.1) 15 (15, 16) times, p.2, leave these sts. on a spare needle, cast off 1, (p.2, k.1) 15 (15, 16) times, p.2. Now take 2 tog. at neck edge on every row 35 (35, 36) times. Cast off rem. 12 (12, 14) sts. Return to sts. on spare needle and complete second shoulder to match first, reversing all shapings.

FRONT

Work as for Back until work measures 6½ in. from beg. Change to No. 11 needles and beg. side shaping.

Next row: work twice into first st., patt. 54 (57, 60) and leave on a spare needle, cast off 1, patt. 55 (58, 61) working twice into last st.: 56 (59, 62) sts.

Next row: patt. to end of row, taking last 2 sts. tog.

Next row: cast off 2, patt. to end of row. Rep. these 2 rows twice more.

7th row: work twice into first st., patt. to end of row, taking last 2 sts. tog.

8th row: cast off 2, patt. to end of row.

9th row: patt. to end of row, taking last 2 sts. tog.

10th row: cast off 2, patt. to end of row.

11th row: as 9th row.

12th row: as 10th row.

Rep. 7th to 12th rows 4 times, then cont. in a similar way until all sts. have been worked off. Return to sts. on spare needle, and work other side to match first, reversing all shapings.

YOKE

With No. 11 needles cast on 3 sts. and k. 1 row. Now work in reversed st.st. (1 row p., 1 row k.) as follows:

1st row: cast on 2, p. to end of row, working twice into last st.

2nd row: cast on 2, k. to end of row, working twice into last st.

Rep. these 2 rows until there are 125 (131, 137) sts. on needle then cont. without further shaping until work measures 8¼ in. from point.

Shape Armhole and for Medallion

1st row: cast off 6 (7, 7), p. 26 (28, 29) and leave on spare needle, cast off 5, p.51 (51, 55) and leave on second spare needle, cast off 5, p.32 (35, 36).

2nd row: cast off 6 (7, 7), k.24 (26, 27), k.2 tog.: 25 (27, 28) sts.

3rd row: p.2 tog. at both ends of row: 23 (25, 26) sts.

4th row: k.21 (23, 24), k.2 tog.: 22 (24, 25) sts.
5th row: p.2 tog. at both ends of row: 20 (22, 23) sts.
6th row: k.2 tog. at end of row: 19 (21, 22) sts.
7th row: p.2 tog. at end of row: 18 (20, 21) sts.
8th row: k.2 tog. at end of row: 17 (19, 20) sts.
9th row: p.2 tog. at both ends of row: 15 (17, 18) sts.
10th row: k.2 tog. at end of row: 14 (16, 17) sts.
11th row: p.2 tog. at both ends of row: 12 (14, 15) sts.
12th row: k.2 tog. at end of row: 11 (13, 14) sts.
13th row: p.2 tog. at end of row: 10 (12, 13) sts.
14th row: k.
15th row: p.2 tog. at end of row: 9 (11, 12) sts.
16th row: k.
17th row: p.2 tog. at end of row: 8 (10, 11) sts.
18th row: k.
19th row: p.2 tog. at end of row: 7 (9, 10) sts.
20th row: k.
Size 34 only. 21st row: p. **Sizes 36 and 38 only. 21st row:** p., taking 2 tog. at end of row. **All sizes:** 7 (8, 9) sts.
22nd row: k., working twice into last st.: 8 (9, 10) sts.
Size 34 only. 23rd row: p. twice into first st. and p. to end of row. **Sizes 36 and 38 only. 23rd row:** p., working twice into first st. and taking 2 tog. at end of row: 9 (9, 10) sts.
24th row: k., working twice into last st.: 10 (10, 11) sts.
25th row: p. twice into first st., p. to end of row: 11 (11, 12) sts.
26th row: k., working twice into last st.: 12 (12, 13) sts.
27th row: p.
Rep. 24th and 25th rows twice more.
32nd row: as 24th row.
33rd row: p.17 (17, 20) sts. Leave on spare needle. Return to the 26 (28, 29) sts. on spare needle and work to match first piece, reversing all shapings. Leave these 17 (17, 18) sts. on another spare needle. Return to the 51 (51, 55) sts. on centre needle and with wrong side facing work as follows:
1st row: k.2 tog. at both ends of row: 49 (49, 53) sts.
2nd row: p.2 tog. at both ends of row: 47 (47, 51) sts. Rep. these 2 rows then rep. first row again. Work one row without shaping: 41 (41, 45) sts.
Rep. these 6 rows: 31 (31, 35) sts.
13th row: k.
14th row: p.
Rep. these 2 rows once more.
17th row: k. twice into first and last sts.: 33 (33, 37) sts.
18th row: p. twice into first and last sts.: 35 (35, 39) sts.
19th row: as 17th row: 37 (37, 41) sts.
20th row: as 18th row: 39 (39, 43) sts.
21st row: as 17th row: 41 (41, 45) sts.
22nd row: p.
23rd row: k. twice into first st., k.19 (19, 21) and leave on a spare needle, cast off 1, k.19 (19, 21), k. twice into last st.
24th row: p. twice into first st., p.18 (18, 20), p.2 tog.; turn. Place rem. 21 (21, 23) sts. on a spare needle.
25th row: k.2 tog., k.18 (18, 20), k. twice into last st.
26th row: p. twice into first st., p.18 (18, 20), p.2 tog.
27th row: k. 2 tog., k.18 (18, 20), k. twice into last st.
28th row: p. to last 2 sts., p.2 tog.
29th row: k.2 tog., k.18 (18, 20); turn. Cast on 5; turn. Now

k.17 (17, 18) sts. from holder: 41 (41, 44) sts.
Cont. to take 2 tog. at neck edge on every row until 12 (12, 14) sts. rem. Cast off. Work opposite side to match reversing shapings.

SLEEVES (make 2 alike)
With No. 13 needles cast on 80 (83, 86) sts. and work in ribbed patt. as for body of work for 1 in. Change to No. 11 needles and cont. in ribbing until work measures 3 (3, 3½) in. from beg. Cast off 6 (7, 7) at beg. of next 2 rows. Take 2 tog. at both ends of next 5 (9, 11) right-side rows, then dec. at both ends of every row 19 (15, 15) times. Cast off rem. 20 (21, 20) sts. ribwise.

MEDALLIONS (make 2 alike)
With crochet hook work 9 ch. and join into a ring with a sl.st.
1st round: 3 ch., then work 17 tr. into ring. Join with a sl.st.
2nd round: (7 ch., 1 d.c. into 2nd st. from hook) 9 times.
3rd round: 9 d.c. into each ch.loop, then join with a sl.st. Now sl.st. up first 4 ch. of loop.
4th round: (6 ch., 1 d.c. into 5th d.c. of loop) 9 times and join with a sl.st.
5th round: (1 d.c., 1 half tr., 6 tr., 1 half tr., 1 d.c.) into space 9 times, join with a sl.st. Fasten off.

TO COMPLETE
Press all pieces under damp cloth. Join yoke to front with neat backstitching. Backstitch shoulder seams. Set in sleeves. Join sleeve and side seams. With crochet hook work a row of d.c. all round neck, taking care to keep it flat and even, then work (1 d.c., 1 ch.) all round, finishing with a sl.st. Stitch medallions over holes in front, making edges very neat and firm. Press again.

Polo-neck sweater with cut-away armholes

illustrated on page 127

MATERIALS
11 (12, 13, 14, 15) balls (25 gr. each) Hayfield Diane. One pair each Nos. 9 and 11 knitting needles (USA sizes 5 and 2).

MEASUREMENTS
To fit bust size 32 (34, 36, 38, 40) in.; length 23½ (24, 24½, 25, 25½) in.

TENSION
6 sts. to 1 in. over pattern on No. 9 needles.

ABBREVIATIONS
See page 11.

BACK
* With No. 11 needles cast on 111 (115, 119, 123, 127) sts. and work 16 rows in k.1, p.1 rib.
Change to No. 9 needles and work in pattern as follows:
1st row: * p.3, k.1; rep. from * to last 3 sts., p.3.
2nd row: * k.3, sl.1 purlwise; rep. from * to last 3 sts., k.3.
These 2 rows form the patt. Cont. in patt. until work measures 15½ in. from beg.

Cast off 4 sts. at start of next 2 rows.
Next row: p.2, p.2 tog., patt. to last 4 sts., p.2 tog. t.b.l., p.2.
Next row: k.2, patt. to last 2 sts., k.2. ** Cont. to dec. keeping pattern correct until 32 (34, 36, 38, 40) sts. rem. Cast off.

FRONT

Work as Back to **. Cont. to dec. for raglan until 49 (55, 57, 63, 65) sts. rem.

Shape Neck
Next row (wrong side): k.2, patt. 18 (20, 21, 23, 24), cast off 9 (11, 11, 13, 13), patt. to end.
Work on these end sts. only. Cont. to dec. on raglan edge as before and at the same time cast off 2 sts. at beg. of next row (neck edge), and 2 sts. at beg. of foll 2 (3, 3, 4, 4) alt. rows, then 1 st. on next 3 (3, 3, 2, 2) alt. rows.
Dec. on raglan edge until all sts. have been worked off.
Rejoin yarn to rem. sts. and work to match first side, reversing shapings.

SHOULDER GUSSETS (make 2 alike)
With No. 9 needles cast on 15 sts. and work in patt. for 4 rows. Cont. in patt. dec. 1 st. at each end of next row and the foll. 6th and 12th rows. Work 3 rows straight. Cast off 4 sts. at start of next row. Work 1 row. Cast off.

TO COMPLETE
Join three raglan seams (i.e. stitching shoulder gussets in positions between back and front of sweater).

Collar
With right side facing and No. 11 needles pick up 125 (125, 129, 129, 133) sts. round neck edge and work 14 rows in k.1, p.1 rib and then 34 rows in patt. Cast off in pattern.
Join other raglan seam.

Armhole Edgings (work both alike)
With right side facing and No. 11 needles pick up 94 (96, 98, 100, 102) sts. round armhole edge and work 6 rows k.1, p.1 rib. Cast off in rib. Join side seams.

MATERIALS
16 (17, 18) oz. Lister Lavenda Double Crêpe in main colour, 1 oz. in a contrasting colour. One pair each Nos. 8 and 10 knitting needles (USA sizes 6 and 3). One set of four No. 10 needles (USA size 3).

MEASUREMENTS
To fit bust size 34 (36, 38) in.

TENSION
6 sts. and 7 rows to I inch on No. 8 needles.

ABBREVIATIONS
See page 11; M., main colour; C., contrasting colour.

Classic V-necked sweater

illustrated in colour on page 143

BACK

With No. 10 needles and M. cast on 109 (115, 121) sts. and work 14 rows in st.st. Join in C., and work foll. stripe patt: 2 rows C., 12 rows M., 2 rows C.

Change to No. 8 needles and work 2 more rows in st.st. in M., then continue in rib pattern as follows:

1st row: k.

2nd row: * k.1, p.1; rep. from * to last st., k.1. These 2 rows form pattern. Continue in patt. until work measures $16\frac{1}{4}$ ($16\frac{1}{2}$, $16\frac{3}{4}$) in. measured from the first C. stripe.

Shape Armholes

Cast off 5 sts. at beg. of next 2 rows. Cast off 2 sts. at beg. of next 2 rows. Cast off 1 st. at beg. of next 10 rows. Continue on these sts. until the armholes measure $6\frac{3}{4}$ (7, 7) in.

Shape Shoulders

Cast off 10 (12, 14) sts. at beg. of next 2 rows, and 12 sts. at beg. of the next 2 rows. Cast off rem. sts.

FRONT

Work as for back until work measures $11\frac{1}{2}$ ($11\frac{3}{4}$, 12) in. from the first C. stripe. Divide in centre for neck: work over 54 (57, 60) sts., turn and finish this side first.

Dec. at neck edge on each 2nd and 4th row alternately, and at the same time when work measures $16\frac{1}{4}$ ($16\frac{1}{2}$, $16\frac{3}{4}$) in. from the first C. stripe shape armhole as follows: starting from the side edge cast off at the beg. of the next 7 rows at this edge, 5 sts. once, 2 sts. once, and 1 st. 5 times.

Continue the decs. at neck edge until 22 (24, 26) sts. rem. and when the armhole measures $6\frac{3}{4}$ (7, 7) in. shape shoulder as follows:

Starting from the armhole edge cast off 10 (12, 14) sts., work to neck edge, turn and work back, turn and cast off rem. sts.

Rejoin yarn at centre front. Cast off the centre stitch, and work the other side to match, reversing shapings.

SLEEVES (make 2 alike)

With No. 10 needles and M. cast on 60 sts. and work 14 rows in st.st.

Join in C. and work foll. stripe patt.: 2 rows C., 12 rows M., 2 rows C.

Change to No. 8 needles and work 2 rows in st.st. in M., then continue in rib pattern, inc. 1 st. at the beg. and end of the 5th (5th, first) row and then each 8th row until there are 84 (86, 88) sts. Cont. in rib patt. until work measures 16 ($16\frac{1}{2}$, 17) in. from the first C. stripe.

Shape Top

Cast off 5 sts. at beg. of next 2 rows. Cast off 1 st. at beg. of next 18 (20, 22) rows. Cast off 3 sts. at beg. of next 2 rows. Cast off 4 sts. at beg. of next 2 rows. Cast off 5 sts. at beg. of next 2 rows. Cast off 6 sts. at beg. of next 2 rows. Cast off 7 sts. at beg. of next 2 rows. Cast off remaining sts.

TO COMPLETE

Press the pieces lightly under a damp cloth. Sew the shoulder side and sleeve seams, and set the sleeves into the armholes. Turn under the first 14 rows of st.st. in M. at the bottom of sweater and end of sleeves and slipstitch to form a hem.

Neck Border
With the set of four No. 10 needles and M., and starting from the centre front pick up and k. 62 (65, 68) sts. along the right side of neck, 38 (40, 42) sts. across the back, and 62 (65, 68) sts. along the left side of neck, turn; p.2 tog., p. to last 2 sts., p.2 tog.; turn; change to C., k.2 tog., k. to last 2 sts., k.2 tog.
Continue in this way, dec. 1 st. at the beg. and end of each row, and working 2 rows in C., 8 rows in M. and 2 in C., then complete neck border in M. and inc. 1 st. at the beg. and end of each row for the neck facing, after the 14th row cast off loosely. Backstitch the 2 sides of neck border together using very small sts. Press the seam, and then turn the last 14 rows of st.st. towards the inside and stitch to the neck edge of the sweater.

MATERIALS
Of Hayfield Gaylon Double Knitting: 7 oz. in cream, 4 oz. in yellow, 7 oz. in dark grey, 1 oz. in light grey, and 1 oz. in brown. One pair each Nos. 9 and 10 knitting needles (USA sizes 5 and 3). A set of four No. 10 needles (USA size 3).

MEASUREMENTS
To fit bust size 34/36 in.; length 26 in.; sleeve seam $17\frac{1}{2}$ in.

TENSION
6 sts. and 8 rows to 1 in. over st.st. on No. 9 needles.

ABBREVIATIONS
See page 11; C., cream; Y., yellow; D.G., dark grey; L.G., light grey; B., brown.

THE COLOUR PATTERN
The pattern consists of the following stripe sequence:
* 4 rows C.; 4 rows Y.; 2 rows B.; 4 rows C.; 4 rows D.G.; 4 rows C.; 4 rows Y.; 2 rows L.G.; 4 rows C.; 4 rows D.G.; 4 rows C.; 4 rows Y.; 2 rows B.; 4 rows C.; 4 rows D.G.; 4 rows C.; 4 rows Y.; 2 rows L.G.; 4 rows C.; ** the centre stripe is worked in 4 rows D.G.

BACK
With No. 9 needles and C. cast on 82 sts. and work in st. st. in the stripe sequence as given above for 8 rows, ending at armhole edge.

Shape Armhole
Keeping in stripe sequence, inc. 1 st. at beg. of next and every foll. alt. row until 87 sts. Work one row back to armhole edge.

Shape Shoulder
Next row: cast on 41 sts., work to end of row: 128 sts. on needle, and first row of C.
At beg. of next 8th row inc. 1 st., and on every following 8th

Striped tunic sweater

illustrated in colour on page 126

row inc. 1 st. until 131 sts. are on needle, then on next 6th row inc. 1 st. at same edge: 132 sts., 3rd row of C. stripe worked. Work 1 row. Work 2 rows of D.G. stripe.

Shape Neck

Keeping in stripe sequence, cast off 6 sts. at beg. of row, work to end. At beg. of next and every foll. alt. row dec. 1 st. until 122 sts. rem. and ending on 3rd row of Y. stripe. Complete this stripe.

Work 2 rows L.G.; work 4 rows C: 68 rows now completed. Work centre stripe in D.G.: centre of back is now reached. Now work in the stripe sequence in reverse (from ** back to *) but when 6 rows have been worked from centre stripe, at beg. of next and every alt. row inc. 1 st. until 126 sts. are on needle.

At beg. of next alt. row cast on 6 sts.: 132 sts. on needle, and first row of D.G. stripe worked.

Cont. in stripe sequence and dec. 1 st. at beg. of next and every foll. 6th row until 128 sts. rem. Work 7 rows straight. At beg. of next row cast off 41 sts.: 87 sts. At beg. of next and every foll. alt. row dec. 1 st. until 82 sts. rem.: 3rd row of Y. stripe worked. Complete this stripe and work the last 4 rows of C. stripe: 68 rows are now completed from centre back stripe. Cast off.

FRONT

Work as for Back until beg. of neck shaping. Cast off 8 sts. then dec. 1 st. at beg. of next and every alt. row until 120 sts. rem.

Work in stripe sequence to centre stripe then work the stripe sequence in reverse from ** back to *, casting on 8 sts. instead of 6 as for back.

SLEEVES (make 2 alike)

Work sleeves in the following colour sequence:
* 2 rows D.G.; 4 rows C.; 4 rows Y.; 2 rows L.G.; 4 rows C.; 4 rows D.G.; 4 rows C.; 4 rows Y.; 2 rows B.; 4 rows C.; 4 rows D.G.; 4 rows C.; 4 rows Y.; 2 rows L.G.; 4 rows C.; **, 52 rows pattern, then centre stripe of 4 rows D.G.

With No. 9 needles and D.G., cast on 72 sts. Working in the stripe sequence as given above, work 6 rows st.st.

*** At beg. of each of next 12 rows cast on 2 sts. At beg. of next k. row cast on 2 sts. Keep k. row edge straight but cont. to inc. 1 st. at beg. of every p. row 8 times: 106 sts. At this top edge inc. 1 st. on every row 10 times: **** 116 sts.

Work 8 rows without shaping: 52 rows of stripe pattern now completed.

Work the centre stripe of sleeve in D.G.

Now working from ** back to * of stripe sequence for sleeves, work 8 rows straight. Cont. in stripes working decs. instead of incs. working from **** back to ***, then work 6 rows ending with 2 rows D.G. and 72 sts. on needle. Cast off.

TO COMPLETE

Press pieces lightly with warm iron over damp cloth. With No. 10 needles and D.G., pick up and k. 104 sts. along lower edge of front and work in k.1, p.1 rib for $2\frac{1}{2}$ in. Cast off.

Work back welt in a similar way. At lower sleeve edge, with No. 10 needles and D.G., pick up and k. 50 sts., work in k.1, p.1 rib for 3 in. Cast off ribwise.

Neck Ribbing

Join shoulder seams of back and front. With set of four No. 10 needles and D.G., and right side of work facing, pick up and k. 110 sts. all round neck edge.
K. one round.
Now work in k.1, p.1 rib for 5 in.
Cast off ribwise.

To Make Up

Join side seams. Join sleeve seams and set in sleeves. Press all seams.

Cable-patterned jacket

MATERIALS

25 (27, 29) oz. Wendy Nylonised Double Knitting Wool. One pair each Nos. 9 and 10 knitting needles (USA sizes 5 and 3), plus circular knitting needles in the same sizes, each 30 in. long. A cable needle. Twelve medium buttons.

MEASUREMENTS

To fit bust size 34 (36, 38) in.; length 26 ($26\frac{1}{2}$, 27) in.; sleeve seam 17 in.

TENSION

6 sts. and 8 rows to 1 in. on No. 9 needles.

ABBREVIATIONS

See page 11; m.1, make 1 st. by picking up the strand between the st. just worked and the foll. st., place it on the left-hand needle and k. it t.b.l.; C.6, cable 6 sts., by sl.3 sts. on to cable needle, leave at back of work, k.3, then k.3 from cable needle.

MAIN PIECE

With No. 10 circular needle cast on 229 (243, 257) sts. Work in

rows. Beg. with a p. row, work 4 rows in st.st. Cast on 25 sts. at beg. of each of the next 2 rows.

Next row: k. into the backs of all sts. to form the hemline. Change to No. 9 circular needle.

Next row: k.12, sl.1, k. to last 13 sts., sl.1, k.12.

Next row: p.

Rep. the last 2 rows 11 times more.

Next row: k.12, sl.1, k.33 (35, 37), * k.2 tog., k.1, sl.1, k.1, p.s.s.o., * k.56 (59, 62); rep. from * to * , k.55 (59, 63); rep. from * to *, k.56 (59, 62); rep. from * to *, k.33 (35, 37), sl.1, k.12.

Keeping the sl. sts. in line up to the neck, work 23 rows.

Next row: k.12, sl.1, k.32 (34, 36), * k.2 tog., k.1, sl.1, k.1, p.s.s.o., * k.54 (57, 60); rep. from * to *, k.53 (57, 61); rep. from * to *, k.54 (57, 60); rep. from * to *, k.32 (34, 36), sl.1, k.12.

Work 15 rows.

Next row: k.12, sl.1, k.31 (33, 35), * k.2 tog., k.1, sl.1, k.1, p.s.s.o., * k.52 (55, 58); rep. from * to *, k.51 (55, 59); rep. from * to *, k.52 (55, 58); rep. from * to *, k.31 (33, 35), sl.1, k.12.

P. one row.

Next row: make a pair of buttonholes: k.4, cast off 4, k.4, sl.1, k.4, cast off 4, k. to last 13 sts., sl.1, k.12.

Next row: in patt., casting on 4 sts. over those cast off in the last row.

Continue to make pairs of buttonholes as for the first at 3 in. intervals until 6 have been made altogether.

Next row: k.12, sl.1, k.12, * p.2, k.2, m.1, k.3; rep. from * to last 27 sts., p.2, k.12, sl.1, k.12.

Beg. cable pattern:

1st row: p.25, * k.2, p.6; rep. from * to last 27 sts., k.2, p.25.

2nd row: k.12, sl.1, k.12, * p.2, C.6; rep. from * to last 27 sts., p.2, k.12, sl.1, k.12.

3rd row: as first row.

4th row: k.12, sl.1, k.12, * p.2, k.6; rep. from * to last 27 sts., p.2, k.12, sl.1, k.12.

5th and 6th rows: as first and 4th rows.

7th row: as first row.

8th row: as 2nd row.

Rep. the last 8 rows 4 times more, then rep. first and 2nd rows.

Next row: p.25, * k.2, p.2, p.2 tog., p.2; rep. from * to last 27 sts., k.2, p.25.

Continue in st.st. until work measures 5 in. above the cable pattern.

Next row: k.12, sl.1, k.55 (58, 61), cast off 10 (12, 14), k.99 (103, 107), cast off 10 (12, 14), k.55 (58, 61), sl.1, k.12.

Front

Work on last set of sts. only for first side of front.

P. one row.

Dec. 1 st. at armhole edge on next and following 7 alternate rows. Continue straight until armhole measures 5¼ (5½, 5¾) in. ending at the front edge.

Shape Neck

Next row: cast off 25 sts., work to the end of the row. Dec.

1 st. at neck edge on every row until 23 (24, 25) sts. remain. Continue if necessary until armhole measures 7 (7½, 8) in. ending at armhole edge.

Shape Shoulder
Cast off at the beg. of next and every following alternate row 7 (8, 8) sts. once, 8 sts. once, 8 (8, 9) sts. once.

Back
Return to the centre sts. and work the back. P. one row. Dec. 1 st. at each end of the next and following 7 alternate rows. Continue straight until armholes measure the same as the front, ending after a p. row.

Shape Shoulders
Cast off 7 (7, 8) sts. at the beg. of the next 2 rows. Cast off 8 sts. at the beg. of the next 2 rows. Cast off 8 (8, 9) sts. at the beg. of the next 2 rows. Cast off the remaining sts.
Return to the remaining set of sts. P. one row.
Complete to match the first side.

SLEEVES (make 2 alike)
With pair of No. 10 needles, cast on 48 (52, 56) sts.
Beg. with a p. row, work 6 rows in st.st.
Next row: k. into the backs of all sts. to form the hemline.
Next row: k.13 (15, 17), * p.2, k.1, m.1, k.2, m.1, k.1, * p.2, k.6; rep. from * to *, p.2, k.13 (15, 17).

Cable Pattern
1st row: p.13 (15, 17), * k.2, p.6; rep. from * twice more, k.2, p.13 (15, 17).
2nd row: k.13 (15, 17), p.2, C.6, p.2, k.6, p.2, C.6; p.2, k.13 (15, 17).
3rd row: as first row.
4th row: k.13 (15, 17), * p.2, k.6; rep. from * twice more, k.2, p.13 (15, 17).
5th and 6th rows: rep. first and 4th rows.
7th row: as first row.
8th row: as 2nd row.
Rep. the last 8 rows 4 times more, then rep. first and 2nd rows and at the same time inc. 1 st. at each end of the 14th row and every following 6th row.
Next row: work to the cable pattern, * k.2, p.1, (p.2 tog.) twice, p.1, * k.2, p.6; rep. from * to *, k.2, work to the end of the row.
Continue in st.st. over all sts. and to inc. as before on every 6th row until there are 84 (88, 92) sts.
Continue straight until sleeve measures 17 in., ending after a p. row.

Shape Top
Cast off 5 (6, 7) sts. at the beg. of the next 2 rows.
Dec. 1 st. at each end of the next 6 (4, 2) rows.
Dec. 1 st. at each end of the next and every following alternate row until 42 sts. remain.
Work one row.
Dec. 1 st. at each end of the next 4 rows.

Cast off 4 sts. at each end of the next 4 rows.
Cast off the remaining sts.

COLLAR

With No. 9 circular needle cast on 212 (212, 226) sts.
Work in rounds.

1st round: sl.1, * p.2, k.6; rep. from * 14 (14, 15) times more, p.2, sl.1, k.90 (90, 96).
2nd round: sl.1, * p.2, C.6; rep. from * 14 (14, 15) times more, p.2, sl.1, k.90 (90, 96).
3rd to 8th rounds: rep. first round 6 times.
Rep. the last 8 rounds once more, then rep. first and 2nd rounds.
Next round: sl.1, * p.2, k.1, (k.2 tog.) twice, k.1; rep. from * 14 (14, 15) times more, p.2, sl.1, k.90 (90, 96).
Cast off as follows: sl. the first 91 (91, 97) sts. on to a double-pointed needle, fold collar in half, so that the points of needles meet. With a third needle, cast off k. wise through double sts.

POCKETS (make 2 alike)

With pair of No. 10 needles cast on 32 sts.
P. one row, then k. one row.
Next row: k. into the backs of all sts. to form the hemline.
Next row: * p.2, k.1, m.1, k.2, m.1, k.1; rep. from * to last 2 sts., p.2.

Cable Pattern

1st row: * k.2, p.6; rep. from * to last 2 sts., k.2.
2nd row: * p.2, C.6; rep. from * to last 2 sts., p.2.
3rd row: as first row.
4th row: * p.2, k.6; rep. from * to last 2 sts., p.2.
5th and 6th rows: as first and 4th rows.
7th row: as first row.
8th row: as 2nd row.
Next row: * k.2, p.1, (p.2 tog.) twice, p.1; rep. from * to last 2 sts., k.2.
Next row: p. into the backs of all sts. to form the hemline.
Beg. with a p. row, work 5 rows in st.st.
Cast off.

TO COMPLETE

Press with a warm iron over a damp cloth avoiding the cables. Sew up shoulder seams. Pin cabled edge of collar round neck, with cable edge to right side of st.st. Back st. and press. Hem down stocking st. Fold under fronts at sl. sts. and hem lightly to inside. Buttonhole stitch the pairs of buttonholes together. Sew up sleeves and sew them into armholes. Turn under hem at lower edge, wrists, and tops and bottoms of pockets. Sew on pockets 1½ in. below cabled waist and 4 in. from the front edge. Press seams, hems and facings, steam collar and pockets lightly. Sew on buttons to correspond with buttonholes, then sew on 3 buttons down each sleeve on st.st. panel between cables.

MATERIALS

Of Templeton's Antler Double Crêpe: 7 (8, 9) balls (1 oz. each) each in a light, medium and dark colour. One pair of No. 8 knitting needles (USA size 6). 1¼ yd. petersham ribbon, 1 in. wide.

MEASUREMENTS

To fit bust size 34 (36, 38) in.; length 34 (34½, 35) in.

TENSION

11½ sts. to 2 in.

ABBREVIATIONS

See page 11; L., light colour; M., medium colour; D., dark colour.

BACK
The First Point

With D., cast on 3 sts. Work in st.st. and stripe patt. of 14 rows D., 14 rows M., and 14 rows L throughout, now inc. 1 st. at beg. of every row until there are 67 (70, 72) sts.

For sizes 36 and 38 only. P. 1 row.

All sizes. Leave sts. on a spare needle and work a second piece in a similar way.

Next row: inc. in first st., k.66 (69, 71), then k. across sts. of first point thus: inc. in first st., k.66 (69, 71).

Next row: inc. in first st., p. to end: 137 (143, 147) sts.

Continue in stripe patt. and work as follows:

1st row: inc. in first st., k.66 (69, 71), sl.1, k.2 tog., p.s.s.o., k. to end.

2nd row: inc. in first st., p. to end.

Rep. these 2 rows until work measures 14½ in. along side edge.

Shape work thus:

Next row: k.67 (70, 72), sl.1, k.2 tog., p.s.s.o., k. to end.

Next row: p.: 135 (141, 145) sts.

Next row: inc. in first st., k.65 (68, 70), sl.1, k.2 tog., p.s.s.o., k. to end.

Next row: inc. in first st., p. to end.

Rep. last 2 rows 8 times more.

Next row: k.66 (69, 71), sl.1, k.2 tog., p.s.s.o., k. to end.

Next row: p.: 133 (139, 143) sts.

Next row: inc. in first st., k.64 (67, 69), sl.1, k.2 tog., p.s.s.o., k. to end.

Next row: inc. in first st., p. to end.

Rep. last 2 rows 8 times more.

Next row: k.65 (68, 70), sl.1, k.2 tog., p.s.s.o., k. to end.

Next row: p.: 131 (137, 141) sts.

Next row: inc. in first st., k.63 (66, 68), sl.1, k.2 tog., p.s.s.o., k. to end.

Next row: inc. in first st., p. to end.

Rep. last 2 rows 8 times more.

Next row: k.64 (67, 69), sl.1, k.2 tog., p.s.s.o., k. to end.

Next row: p.: 129 (135, 139) sts.

Next row: inc. in first st., k.62 (65, 67), sl.1, k.2 tog., p.s.s.o., k. to end.

Red, white and blue dress

illustrated in colour on page 126

Next row: inc. in first st., p. to end.

Rep. last 2 rows until work measures 34 (34½, 35) in. along side edge.

Next row: k.2 tog., k.61 (64, 66) (*Note.* k.2 sts. less here on each rep. of this row), sl.1, k.2 tog., p.s.s.o., k. to end.

Next row: p.2 tog., p. to end.

Rep. these 2 rows 13 (14, 15) times more: 73 (75, 75) sts. Mark both ends of last row with a thread. **

Next row: k.2 tog., k.33 (34, 34) (*Note.* k.3 sts. less here on each rep. of this row), sl.1, k.2 tog., p.s.s.o., k. to last 2 sts., k.2 tog.

Next row: p.2 tog., p. to last 2 sts., p.2 tog.

Rep. last 2 rows until 7 (9, 9) sts. remain.

For size 34 only. Next row: k.2 tog., sl.1, k.2 tog., p.s.s.o., k.2 tog. Cast off.

For sizes 36 and 38 only. Next row: (sl.1, k.2 tog., p.s.s.o) 3 times. Cast off.

FRONT

Work as for back to **.

Neck Facing

Next row: k. across 73 (75, 75) sts. of front, then with same needle and beg. and ending at markers, pick up and k.55 (57, 57) sts. along back neck edge.

Next row: k. to mark hemline.

Continue thus:

1st row: inc. in first st., k.35 (36, 36), work 3 sts. into next st., k.35 (36, 36), inc. into each of next 2 sts., k. to last st., inc. in last st.

2nd and following 2 alternate rows: p. increasing 1 st. at both ends of row.

3rd row: inc. in first st., k.38 (39, 39), work 3 sts. into next st., k.37 (38, 38), inc. into each of next 2 sts., k. to last st., inc. in last st.

5th row: inc. in first st., k.41 (42, 42), work 3 sts. into next st., k.39 (40, 40), inc. into each of next 2 sts., k. to last st., inc. in last st.

Cast off.

TO COMPLETE

Press lightly with a warm iron. Join shoulder seams and ends of neck facing.

Arm Facings (make both alike)

With D. and right side of work facing and beg. and ending 6 in. each side of shoulder seam, pick up and k.66 sts. along side edge. Beg. with p., work 5 rows in st.st.
Cast off.

To Make Up

Join side seams and ends of arm facings. Fold neck and arm facings to wrong side and slipstitch in position. Mark a straight line along lower edge of dress by running a thread across work. With right side of work facing, sew petersham along this line, then fold ribbon under and slipstitch to wrong side of work. Press seams, facings and hem.

Wrap-over jacket

MATERIALS
34 oz. Hayfield Croft Double Knitting. One pair each Nos. 9 and 11 knitting needles (USA sizes 5 and 2).

MEASUREMENTS
To fit bust size 38/40 in.; length 30½ in.; sleeve seam 17½ in.

TENSION
11 sts. to 2 in. and 8 rows to 1 inch over pattern on No. 9 needles.

ABBREVIATIONS
See page 11.

BACK
With No. 11 needles cast on 144 sts. and work in k.1, p.1 rib for 1 in.
Change to No. 9 needles and work in the following patt.:
1st row: * k.2, p.2; rep. from * to end.
2nd row: as first row.
3rd row: * p.2, k.2; rep. from * to end.
4th row: as 3rd row.
These 4 rows form patt. throughout. Work 14 patt. rows.
On next row and every following 8th row dec. 1 st. at both ends of row until 116 sts. rem. Now work straight until back measures 23 in. from cast-on edge, ending on wrong side of work.

Shape Armholes
At beg. of each of next 2 rows cast off 5 sts. Dec. 1 st. at both ends of next and alt. rows until 92 sts. rem. Work straight in patt. until armholes measure 5 in. from beg. of armhole shaping ending on wrong side of work.

Shape Neck

Patt. 29 sts., turn and cont. on these sts. only. At neck edge of next row cast off 2 sts. At end of next row dec. 1 st. At beg. of next row cast off 2 sts., work to end. At neck edge of each of next 2 rows dec. 1 st.: 22 sts. rem. Work straight on these sts. until armhole measures $7\frac{1}{2}$ in. from beg. of armhole shaping ending at side edge.

Shape Shoulder

At beg. of next and alt. row cast off 7 sts. Work one row.
Cast off rem. 8 sts.
Rejoin yarn to rem. sts. at neck edge and cast off first 34 sts. Work on rem. 29 sts. to match other side.

RIGHT FRONT

With No. 11 needles cast on 83 sts. Work in k.1, p.1 rib for 1 in., ending on wrong side of work.
Next row: slip first 9 sts. on to a stitch holder and leave for front band, work in the patt. rows as for back on No. 9 needles across the rem. 74 sts. Dec. 1 st. at end of 15th row and on following 8th rows until 61 sts. rem.
Work straight until front measures 23 in. from cast-on edge ending at side edge.

Shape Armhole

At beg. of next row cast off 5 sts. At beg of armhole edge rows dec. 1 st. until 49 sts. rem. Work straight until armhole measures 5 in. from beg. of armhole shaping, ending at front edge.

Shape Neck

Cast off 22 sts., work across rem. 27 sts. Cont. in patt. on these 27 sts. Dec. 1 st. at neck edge of next and every foll. alt. row until 22 sts. rem.
Patt. straight on these sts. until armhole measures $7\frac{1}{2}$ in. from beg. of armhole shaping, ending at side edge.

Shape Shoulder

At beg. of next and alt. row cast off 7 sts. Work one row.
Cast off rem. 8 sts.

LEFT FRONT

Work as for Right Front, reversing all shapings.

SLEEVES (make 2 alike)

With No. 11 needles cast on 62 sts. and work in k.1, p.1 rib for 2 rows.
Change to No. 9 needles and beg. with 2nd row of patt. given for back work in patt. for $3\frac{1}{2}$ in. This is end of turn-back cuff. Cont. in patt. and work dec. rows as follows: dec. 1 st. at both ends of next and every foll. alt. row until 54 sts. rem.
Now inc. 1 st. at both ends of every foll. 8th row until 82 sts. are on needle.
Patt. straight until sleeve is $17\frac{1}{2}$ in. from turned-back row of cuff.

Shape Top

At beg. of next 2 rows cast off 5 sts. then dec. 1 st. at both ends

Classic navy and white sweater worked in a broken rib pattern (see page 131).

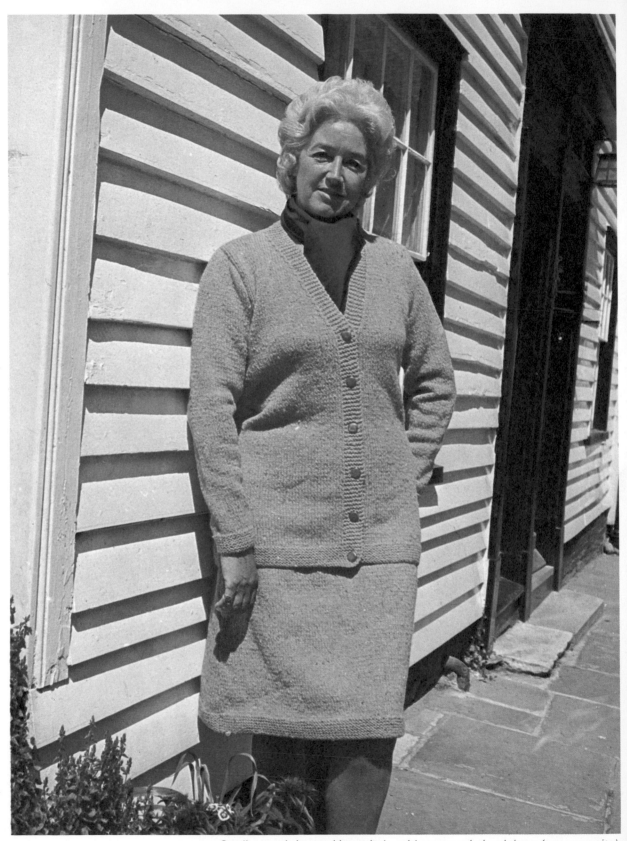

Cardigan suit in stocking stitch, with garter stitch edgings (see opposite).

of next and every foll. alt. rows until 42 sts. rem. At both ends of every row dec. 1 st. until 18 sts. rem.
Cast off.

COLLAR
With No. 9 needles cast on 94 sts. and keeping 1 st. at each end of every right-side row in k.1, and on wrong-side rows in p.1, work the 4-row patt. as for back until collar measures 4½ in. from cast-on edge ending on right side of work. P. one row on wrong side of collar. Leave sts.

FRONT BANDS (make 2 alike)
Slip the 9 sts. left on stitch holder at right front on to a No. 11 needle and cont. in rib until the band fits up to the 22 sts. cast off at neck edge, slightly stretched. Leave sts.

BELT
With No. 9 needles cast on 36 sts. and work in the patt. rows as for back until work is 60 in. Dec. 1 st. at both ends of every row until 8 sts. rem. Cast off.

POCKETS (make 2 alike)
With No. 9 needles cast on 26 sts. and work in patt. as for back until piece measures 6½ in. from beg. Cast off. Turn over one corner of pocket 1½ in. and stitch down. This folded edge forms side of pocket.

TO COMPLETE
Press all pieces of work.
With No. 11 needles k. up 30 sts. along one short edge of collar, then slip the 94 sts. left at long edge of collar on to needle and k. up 30 sts. from other short edge of collar. Now work in k.1, p.1 rib, inc. 1 st. each side of the 30 sts. at corner of collar on every right-side row until rib is same width as ribbing on front bands. Cast off. Slip the 9 sts. from one front band on to a No. 11 needle and pick up and k. 18 sts. along top edge of rever where the 22 sts. were cast off for neck. Work in k.1, p.1 rib until same width as rib round collar edge. Cast off. Work other front band in a similar way.
Join shoulder seams. Join side seams and sleeve seams and set in sleeves. Sew ribbing to each front and also along top edge of revers. Sew on collar to neck edge and join it to turned-back revers for about ½ in. Turn back cuffs at sleeve edges. Press all seams. Sew on pockets to each front. Fold belt in half lengthwise with right sides together then seam. Turn to right side and press flat.

Cardigan suit
illustrated opposite

MATERIALS
15 (16, 17) balls (50 gr. each) Mahony's Blarney Heatherspun for cardigan, 9 (10, 10) balls for skirt. One pair each Nos. 7 and 8 knitting needles (USA sizes 7 and 6). Six medium buttons. A waist length of elastic, ¾ in. wide. A 2-in. buckle.

MEASUREMENTS
To fit bust size 36 (38, 40) in.; hip size 38 (40, 42) in.; length of

cardigan 28 (28¼, 28½) in.; sleeve seam 18 in.; length of skirt 25 in.

TENSION
19 sts. to 4 in. in width and 13 rows to 2 in. in depth over st.st. on No. 7 needles.

ABBREVIATIONS
See page 11; k.f.b., knit into front and back of next st.

CARDIGAN BACK
With No. 8 needles cast on 83 (87, 91) sts. and work 12 rows in garter st.
Inc. row: k.6 (8, 10), * k.f.b., k.6; rep. from * to last 7 (9, 11) sts., k.f.b., k. to end: 94 (98, 102) sts.
Change to No. 7 needles and beg. with a k. row work in st.st. but dec. 1 st. at both ends of every following 10th row until 82 (86, 90) sts. remain. Continue without shaping until work measures 11½ in. from beg. Inc. 1 st. at both ends of next row and every following 12th row until there are 90 (94, 98) sts., then continue without shaping until work measures 20½ in. from beg.

Armhole Shaping
Cast off 4 sts. at beg. of next 2 rows and 2 sts. at beg. of next 4 rows then cast off 1 st. at beg. of next 8 (10, 12) rows: 66 (68, 70) sts.
Continue without shaping until work measures 28 (28¼, 28½) in. from beg.

Shoulder Shaping
Cast off 6 sts. at beg. of next 4 rows and 6 (7, 8) sts. at beg. of next 2 rows. Cast off remaining 30 sts.

CARDIGAN RIGHT FRONT
With No. 8 needles cast on 49 (52, 55) sts. and work 5 rows in garter st., then make buttonhole as follows.
6th row (buttonhole row): k.2, k.2 tog., wind yarn twice round right-hand needle, k.2 tog. t.b.l., k. to end.
7th row: k. until the double loop is reached, drop 1 loop to make a long st. and work k.1, p.1 into this loop, k.3.
Work 5 more rows in garter st.
Inc. row: k.7 (9, 11), * k.f.b., k.6; rep. from * to last 7 (8, 9) sts., k. to end: 54 (57, 60) sts. Change to No. 7 needles and work in st.st. with garter st. border thus.
1st row: k.
2nd row: p. to last 7 sts., k.7.
Continue in this way for 7 more rows, then dec. 1 st. at side edge on next row and every following 10th row until 48 (51, 54) sts. remain, but at same time work further buttonholes when work measures 4 in., 7¼ in., 10½ in., 13¾ in., and 17 in. from beg. taking these and all measurements on main part, not on border. Meanwhile when last side dec. has been worked continue without shaping until work measures 11½ in. from beg., then inc. 1 st. at side edge on next row and every following 12th row until there are 52 (55, 58) sts. Continue without shaping until work measures 18 in. from beg., ending at front

146

edge. Start front shaping as follows.
1st row: k.7, k.2 tog. t.b.l., k. to end.
Continue to dec. in this position on every following 4th row 15 (16, 17) times in all and at same time keep side edge straight until work measures 20½ in. from beg., ending at side.

Armhole Shaping
Cast off 4 sts. at beg. of next row and 2 sts. at same edge on next 2 alternate rows then dec. 1 st. at same edge on next 4 (5, 6) alternate rows. Now keeping side edge straight continue with front decs. until all are complete and 25 (26, 27) sts. remain. Continue without shaping until work measures 28 (28¼, 28½) in. from beg., ending at side edge.

Shoulder Shaping
Cast off 6 sts. at beg. of next row and next alternate row and 6 (7, 8) sts. at beg. of next alternate row. You have thus ended at outer edge, with 7 sts. remaining. Change to No. 8 needles.
Next row: k.6, k.f.b.
Continue in garter st. on these 8 sts. for 3¼ in. Cast off.

CARDIGAN LEFT FRONT
With No. 8 needles cast on 49 (52, 55) sts. and work 12 rows in garter st.
Inc. row: k.7 (8, 9), * k.6, k.f.b.; rep. from * to last 7 (9, 11) sts., k. to end: 54 (57, 60) sts. Change to No. 7 needles.
1st row: k.
2nd row: k.7, p. to end.
Continue thus in st.st. with front border in garter st. and work side decs. and incs. in same positions as those of right front, then continue without shaping until work measures 18 in. from beg., ending at side edge. Start front shaping as follows.
1st row: k. to last 9 sts., k.2 tog., k.7.
Continue to dec. in this position on every following 4th row 15 (16, 17) times in all and at the same time complete to match right front working armhole and shoulder shapings at opposite edge.

CARDIGAN SLEEVES (make 2 alike)
With No. 8 needles cast on 35 (37, 40) sts. and work 12 rows in garter st.
Inc. row: k.3 (4, 6), * k.f.b., k.6; rep. from * to last 4 (5, 6) sts., k.f.b., k. to end: 40 (42, 45) sts.
Change to No. 7 needles and work in st.st. but inc. 1 st. at both ends of every following 7th row until there are 68 (70, 73) sts. Continue without shaping until work measures 18 in. from beg. Place marker loops of contrast wool at each end of last row, then work 6 rows straight. Cast off 1 st. at beg. of next 6 rows, 2 sts. at beg. of next 6 (8, 10) rows and 4 sts. at beg. of next 8 rows. Cast off remaining 18 (16, 15) sts.

TO COMPLETE CARDIGAN
Press st.st. sections lightly on wrong side with warm iron and damp cloth. Join shoulder seams. Press seams. Join ends of front border extensions and sew inner edge of this strip to back neck. Press seam using point of iron. Sew in sleeves matching markers to beg. of armhole casting-off. Press seams. Remove

markers. Join side and sleeve seams and press. Sew on buttons to correspond with buttonholes.

SKIRT BACK
With No. 8 needles cast on 108 (113, 118) sts. and work 12 rows in garter st.

Inc. row: k.10 (12, 14), * k.f.b., k.7; rep. from * to last 10 (13, 16) sts., k.f.b., k. to end: 120 (125, 130) sts.

Change to No. 7 needles and beg. with a k. row work in st.st. but dec. 1 st. at both ends of every 10th row until 100 (105, 110) sts. remain. Continue without shaping until work measures $17\frac{1}{4}$ in. from beg., ending with a p. row, and then continue as follows.

1st row: k.2 tog. t.b.l., k. to last 2 sts., k.2 tog.
Work 5 rows straight. Rep. last 6 rows twice more.

19th row: k.2 tog. t.b.l., k.22 (23, 24), k.2 tog., k.2 tog. t.b.l., k.38 (41, 44), k.2 tog., k.2 tog. t.b.l., k.22 (23, 24), k.2 tog.
Work 5 rows straight.

25th row: k.2 tog. t.b.l., k.20 (21, 22), k.2 tog., k.2 tog. t.b.l., k.36 (39, 42), k.2 tog., k.2 tog. t.b.l., k.20 (21, 22), k.2 tog.
Work 5 rows straight.

31st row: k.2 tog. t.b.l., k.18 (19, 20), k.2 tog., k.2 tog. t.b.l., k.34 (37, 40), k.2 tog., k.2 tog. t.b.l., k.18 (19, 20), k.2 tog.
Work 5 rows straight.

37th row: k.2 tog. t.b.l., k.16 (17, 18), k.2 tog., k.2 tog. t.b.l., k.32 (35, 38), k.2 tog., k.2 tog. t.b.l., k.16 (17, 18), k.2 tog.
Work 5 rows straight.

43rd row: k.2 tog. t.b.l., k.14 (15, 16), k.2 tog., k.2 tog. t.b.l., k.30 (33, 36), k.2 tog., k.2 tog. t.b.l., k.14 (15, 16), k.2 tog.
Continue on remaining 64 (69, 74) sts. for 8 rows. Cast off.

SKIRT FRONT
Work exactly as given for Back.

TO COMPLETE SKIRT
Press st.st. parts lightly on wrong side with warm iron and damp cloth. If lower border seems to pull in press it lightly. Backstitch side seams and press. Cut elastic to your waist measurement, overlap ends $\frac{1}{2}$ in. to form a ring, and sew securely. Pin elastic inside waist edge of skirt and hold in place with a row of herringbone sts.

Belt (optional)
With No. 9 needles cast on 11 sts.
1st row: k.2, * p.1, k.1; rep. from * to last st., k.1.
2nd row: k.1, * p.1, k.1; rep. from * to end.
Rep. these 2 rows until work measures 32 (34, 36) in. Cast off leaving an end about $\frac{1}{4}$ yard. Using this end oversew cast-off edge to bar of buckle.

MATERIALS

17 (18, 19, 20, 21) balls (50 gr. each) Mahony's Blarney Bainin (USA Blarneyspun) for version with neck border; one extra ball for each size for version with polo collar. One pair each Nos. 7, 9 and 10 knitting needles (USA sizes 7, 5 and 3). A medium cable needle.

MEASUREMENTS

To fit bust/chest size 34 (36, 38, 40, 42) in.; centre back length 26½ (27, 27¼, 29, 29½) in.; sleeve seam 16½ (16½, 16½, 18½, 18½) in.

TENSION

5 sts. and 6½ rows to 1 inch measured over st.st.

ABBREVIATIONS

See page 11; c.n., cable needle; C.4 B., sl. next 2 sts. on c.n. and hold at back of work, k.2 then k.2 from c.n.; C.4 F., as C.4 B. but leave the 2 sts. at front of work; C.6 F. and C.6 B., as C.4 F. and C.4 B. but slip 3 sts. on to c.n. and k. next 3 sts.; tw.3r., slip next 2 sts. on to c.n. and hold at back of work, k.1, then k.2 from c.n.; tw.3l., slip next st. on to c.n. and hold at front of work, k.2 then k.1 from c.n.; C.3 R., sl. next st. on c.n. at back, k.2, then p.1 from c.n.; C.3 L., sl. next 2 sts. on c.n. at front, p.1, then k.2 from c.n.; inc. in loop, pick up loop between needles, place on left-hand needle and p. into the back of it.

THE PATTERNS
PANEL ONE: Ladder of life
Worked on 5, 6, 7 or 8 sts. (for Front and Back).
1st row: k.
2nd row: p.
3rd and 4th rows: k.
These 4 rows form the patt.

PANEL TWO: Double cable
Worked on 9 sts.
1st row: k.
2nd row: p.
3rd row: C.4 B., k.1, C.4 F.
4th row: p.
These 4 rows form the patt.

PANEL THREE: Honeycomb
Worked on 12 (12, 12, 18, 18) sts.
1st row: k.
2nd row: p.
3rd row: (tw.3r., tw.3l.) 2 (2, 2, 3, 3) times.
4th row: p.
5th and 6th rows: rep. first and 2nd rows.
7th row: (tw.3l., tw.3r.) 2 (2, 2, 3, 3) times.
8th row: p.
These 8 rows form the patt.

PANEL FOUR: Diamond and cable
Worked on 28 sts.
1st row: k.6, p.6, C.4 F., p.6, k.6.

His and hers Aran sweaters
illustrated in colour on page 125

2nd row: p.6, k.6, p.4, k.6, p.6.
3rd row: C.6 F., p.5, C.3 R., C.3 L., p.5, C.6 B.
4th row: p.6, k.5, p.2, k.2, p.2, k.5, p.6.
5th row: k.6, p.4, C.3 R., p.2, C.3 L., p.4, k.6.
6th row: p.6, (k.4, p.2) twice, k.4, p.6.
7th row: k.6, p.3, C.3 R., p.4, C.3 L., p.3, k.6.
8th row: p.6, k.3, p.2, k.6, p.2, k.3, p.6.
9th row: C.6 B., p.2, C.3 R., p.6, C.3 L., p.2, C.6 F.
10th row: p.6, k.2, p.2, k.8, p.2, k.2, p.6.
11th row: k.6, p.1, C.3 R., p.8, C.3 L., p.1, k.6.
12th row: p.6, k.1, p.2, k.10, p.2, k.1, p.6.
13th row: k.6, p.1, k.2, p.10, k.2, p.1, k.6.
14th row: as 12th row.
15th row: C.6 F., p.1, C.3 L., p.8, C.3 R., p.1, C.6 B.
16th row: as 10th row.
17th row: k.6, p.2, C.3 L., p.6, C.3 R., p.2, k.6.
18th row: as 8th row.
19th row: k.6, p.3, C.3 L., p.4, C.3 R., p.3, k.6.
20th row: as 6th row.
21st row: C.6 B., p.4, C.3 L., p.2, C.3 R., p.4, C.6 F.
22nd row: as 4th row.
23rd row: k.6, p.5, C.3 L., C.3 R., p.5, k.6.
24th row: as 2nd row.
These 24 rows form the patt.

BACK

With No. 10 needles cast on 98 (102, 106, 110, 114) sts. and work in p.2, k.2 rib.
1st row: * p.2, k.2; rep. from * to last 2 sts., p.2.
2nd row: * k.2, p.2; rep. from * to last 2 sts., k.2.
Rep. these 2 rows 5 (5, 5, 7, 7) times more then first row again. Change to No. 7 needles.
Inc. row: p.4 (7, 9, 3, 4), * inc. in loop, p.10 (8, 8, 8, 7); rep. from * but end last rep. p.4 (7, 9, 3, 5).
Cont. in patt. on 108 (114, 118, 124, 130) sts. working first row of each panel with p.1 at side edges and p.2 between panels thus:
1st row: p.1, Panel One across 5 (7, 8, 6, 8) sts., p.2, Panel Two across 9 sts., p.2, Panel Three across 12 (12, 12, 18, 18) sts., p.2, Panel One across 5 (6, 7, 6, 7) sts., p.2, Panel Four across 28 sts., p.2, Panel One across 5 (6, 7, 6, 7) sts., p.2, Panel Three across 12 (12, 12, 18, 18) sts., p.2, Panel Two across 9 sts., p.2, Panel One across 5 (7, 8, 6, 8) sts., p.1.
2nd row: work 2nd row of each panel with k.1 at side edges and k.2 between panels.
Cont. in patt. until work measures 17½ (17½, 17½, 19, 19) in. ending on wrong side.

Shape Armholes

Cast off 2 (3, 3, 3, 4) sts. at beg. of next 2 rows. Dec. 1 st. at both ends of next 7 (8, 9, 7, 8) right-side rows.
Cont. thus:
1st row: work straight.
2nd and 3rd rows: dec. 1 st. at both ends of each row.
Rep. these 3 rows 9 (9, 9, 13, 13) times more. Now dec. 1 st. at both ends of the next 8 (9, 9, 6, 6) right-side rows. Leave rem. 34 (34, 36, 36, 38) sts. on a holder.

FRONT

Work as for Back until 46 (46, 48, 48, 50) sts. rem. in armhole shaping ending on wrong side.

Shape Neck

Next row: k.2 tog., patt. 9, k.2 tog., turn.

Work on these sts. only, dec. at armhole edge on every right-side row and at the same time dec. at neck edge on the next 2 rows, then on next 2 right-side rows (4 sts. rem.). Now dec. at neck edge on the next 2 rows, then on next 2 right-side rows (4 sts. rem.). Now dec. at armhole edge only on next 2 right-side rows. Work 1 row on rem. 2 sts. Cast off.

With right side facing, sl. next 20 (20, 22, 22, 24) sts. on holder, rejoin yarn at neck edge and k.2 tog., k.9, k.2 tog. Complete to match other side.

SLEEVES (make 2 alike)

With No. 10 needles cast on 46 (46, 50, 50, 54) sts. and work in p.2, k.2 rib for 2½ in. ending with a first row.
Change to No. 7 needles.

Inc. row: p.3 (3, 1, 4, 3), * inc. in loop, p.5 (4, 6, 3, 4); rep. from * ending last rep. p.3 (3, 1, 4, 3): 55 (57, 59, 65, 67) sts.

Cont. in patt. with double cable at centre and ladder of life and honeycomb each side thus:

For sizes 34, 36 and 38 only. 1st row: p.2, k.12, p.2, k.5 (6, 7), p.2, k.9, p.2, k.5 (6, 7), p.2, k.12, p.2.

2nd row: k.2, p.12, k.2, p.5 (6, 7), k.2, p.9, k.2, p.5 (6, 7), k.2, p.12, k.2.

3rd row: p.2, (tw.3r., tw.3l.) twice, p.2, k.5 (6, 7), p.2, C.4 B., k.1, C.4 F., p.2, k.5 (6, 7), p.2, (tw.3r., tw.3l.) twice, p.2.

4th row: k.2, p.12, k.9 (10, 11), p.9, k.9 (10, 11), p.12, k.2.
(These 4 rows set the patts. but honeycomb panels will be tw.3l., tw.3r., on 7th row.)

For sizes 40 and 42 only. 1st row: k.18, p.2, k.6 (7), p.2, k.9, p.2, k.6 (7), p.2, k.18.

2nd row: p.18, k.2, p.6 (7), k.2, p.9, k.2, p.6 (7), k.2, p.18.

3rd row: (tw.3r., tw.3l.) 3 times, p.2, k.6 (7), p.2, C.4 B., k.1, C.4 F., p.2, k.6 (7), p.2, (tw.3r., tw.3l.) 3 times.

4th row: p.18, k.10 (11), p.9, k.10 (11), p.18.

For all sizes. Cont. in patts. as set, but inc. 1 st. both ends of the next and every foll. 6th (5th, 5th, 6th, 6th) row working all inc. sts. into ladder patt. for sizes 34, 36 and 38, but for sizes 40 and 42 work first 2 inc. sts. into a p.2 rib and rem. sts. into ladder patt.

Cont. inc. thus until there are 81 (87, 91, 95, 99) sts. then cont. straight until sleeve measures 16½ (16½, 16½, 18½, 18½) in. ending on wrong side.

Shape Top

Cast off 2 (3, 3, 3, 4) sts. at beg. of next 2 rows. Cont. thus:
1st row: dec. 1 st. at both ends of row.
2nd row: work straight.
3rd and 4th rows: as first and 2nd rows.
5th and 6th rows: work straight.
Rep. these 6 rows once (once, once, twice, twice) more. Now dec. 1 st. at both ends of the next 7 (8, 9, 4, 5) right-side rows. Cont. thus:

1st row: work straight.

2nd and 3rd rows: dec. 1 st. at both ends of each row.

Rep. these 3 rows 5 (5, 5, 9, 9) times more, then dec. both ends of the next 8 (9, 9, 6, 6) right-side rows. Work 1 row on rem. 15 (15, 17, 17, 17) sts., but across cable sts. work p.2 tog. twice, p.1, p.2 tog. twice. Leave rem. 11 (11, 13, 13, 13) sts. on holder.

TO COMPLETE

First pin out and press work on wrong side with a damp cloth and hot iron. Join raglan shaping leaving right back seam open.

Neck Border or Polo Collar

Now with right side facing and No. 10 needles, k. across back neck sts., then sts. of one sleeve, pick up and k.12 sts. down front neck, k. sts. from holder, pick up and k.12 sts. up other side, then sts. of second sleeve: 100 (100, 108, 108, 112) sts.

For neck border. 1st row: k.1, * p.2, k.2; rep. from * to last 3 sts., p.2, k.1.

2nd row: p.1, * k.2, p.2; rep. from * to last 3 sts., k.2, p.1.

Rep. these 2 rows 4 times more. Cast off in rib.

For polo collar. 1st row: p.1, * k.2, p.2; rep. from * to last 3 sts., k.2, p.1.

2nd row: k.1, * p.2, k.2; rep. from * to last 3 sts., p.2, k.1.

Cont. in the k.2, p.2 rib for $2\frac{1}{2}$ in., then change to No. 9 needles and cont. until collar measures $6\frac{1}{2}$ in. Cast off loosely in rib.

To Make Up

Join remaining raglan seam including neck border but join collar on reverse side to turn over. Join sleeves and side seams. Press seams.

Classic pullover

MATERIALS

23 (25, 26) balls (25 gr. each) Wendy Courtellon Double Knit. One pair each Nos. 9 and 10 knitting needles (USA sizes 5 and 3).

MEASUREMENTS

To fit chest size 36 (40, 44) in.

TENSION

1 patt. rep. (i.e. 18 sts.) to $2\frac{1}{2}$ in., when lightly pressed.

ABBREVIATIONS

See page 11.

FRONT

With No. 10 needles cast on 127 (145, 163) sts.

1st and 3rd sizes only. 1st row: p.1, k.2, p.2, k.2, p.2, k.1, * p.2, k.2, p.2, k.2, p.1, k.2, p.2, k.2, p.2, k.1; rep. from * to last 9 sts., p.2, k.2, p.2, k.2, p.1.

2nd size only. 1st row: k.1, * p.2, k.2, p.2, k.2, p.1, k.2, p.2, k.2, p.2, k.1; rep. from * to end of row.

All sizes. 2nd row: p. over the k. and k. over the p. sts. of row before.

Rep. last 2 rows 7 (8, 9) times more.
Beg. main pattern:
1st row: * p.2, k.2, p.2, k 2, p.1; rep. from * to last st., p.1.
2nd row: k. over the p. and p. over the k. sts. of row before.
3rd and 4th rows: as first and 2nd rows.
5th to 8th rows: rep. the two welt rows twice.
9th row: * k.2, p.2, k.2, p.2, k.1; rep. from * to last st., k.1.
10th row: as 2nd row.
11th and 12th rows: as 9th and 10th rows.
1st and 3rd sizes only. 13th row: k.1, p.2, k.2, p.2, k.2, p.1,
* k.2, p.2, k.2, p.2, k.1, p.2, k.2, p.2, k.2, p.1; rep. from * to last 9
sts., k.2, p.2, k.2, p.2, k.1.
2nd size only. 13th row: p.1, * k.2, p.2, k.2, p.2, k.1, p.2, k.2,
p.2, k.2, p.1; rep. from * to end of row.
All sizes. 14th row: as 2nd row.
15th and 16th rows: as 13th and 14th rows. **
Rep. last 16 rows 4 (5, 5) times more, then rep. rows 1 to 4
inclusive.

Divide for Neck
Work as for 5th row over 61 (70, 79) sts., p.2 tog., turn and work
on this set of sts.
*** Work 3 rows.
Dec. 1 st. on inner edge on next and following 4th row. Work
one row thus ending on outer edge.

Shape Armhole
Cast off 8 (10, 12) sts. at beg. of next row. Work to end of row.
Work one row.
Dec. 1 st. at both ends of next row.
Dec. 1 st. on alternate rows on armhole edge 6 (8, 10) times
more and at same time continue to dec. on inner edge on 4th

row from last dec. and every following 4th row until 33 (36, 39) sts. remain, end on outer edge.

Shape Shoulder
Cast off at beg. of next and every following alternate row 8 (9, 9) sts. once, 8 (9, 10) sts. twice, 9 (9, 10) sts. once.
Return to remaining sts., place the first st. on a safety pin, rejoin yarn at inner edge, p.2 tog., work in pattern to end of row.
Complete as for first side from ***.

BACK
Work as front to **.
Rep. last 16 rows 4 (5, 5) times more, then rep. rows 1 to 12 inclusive.

Shape Armholes
Cast off 8 (10, 12) sts. at beg. of next 2 rows.
Dec. 1 st. at both ends of next and following 6 (8, 10) rows.
Continue straight until armholes measure same as front.

Shape Shoulders
Cast off 8 (9, 9) sts. at beg. of next 2 rows. Cast off 8 (9, 10) sts. at beg. of next 4 rows. Cast off 9 (9, 10) sts. at beg. of next 2 rows. Leave remaining sts. on a stitch holder.

SLEEVES (make 2 alike)
With No. 10 needles cast on 52 (56, 60) sts.
1st row: p.1, * k.2, p.2; rep. from * to last 3 sts., k.2, p.1.
2nd row: k.1, * p.2, k.2; rep. from * to last 3 sts., p.2, k.1.
Rep. last 2 rows until work measures 2 in.
Change to No. 9 needles, continue in rib, inc. 1 st. at both ends of first and every following 6th row until there are 88 (96, 100) sts.
Continue straight until sleeve measures 17 (19, 19) in.

Shape Top
Cast off 8 (10, 12) sts. at beg. of next 2 rows.
Dec. 1 st. at both ends of next 6 (2, 2) rows.
Dec. 1 st. at both ends of next and every following alternate row until 36 sts. remain.
Work one row.
Dec. 1 st. at both ends of next 2 rows.
Cast off 3 sts. at beg. of next 4 rows.
Work 4 (4½, 5) in. on remaining sts.
Leave sts. on a stitch holder.

TO COMPLETE
Sew extensions of sleeve tops along cast-off sts. of fronts, also right-hand side of back.

Neckband
With No. 10 needles rib along sts. of left sleeve top, pick up and k.69 (77, 81) sts. down left side of neck, k. st. on safety pin, pick up and k.69 (77, 81) up right side of neck, rib across sts. of second sleeve top, k. across sts. of back.
1st rib row: k.1, * p.2, k.2; rep. from * to centre st., p. this

st. ** k.2, p.2; rep. from ** to last st., k.1. Keeping rib as set, dec. 1 st. on each side of the sts. picked up from safety pin (k. this st. on right-side rows and p. it on wrong-side rows) in every row until ribbing measures 1½ in.
Cast off ribwise.

To Make Up
Sew sleeve extension to left side of back. Continue up neck ribbing. Press very lightly with a warm iron over a dry cloth. Sew up side and sleeve seams. Press seams.

Chevron sweater

MATERIALS
21 (23, 26) oz. Wendy Nylonised Double Knit. One pair each Nos. 12 and 9 knitting needles (USA sizes 1 and 5).

MEASUREMENTS
To fit chest size 36 (40, 44) in.; length at side 24 (25½, 26) in.; length of sleeve seam 17½ (18½, 19½) in.

TENSION
6 sts. and 8 rows to 1 in. with No. 9 needles.

ABBREVIATIONS
See page 11.

BACK
With No. 12 needles cast on 114 (126, 138) sts. Work 2½ (2¾, 3) in. in k.1, p.1 rib.
Change to No. 9 needles and patt.
1st row: * p.6, k.6 (7, 8), p.6 (7, 8), k.1, p.1, k.6 (7, 8), p.6

(7, 8), k.6; rep. from * twice.

2nd row: * p.5, k.6 (7, 8), p.6 (7, 8), k.2, p.2, k.6 (7, 8), p.6 (7, 8), k.5; rep. from * twice.

3rd row: * p.4, k.6 (7, 8), p.6 (7, 8), k.3, p.3, k.6 (7, 8), p.6 (7, 8), k.4; rep. from * twice.

4th row: * p.3, k.6 (7, 8), p.6 (7, 8), k.4, p.4, k.6 (7, 8), p.6 (7, 8), k.3; rep. from * twice.

5th row: * p.2, k.6 (7, 8), p.6 (7, 8), k.5, p.5, k.6 (7, 8), p.6 (7, 8), k.2; rep. from * twice.

6th row: * p.1, k.6 (7, 8), p.6 (7, 8), k.6, p.6, k.6 (7, 8), p.6 (7, 8), k.1; rep. from * twice.

7th row: * k.6 (7, 8), p.6 (7, 8), k.6 (7, 7), p.1 (0, 0), k.1 (0, 0), p.6 (7, 7), k.6 (7, 8), p.6 (7, 8); rep. from * twice.

8th row: * k.5 (6, 7), p.6 (7, 8), k.6 (7, 8), p.2 (1, 0), k.2 (1, 0), p.6 (7, 8), k.6 (7, 8), p.5 (6, 7); rep. from * twice.

9th row: * k.4 (5, 6), p.6 (7, 8), k.6 (7, 8), p.3 (2, 1), k.3 (2, 1), p.6 (7, 8), k.6 (7, 8), p.4 (5, 6); rep. from * twice.

10th row: * k.3 (4, 5), p.6 (7, 8), k.6 (7, 8), p.4 (3, 2), k.4 (3, 2), p.6 (7, 8), k.6 (7, 8), p.3 (4, 5); rep. from * twice.

11th row: * k.2 (3, 4), p.6 (7, 8), k.6 (7, 8), p.5 (4, 3), k.5 (4, 3), p.6 (7, 8), k.6 (7, 8), p.2 (3, 4); rep. from * twice.

12th row: * k.1 (2, 3), p.6 (7, 8), k.6 (7, 8), p.6 (5, 4), k.6 (5, 4), p.6 (7, 8), k.6 (7, 8), p.1 (2, 3); rep. from * twice.

For size 36 only. These 12 rows form patt.

For sizes 40 and 44 only. 13th row: * k.1 (2), p.7 (8), k.7 (8), p.6 (5), k.6 (5), p.7 (8), k.7 (8), p.1 (2); rep. from * twice.

14th row: * k.0 (1), p.7 (8), k.7 (8), p.7 (6), k.7 (6), p.7 (8), k.7 (8), p.0 (1); rep. from * twice.

For size 40 only. These 14 rows form patt.

For size 44 only. 15th row: * p.8, k.8, p.7, k.7, p.8, k.8; rep. from * twice.

16th row: * p.7, k.8, p.8, k.8, p.8, k.7; rep. from * twice.
These 16 rows form patt.

For all sizes. Cont. in patt. as set. Cont. straight until work measures 15 (16, 17) in. from cast-on edge, ending with a wrong-side row.

Shape Armholes

Keeping patt. correct, cast off 5 (6, 7) sts. at beg. of each of the next 2 rows, then dec. 1 st. at each end of next 4 (6, 8) alt. rows: 96 (102, 108) sts. **

Cont. straight until work measures 24 ($25\frac{1}{2}$, 27) in. from cast-on edge, ending with a wrong-side row.

Shape Shoulders

Cast off 8 (8, 9) sts. at beg. of next 4 rows and 8 (9, 9) sts. at beg. of next 4 rows.
Leave rem. 32 (34, 36) sts. on st. holder.

FRONT

Work as Back to ** Work straight until Front measures 22 ($23\frac{1}{2}$, 25) in. from cast-on edge, ending with a wrong-side row.

Shape Neck

Next row: patt. 37 (39, 41), patt. 2 tog., slip next 18 (20, 22) sts. on to one st. holder, and rem. 39 (41, 43) sts. on to 2nd st. holder. Working on first sts. only, dec. 1 st. at neck edge on each of next 2 rows then on every alt. row until 32 (34, 36) sts. remain. Cont. straight until this side of Front is same length as Back to beg. of shoulder shaping, ending at armhole edge.

Shape Shoulder

Cast off 8 (8, 9) sts. at beg. of next 2 alt. rows and 8 (9, 9) sts. at beg. of next 2 alt. rows.
Rejoin yarn to inner edge of the sts. on 2nd st. holder, patt. 2 tog. then patt. to end.
Work this side to match first, reversing all shapings.

SLEEVES (make 2 alike)

With No. 12 needles cast on 56 (60, 64) sts. Work $2\frac{1}{2}$ ($2\frac{3}{4}$, 3) in. in k.1, p.1 rib.
Change to No. 9 needles and patt., with centre 38 (42, 46) sts. in patt. as given for Back and 9 extra sts. at each end of needle as follows.
1st sleeve patt. row: p.3, k.6, work rep. of first row of Back patt., p.6, k.3.
2nd sleeve patt. row: p.4, k.5, work rep. of 2nd row of Back patt., p.5, k.4.
3rd sleeve patt. row: p.5, k.4, work rep. of 3rd row of Back patt., p.4, k.5.
Cont. in patt. in this way, inc. 1 st. at each end of 7th patt. row then every foll. 6th row, taking extra sts. into patt., until there are 92 (98, 104) sts.
Work 1 row after last inc., or cont. straight until side edge measures $17\frac{1}{2}$ ($18\frac{1}{2}$, $19\frac{1}{2}$) in., ending with a wrong-side row.

Shape Top

Keeping patt. correct, cast off 4 (5, 6) sts. at beg. of next 2 rows, then dec. 1 st. at each end of next 3 rows. Dec. 1 st. at each end of next 8 (9, 10) alt. rows. Dec. 1 st. at each end of next and every row 9 (13, 17) times. Cast off rem. sts.

TO COMPLETE

Pin out pieces, wrong side up, to required measurements and press lightly with damp cloth and warm iron, avoiding ribbing. Join right shoulder seam and press seam.

Polo Collar

With right side of work facing and No. 12 needles, pick up and k.21 (25, 29) sts. round left front neck, the sts. from centre front st. holder, 21 (25, 29) sts. round right front neck to seam, and the sts. from back neck st. holder.
Work in k.1, p.1 rib across all sts. for $2\frac{1}{2}$ in. Change to No. 9 needles and cont. in rib until polo collar measures $4\frac{1}{2}$ (5, $5\frac{1}{2}$) in. ending with a right-side row. Cast off loosely in rib. Join polo collar and left shoulder seam; press seam.
Sew in sleeves and press seams. Join side and sleeve seams and press seams.

Belted sweater

MATERIALS

26 (28, 29) oz. Hayfield Gaylon Double Knitting. One pair each Nos. 11, 10 and 9 knitting needles (USA sizes 2, 3 and 5). One set of four each Nos. 11 and 10 needles (USA sizes 2 and 3) with points at both ends. Six buttons $\frac{1}{2}$ in. in diameter. One buckle 2 in. wide.

MEASUREMENTS

To fit chest size 40 (42, 44) in.; length $29\frac{1}{4}$ ($29\frac{1}{2}$, $29\frac{3}{4}$) in.; sleeve seam 20 ($20\frac{1}{2}$, 21) in.

TENSION

6 sts. to 1 in. over st.st. with No. 9 needles.

ABBREVIATIONS

See page 11; k.1 below, k. next st. through st. in row below.

BACK

With No. 11 needles cast on 131 (137, 143) sts.
1st row: sl.1, * k.1 t.b.l., p.1; rep. from * to last 2 sts., k.2 t.b.l.
2nd row: sl.1, * p.1, k.1 t.b.l.; rep. from * to end. These 2 rows form twisted rib patt. Work straight in twisted rib for $1\frac{1}{4}$ in. dec. 1 st. at end of last rib row: 130 (136, 142) sts. Change to No. 9 needles and st. st. **
Work straight for $3\frac{1}{2}$ in., ending with a p. row.
Next (dec.) row: k.5, k.2 tog. t.b.l., k. to last 7 sts., k.2 tog., k.5.
Cont. in st.st., rep. this last row on every foll. 6th row until 108 (114, 120) sts. remain.
*** Work straight for a few rows until Back measures 13 in. from cast-on edge, ending with a p. row.

Next (inc.) row: k.5, k. into front and back of next st., k. to last 6 sts., k. into front and back of next st., k.5.
Cont. in st.st. rep. this last row on every foll. 10th row until there are 120 (126, 132) sts. Work straight until Back measures 20 in. from cast-on edge, ending with a p. row.

Shape Armholes
Cast off 6 (7, 8) sts. at beg. of the next 2 rows, then dec. 1 st. at each end of every foll. row until 96 (100, 104) sts. remain. ***
Work straight until armholes measure $8\frac{1}{2}$ ($8\frac{3}{4}$, 9) in., ending with a p. row.

Shape Shoulders
Cast off 10 (11, 12) sts. at the beg. of the next 4 rows, then 10 sts. at the beg. of the next 2 rows. Put rem. 36 sts. on to a st. holder.

POCKET LININGS (make 2 alike)
With No. 9 needles cast on 29 sts. Work straight in st.st. until Pocket Lining measures 6 in., ending with a p. row. Leave sts. on a st. holder.

FRONT
Cast on and work as Back to **. Working in st.st. with No. 9 needles work straight for 1 in., ending with a p. row.
Next row: k.17; turn.
Transfer rem. sts. on to a st. holder. Working on these 17 sts. cont. straight in st.st. for a further $2\frac{1}{2}$ in., ending with a p. row.
Next (dec.) row: k.5, k.2 tog. t.b.l., k. to end. Rep. this last row on every foll. 6th row until 13 sts. remain. Work one row straight. Leave sts. on a safety pin for time being without breaking yarn.
With right side facing, transfer the next 29 sts. from st. holder on to a different st. holder, then join yarn to rem. sts. and k.38 (44, 50) sts.; turn. Leave the 46 sts. on the st. holder.
Working on these centre sts. cont. straight in st.st. until centre measures the same length as side edge, ending with a p. row. Break yarn and leave these sts. on st. holder.
With right side of work facing transfer the next 29 sts. from st. holder on to another st. holder then join in new ball of yarn and k. rem. 17 sts. Now work to match first side edge of 17 sts. with dec. row as: k. to last 7 sts., k.2 tog., k.5.
Break yarn.
With right side of work facing return to first set of 13 side sts.
Next row: k.13, with right side facing k. across one set of 29 Pocket Lining sts., k.38 (44, 50) centre sts., k. across 2nd set of 29 pocket lining sts., k. across rem. 13 sts.: 122 (128, 134) sts.
Cont. in st.st., work 3 rows straight, beg. with a p. row.
Next row: k.5, k.2 tog. t.b.l., k. to last 7 sts., k.2 tog., k.5. Rep. this last dec. row on every foll. 6th row until 108 (114, 120) sts. remain.
Now work as Back from *** to ***: 96 (100, 104) sts. Work straight until armholes measure $6\frac{1}{2}$ ($6\frac{3}{4}$, 7) in., ending with a p. row.

Shape Neck
Next row: k.40 (42, 44) sts.; turn and leave rem. 56 (58, 60)

sts. on a st. holder. Working on first set of sts. dec. 1 st. at neck edge on the next and every foll. row until 30 (32, 34) sts. remain. Now cont. straight until armhole measures 8½ (8¾, 9) in., ending at armhole edge.

Shape Shoulder

Cast off 10 (11, 12) sts. at the beg. of the next and foll. alt. row. Cast off 10 sts. at the beg. of the next alt. row.

With right side of Front facing, return to rem. sts. Slip the centre 16 sts. on to a st. holder then k. to end of row: 40 (42, 44) sts. Now work to match first side of neck, reversing all shapings.

Top Pockets (make both alike)

With right side facing and No. 10 needles, rejoin yarn to one set of 29 sts.

1st row: sl.1, k. to end.

2nd row: sl. 1, * k.1 below, p.1; rep. from * to last 2 sts., k.1 below, k.1.

Rep. these 2 rows until top pocket measures same as edges of centre and side panels to the point where pocket lining sts. were joined, ending with a right-side row.

Now reverse patt. for pocket flap by working next row as a first patt. row, then next row as 2nd patt. row. Now cont. as set in patt. for 1 in. Cast off in patt.

SLEEVES (make 2 alike)

With No. 11 needles cast on 59 (63, 67) sts.

Work 4 in. in twisted rib.

Change to No. 9 needles and st.st. Work 2 rows straight.

Next row: k.2, k. into front and back of next st., k. to last 3 sts., k. into front and back of next st., k.2. Rep. this last row on every foll. 6th row until there are 91 (95, 99) sts. Work straight until Sleeve measures 20 (20½, 21) in., ending with a p. row.

Shape Top

Cast off 6 (7, 8) sts. at the beg. of the next 2 rows, then dec. 1 st. at each end of the next and every foll. alt. row until 47 sts. remain. Cast off 2 sts. at the beg. of the next 2 rows, 3 sts. at the beg. of the next 2 rows, 4 sts. at the beg. of the next 2 rows, 5 sts. at the beg. of the next 2 rows, 6 sts. at the beg. of the next 2 rows. Cast off the rem. 7 sts.

BELT

With No. 11 needles cast on 13 sts. Work in twisted rib. Work straight until Belt measures 38 (39, 40) in. Now dec. 1 st. at each end of every row until 3 sts. remain. Fasten off these 3 sts.

TO COMPLETE

Baste shoulder seams.

Collar

With right side of back facing and with set of four No. 11 needles with points at both ends k. across the 36 sts. left at back of neck, inc. 1 st. in first and last sts., pick up and k. 22 sts. down side of front neck, k. across centre 16 sts. inc. 1 st. in first and last sts. then pick up and k. 22 sts. up other side of front neck: 100 sts.

Work in rounds of k.2, p.2 rib. Work 6 in., finishing at end of round.
Change to a set of four No. 10 needles. Cont. in k.2, p.2 rib until collar measures 11 in. Cast off fairly loosely in rib.

To Make Up

Press all pieces using a warm iron and a damp cloth. Join side and shoulder seams. Sew sleeve seams and set sleeves into armholes.
Sew side edges of fisherman rib pockets into front, turn pocket flaps over to right side and slip st. down at side edges. Sew linings into position beneath pockets. Sew a button to the centre of each pocket flap, and sew four buttons, evenly spaced, along left shoulder seam. Attach buckle to unshaped end of belt. Make a slot at each side of waist to hold belt in position. Give a final light press.

MATERIALS

3 balls (25 gr. each) Twilleys Cortina in main colour, and 1 ball each in lavender, mauve, light pink and dark pink. One pair of No. 5 knitting needles (USA size 9).

MEASUREMENTS

To fit an average-sized head.

TENSION

5 sts. to 1 in.

ABBREVIATIONS

See page 11.

TO MAKE

Note. Use yarn double throughout.
With main colour cast on 100 sts., and work 2 rows in k.1, p.1 rib. Cont. in st.st., working in patt as chart, right, until 24th row is completed. The design is repeated over 10 sts., and the chart shows one complete repeat. Continue with main colour for 1 in., ending with a p. row.

Shape Top

1st row: * k.8, k.2 tog.; rep from * to end. Work 3 rows.
5th row: * k.7, k.2 tog.; rep. from * to end. Work 3 rows.
9th row: * k.6, k.2 tog.; rep. from * to end. Work 3 rows.
13th row: * k.5, k.2 tog.; rep. from * to end. Work 3 rows.
17th row: * k.4, k.2 tog.; rep. from * to end. Work 3 rows.
21st row: * k.3, k.2 tog.; rep. from * to end. Work 3 rows.
25th row: * k.2, k.2 tog.; rep. from * to end. Work one row.
27th row: * k.1, k.2 tog.; rep. from * to end.
Break yarn, run end through rem. sts., draw up and fasten off.

TO COMPLETE

Press work on the wrong side. Join back seam of cap. Press seam.

Fair Isle cap

illustrated in colour on page 72

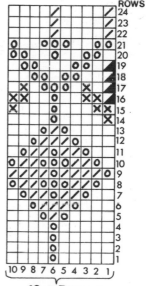

ROWS
10st. Repeat

☐ MAIN
◪ LAVENDER
☒ MAUVE
◿ DARK PINK
⊙ LIGHT PINK

Cable-patterned cap

MATERIALS

5 balls (25 gr. each) Twilleys Cortina. One pair of No. 6 knitting needles (USA size 8). A cable needle.

MEASUREMENTS

To fit an average-sized head.

TENSION

17 sts. to 3 in. over cable pattern.

ABBREVIATIONS

See page 11.

TO MAKE

Note. Use yarn double throughout.

Cast on 101 sts., and k. 6 rows, then work in patt. as follows:

1st row: k. **2nd row:** p.

3rd row: k.1, * sl. next 3 sts. on to cable needle and place at back of work, k. next 3 sts., k.3 from cable needle; rep. from * to last 4 sts., k.4.

4th row: p.

5th row: k.

6th row: p.

7th row: k.4, * sl. next 3 sts. on to cable needle and place at front of work, k. next 3 sts., then k. 3 from cable needle; rep. from * to last st., k.1.

8th row: p.

Rep. last 8 rows once, then k.4 rows. Change to k.1, p.1 rib, beg. 2nd row with p.1, and cont. until work measures 7 in. from beg., ending with a wrong-side row.

Next row: * rib 7, p.3 tog.; rep. from * to last st., rib 1. Work 2 rows.

Next row: * rib 5, p.3 tog.; rep. from * to last st., rib 1. Work 2 rows.

Next row: * rib 3, p.3 tog.; rep. from * to last st., rib 1. Work 2 rows.

Next row: * rib 1, p.3 tog.; rep. from * to last st., rib 1. Break yarn. Run end through rem. sts., draw up and fasten off.

TO COMPLETE

Join back seam of cap. Make pompon and sew to top of cap.

Bedroom bootees

illustrated in colour on page 72

MATERIALS

2 oz. double knitting yarn in main colour, 1 oz. in a contrast shade. One pair of No. 5 knitting needles (USA size 9). A medium crochet hook.

MEASUREMENTS

To fit an average-sized foot; 15½ in. long.

TENSION

4 sts. and 10 rows to 1 in.

ABBREVIATIONS

See page 11; M., main shade; C., contrast shade.

TO MAKE (make 2 alike)

With C., cast on 62 sts. Work 2 rows in g.st.

3rd row: * k.2, m.1 (by putting yarn over needle), k.2 tog.; rep. from * to end of row.

4th and 5th rows: work in g.st.

Change to M., and work 43 rows in g.st.

Change to C., and work 2 rows in g.st.

49th row: as 3rd row.

50th and 51st rows: work in g.st.

Cast off fairly loosely.

TO COMPLETE

Lay work on a flat surface, then fold both long edges over to meet at the centre. Stitch across one short end: this will form toe of bootee. With C. and crochet hook, crochet a chain 1½ yd. long for each bootee. Thread this chain through holes in C. panels to form a criss-cross lace-up fastening at centre front. Finish chains with tassels, if wished.

Blue bathmat

illustrated in colour on page 72

MATERIALS

4 hanks (4 oz. each) Twilleys '747' Orlon. One pair ½-in. wooden knitting needles. Medium crochet hook.

MEASUREMENTS

42 in. by approx 20 in.

TENSION

3 sts. to 2 in.

ABBREVIATIONS

See page 11.

TO MAKE

Cast on 29 sts.

1st row: k.1, *p.1, k.1; rep. from * to end.

2nd row: p.1, *k.1, p.1; rep. from * to end.

These 2 rows form the patt. Rep. them until work measures 34 in. Cast off.

TO COMPLETE

Cut. rem. yarn into 8-in. lengths, and using crochet hook make a fringe at each narrow end of mat, pulling one double strand of yarn through every stitch.

Pink bathmat

illustrated in colour on page 72

MATERIALS

4 hanks (4 oz. each) Twilleys '747' Orlon. One pair ½-in. wooden knitting needles. Medium crochet hook.

MEASUREMENTS

40 in. by 20 in.

TENSION

3 sts. to 2 in.

TO MAKE

Cast on 30 sts.
1st row: * k.1, p.1; rep. from * to end.
2nd row: * k.1, p.1; rep. from * to end.
3rd row: * p.1, k.1; rep. from * to end.
4th row: * p.1, k.1; rep. from * to end.
These 4 rows form the patt. Rep. them until work measures 32 in. Cast off.

TO COMPLETE

Cut rem. yarn into 8-in. lengths, and using the crochet hook make a fringe at each narrow end of mat. Knot one double strand of yarn through every stitch.

Oval cushion

instructions for rectangular cushion start on page 166, for round cushion on page 168

MATERIALS

2 balls (20 gr. each) Coats Mercer-Crochet No. 20. One set of four No. 12 knitting needles (USA size 1). One steel crochet hook International Standard Size 1·75. An oval cushion pad, approximately 18 in. by 12 in.

MEASUREMENTS

Finished cushion measures approx. 18 in. long by 12 in. wide, at widest point.

ABBREVIATIONS

See page 11.

TO MAKE
First Section

Cast on 68 sts. (23 sts. on each of 2 needles and 22 sts. on 3rd needle) and work in rounds as follows:

1st and alternate rows: k.
2nd row: * y.f., k.31, y.f., k.1 t.b.l., y.f., k.1, y.f., k.1 t.b.l.; rep.

from * once more.

4th row: * y.f., k.33, y.f., k.1 t.b.l., y.f., k.3, y.f., k.1 t.b.l.; rep. from * once more.

6th row: * y.f., k.35, y.f., k.1 t.b.l., y.f., k.5, y.f., k.1 t.b.l.; rep. from * once more.

8th row: * y.f., k.37, y.f., k.1 t.b.l., y.f., k.7, y.f., k.1 t.b.l.; rep. from * once more. ·

10th row: * y.f., k.39, y.f., k.1 t.b.l., y.f., k.9, y.f., k.1 t.b.l.; rep. from * once more.

12th to 15th rows: k.

16th row: * y.r.n. twice, sl.1, k.1, p.s.s.o., k.1; rep. from * to end.

17th and alternate rows: k., working k.1, p.1 into each 2 y.r.n.

18th row: k.5, * y.r.n. twice, k.12; rep. from * to last 7 sts., y.r.n. twice, k.7.

20th row: before commencing row, slip last st. off right-hand needle on to left-hand needle, * sl.1, k.1, p.s.s.o., k.5, y.r.n. twice, k.5, k.2 tog.; rep. from * to end.

22nd row: * sl.1, k.1, p.s.s.o., k.5, y.r.n. twice, k.5, k.2 tog.; rep. from * to end.

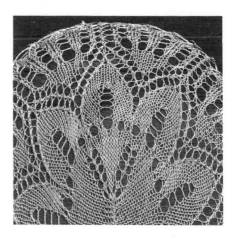

24th row: * y.f., sl.1, k.1, p.s.s.o., k.5, y.r.n. twice, k.5, k.2 tog.; rep. from * to end.

26th row: * y.f., k.1 t.b.l., y.f., sl.1, k.1, p.s.s.o., k.10, k.2 tog.; rep. from * to end.

28th row: * y.f., k.3, y.f., sl.1, k.1, p.s.s.o., k.8, k.2 tog.; rep. from * to end.

30th row: * y.f., k.2 tog., y.f., k.1 t.b.l., (y.f., sl.1, k.1, p s s.o.) twice, k.6, k.2 tog.; rep. from * to end.

32nd row: * y.f., k.2 tog., y.f., k.3, (y.f., sl.1, k.1, p.s.s.o.) twice, k.4, k.2 tog.; rep. from * to end.

34th row: * y.f., k.2 tog., y.f., k.5, (y.f., sl.1, k.1, p.s.s.o.) twice, k.2, k.2 tog.; rep. from * to end.

36th row: * y.f., k.2 tog., y.f., k.7, (y.f., sl.1, k.1, p.s.s.o.) twice, k.2 tog.; rep. from * to end.

38th row: * y.f., k.2 tog., y.f., k.9, (y.f., sl.1, k.1, p.s.s.o.) twice; rep. from * to end.

40th row: * k.2 tog., y.f., sl.1, k.1, p.s.s.o., y.r.n. twice, k.2, y.r.n. twice, sl.1, k.1, p.s.s.o., k.1, y.r.n. twice, k.2, y.r.n. twice, k.2 tog., y.f., sl.1, k.1, p.s.s.o., k.1; rep. from * to end.

42nd row: before commencing row, k.1, then slip this st. on to end of right-hand needle, * sl.1, k.1, p.s.s.o., k.1, (y.r.n. twice, k.4) 3 times, y.r.n. twice, k.1, k.2 tog., y.f., sl.1, k.2 tog., p.s.s.o. y.f.; rep. from * to end.

44th to 46th rows: * (sl.1, k.1, p.s.s.o., k.1, y.r.n. twice, k.1, k.2 tog.) 4 times, y.f., sl.1, k.2 tog., p.s.s.o., y.f.; rep. from * to end.

48th row: * k.24, y.f., sl.1, k.2 tog., p.s.s.o., y.f.; rep. from * to end.

50th row: * (sl.1, k.1, p.s.s.o., k.2, k.2 tog.) 4 times, y.f., sl.1, k.2 tog., p.s.s.o., y.f.; rep. from * to end.

52nd row: * (sl.1, k.1, p.s.s.o., k.2 tog., y.r.n. twice) 3 times, sl.1, k.1, p.s.s.o., k.2 tog., y.f., sl.1, k.2 tog., p.s.s.o., y.f.; rep. from * to end.

53rd row: k., working k.1, p.1 into each 2 y.r.n.

With crochet hook, work * 1 d.c. into next 3 sts., 12 ch., (1 d.c. into next 4 sts., 12 ch.) twice, (1 d.c. into next 3 sts., 12 ch.) twice; rep. from * all round, 1 s.s. into first d.c. Fasten off.

With wrong side facing, crochet or sew together the cast-on sts. in centre of section.
Work second section exactly as for first section.
Damp and pin out to measurements.

TO JOIN SECTIONS

Attach thread into any loop on last row of first section, 1 d.c. into same place, 6 ch., 1 d.c. into corresponding loop of second section, 6 ch., 1 d.c. into next loop on first section. Continue in this manner leaving sufficient opening to insert cushion pad then complete joining as before, ending with 1 s.s. into first d.c. Fasten off.

Rectangular cushion

illustrated on page 164

MATERIALS

2 balls (20 gr.) each Coats Mercer-Crochet No. 20. One set of four No. 12 knitting needles (USA size 1). One steel crochet hook International Standard Size 1·75. A cushion pad, approximately 9 in. by 13 in.

MEASUREMENTS

Finished cushion measures approx. 13 in. by 9 in.

ABBREVIATIONS

See page 11.

TO MAKE
First Section

Cast on 48 sts. (16 sts. on each of 3 needles) and work in rounds as follows:

1st row: k.

2nd row: * (y.f., k.1, y.f. sl.1, k.2 tog., p.s.s.o.) 5 times, (y.f., k.1, y.f., k.1 t.b.l.) twice; rep. from * once more.

3rd and alternate rows: k. **4th row:** * y.f., k.23, y.f., k.1 t.b.l., y.f., k.3, y.f., k.1 t.b.l.; rep. from * once more.

6th row: * (y.f., k.1, y.f., sl.1, k.2 tog., p.s.s.o.) 6 times, y.f., k.1, y.f., k.1 t.b.l., y.f., k.1, y.f., sl.1, k.2 tog., p.s.s.o., y.f., k.1, y.f., k.1 t.b.l.; rep. from * once more.

8th row: * y.f., k.27, y.f., k.1 t.b.l., y.f., k.7, y.f., k.1 t.b.l.; rep. from * once more.

10th row: * (y.f., k.1, y.f., sl.1, k.2 tog., p.s.s.o.) 7 times, y.f., k.1, y.f., k.1 t.b.l., (y.f., k.1, y.f., sl.1, k.2 tog., p.s.s.o.) twice, y.f., k.1, y.f., k.1 t.b.l.; rep. from * once more.

12th row: * y.f., k.31, y.f., k.1 t.b.l., y.f., k.11, y.f., k.1 t.b.l.; rep. from * once more.

14th row: * (y.f., k.1, y.f., sl.1, k.2 tog., p.s.s.o.) 8 times, y.f., k.1, y.f., k.1 t.b.l., (y.f., k.1, y.f., sl.1, k.2 tog., p.s.s.o.) 3 times, y.f., k.1, y.f., k.1 t.b.l.; rep. from * once more.

16th row: * y.f., k.35, y.f., k.1 t.b.l., y.f., k.15, y.f., k.1 t.b.l.; rep. from * once more.

18th row: * (y.f., k.1, y.f., sl.1, k.2 tog., p.s.s.o.) 9 times, y.f., k.1, y.f., k.1 t.b.l., (y.f., k.1, y.f., sl.1, k.2 tog., p.s.s.o.) 4 times, y.f., k.1, y.f., k.1 t.b.l.; rep. from * once more.

20th row: * y.f., k.39, y.f., k.1 t.b.l., y.f., k.19, y.f., k.1 t.b.l.; rep. from * once more.

22nd row: * (y.f., k.1, y.f., sl.1, k.2 tog., p.s.s.o.) 10 times, y.f., k.1, y.f., k.1 t.b.l., (y.f., k.1, y.f., sl.1, k.2 tog., p.s.s.o.) 5 times, y.f., k.1, y.f., k.1 t.b.l.; rep. from once more.

24th row: * (y.f., k.3, y.f., sl.1, k.1, p.s.s.o., k.13, k.2 tog.) twice, y.f., k.3, y.f., k.1 t.b.l., y.f., k.3, y.f., sl.1, k.1, p.s.s.o., k.13, k.2 tog., y.f., k.3, y.f., k.1 t.b.l.; rep. from * once more.

26th row: * y.f., k.5, (y.f., sl.1, k.2 tog., p.s.s.o., y.f., k.1) 3 times, y.f., sl.1, k.2 tog., p.s.s.o.; rep. from * once more, y.f., k.5, y.f., k.1 t.b.l.; rep. from * to * once more, y.f., k.5, y.f., k.1 t.b.l.; rep. from first * once more.

28th row: * y.f., sl.1, k.1, p.s.s.o., k.5, * * y.f., sl.1, k.1, p.s.s.o., k.9, k.2 tog., y.f., * * k.7; rep. from * * to * * once more, k.5, k.2 tog., y.f., k.1 t.b.l., y.f., sl.1, k.1, p.s.s.o., k.5; rep. from ** to ** once more, k.5, k.2 tog., y.f., k.1 t.b.l.; rep. from * once more.

30th row: * y.f., sl.1, k.2 tog., p.s.s.o., k.5, ** y.f., sl.1, k.2 tog., p.s.s.o., y.f., k.1; rep. from ** once more, y.f., sl.1, k.2 tog., p.s.s.o., y.f., k.5, y.f., k.4; rep. from ** to ** twice more, y.f., sl.1, k.2 tog., p.s.s.o., y.f., k.5, sl.1, k.2 tog., p.s.s.o., y.f., k.1 t.b.l., y.f., sl.1, k.2 tog., p.s.s.o., k.5; rep. from ** to ** twice more, y.f., sl.1, k.2 tog., p.s.s.o., y.f., k.5, sl.1, k.2 tog., p.s.s.o., y.f., k.1 t.b.l.; rep. from * once more.

32nd row: * y.f., k.1 t.b.l., (y.f., sl.1, k.1, p.s.s.o., k.5) twice, k.2 tog., y.f., k.6, y.f., k.1 t.b.l., y.f., k.5, y.f., sl.1, k.1, p.s.s.o., (k.5, k.2 tog., y.f.) twice, (k.1 t.b.l., y.f.) 3 times, sl.1, k.1, p.s.s.o., k.5, y.f., sl.1, k.1, p.s.s.o., (k.5, k.2 tog., y.f.) twice, k.1 t.b.l., y.f., k.1 t.b.l.; rep. from * once more.

34th row: * y.f., k.3, y.f., sl.1, k.1, p.s.s.o., k.5, y.f., sl.1, k.2 tog., p.s.s.o., y.f., k.1, y.f., sl.1, k.2 tog., p.s.s.o., y.f., k.5, k.2 tog., y.f., k.3, y.f., * k.6, y.f., sl.1, k.2 tog., p.s.s.o., y.f., k.1, y.f., sl.1, k.2 tog., p.s.s.o., y.f., k.5, k.2 tog., y.f., k.3, y.f., k.1 t.b.l.; rep. from * to * once more, k.1 t.b.l.; rep. from first * once more.

36th row: * y.f., sl.1, k.1, p.s.s.o., y.f., k.1 t.b.l., y.f., k.2 tog., y.f., sl.1, k.1, p.s.s.o., k.5, y.f., sl.1, k.1, p.s.s.o., k.1, k.2 tog., y.f., k.5, k.2 tog.; rep. from * once more, y.f., sl.1, k.1, p.s.s.o., y.f., k.1 t.b.l., y.f., k.2 tog., y.f., k.1 t.b.l.; rep. from * to * once more, y.f., sl.1, k.1, p.s.s.o., y.f., k.1 t.b.l., y.f., k.2 tog., y.f., k.1 t.b.l.; rep. from first * once more.

38th row: * y.f., sl.1, k.1, p.s.s.o., k.1, y.f., k.1 t.b.l., y.f., k.1, k.2 tog., y.f., sl.1, k.1, p.s.s.o., k.5, y.f., sl.1, k.2 tog., p.s.s.o., y.f., k.5, k.2 tog.; rep. from * once more, y.f., sl.1, k.1, p.s.s.o., k.1, y.f., k.1 t.b.l., y.f., k.1, k.2 tog., y.f., k.1 t.b.l.; rep. from * to * once more, y.f., sl.1, k.1, p.s.s.o., k.1, y.f., k.1 t.b.l., y.f., k.1, k.2 tog., y.f., k.1 t.b.l.; rep. from first * once more.

40th row: * y.f., sl.1, k.1, p.s.s.o., k.2, y.f., k.1 t.b.l., y.f., k.2, k.2 tog., y.f., sl.1, k.1, p.s.s.o., k.4, k.2 tog., y.f., k.5, k.2 tog.; rep. from * once more, y.f., sl.1, k.1, p.s.s.o., k.2, y.f., k.1 t.b.l., y.f., k.2, k.2 tog., y.f., k.1 t.b.l.; rep. from * to * once more, y.f., sl.1, k.1, p.s.s.o., k.2, y.f., k.1 t.b.l., y.f., k.2, k.2 tog., y.f., k.1 t.b.l.; rep. from first * once more.

42nd row: * y.f., sl.1, k.1, p.s.s.o., k.3, y.f., k.1 t.b.l., y.f., k.3, k.2 tog., y.f., sl.1, k.1, p.s.s.o., k.9, k.2 tog.; rep. from * once more, y.f., sl.1, k.1, p.s.s.o., k.3, y.f., k.1 t.b.l., y.f., k.3, k.2 tog., y.f., k.1 t.b.l.; rep. from * to * once more, y.f., sl.1, k.1, p.s.s.o., k.3, y.f., k.1 t.b.l., y.f., k.3, k.2 tog., y.f., k.1 t.b.l.; rep. from first * once more.

44th row: * (y.f., k.1 t.b.l., y.f., sl.1, k.1, p.s.s.o., k.7, k.2 tog.) 5 times, (y.f., k.1 t.b.l.) twice, (y.f., k.1 t.b.l., y.f., sl.1, k.1, p.s.s.o., k.7, k.2 tog.) 3 times, (y.f., k.1 t.b.l.) twice; rep. from * once more.

46th row: * (y.f., k.3, y.f., sl.1, k.1, p.s.s.o., k.5, k.2 tog.) 5 times, y.f., k.3, y.f., k.1 t.b.l., (y.f., k.3, y.f., sl.1, k.1, p.s.s.o., k.5, k.2 tog.) 3 times, y.f., k.3, y.f., k.1 t.b.l.; rep. from * once more.
48th row: * (y.f., k.1, y.f., sl.1, k.2 tog., p.s.s.o., y.f., k.1, y.f., sl.1, k.1, p.s.s.o., k.3, k.2 tog.) 5 times, y.f., k.1, y.f., sl.1, k.2 tog., p.s.s.o., y.f., k.1, y.f., k.1 t.b.l., (y.f., k.1, y.f., sl.1, k.2 tog., p.s.s.o., y.f., k.1, y.f., sl.1, k.1, p.s.s.o., k.3, k.2 tog.) 3 times, y.f., k.1, y.f., sl.1, k.2 tog., p.s.s.o., y.f., k.1, y.f., k.1 t.b.l.; rep. from * once more.
50th row: * (y.f., k.7, y.f., sl.1, k.1, p.s.s.o., k.1, k.2 tog.) 5 times, y.f., k.7, y.f., k.1 t.b.l., (y.f., k.7, y.f., sl.1, k.1, p.s.s.o., k.1, k.2 tog.) 3 times, y.f., k.7, y.f., k.1 t.b.l.; rep. from * once more.
51st row: k.
Next row: k.1 st. from left-hand needle on to right-hand needle and with crochet hook, work * 1 d.c. into next 2 sts., 10 ch., (1 d.c. into next 3 sts., 10 ch.) 21 times, 1 d.c. into next 2 sts., 10 ch., 1 d.c. into next 3 sts., 10 ch., 1 d.c. into next 2 sts., 10 ch., (1 d.c. into next 3 sts., 10 ch.) 13 times, 1 d.c. into next 2 sts., 10 ch., 1 d.c. into next 3 sts., 10 ch.; rep. from * once more, 1 s.s. into first d.c. Fasten off.
With wrong side facing, crochet or sew together the cast-on sts. in centre of section.
Work second section exactly as for first section.
Damp and pin out to measurements.

TO JOIN SECTIONS

Attach thread into any loop on last row of first section, 5 ch., 1 d.c. into corresponding loop on second section, 5 ch., 1 d.c. into next loop on first section. Continue in this manner leaving sufficient opening to insert cushion pad, then complete joining as before ending with 1 s.s. into first d.c. Fasten off.

Round cushion

illustrated on page 164

MATERIALS
2 balls (20 gr. each) Coats Mercer-Crochet No. 20. One set of four No. 12 knitting needles (USA size 1). One steel crochet hook International Standard Size 1·75. A circular cushion pad with a diameter of 12 in.

MEASUREMENTS
Finished cushion has a diameter of approx. 12 in.

ABBREVIATIONS
See page 11.

TO MAKE
First Section
Cast on 9 sts. (3 sts. on each of 3 needles) and work in rounds as follows.
1st row: k.
2nd row: * y.f., k.1; rep. from * to end.
3rd and 4th rows: as first and 2nd rows.
5th row: * k.3, y.r.n. twice, k.1, y.r.n. twice; rep. from * to end.
6th to 12th rows: work only 1 st. into each 2 y.r.n. of 5th and following rows, * k.3, y.r.n. twice, sl.1, k.2 tog., p.s.s.o., y.r.n. twice; rep. from * to end.

13th row: * sl.1, k.2 tog., p.s.s.o., y.r.n. twice, k.3, y.r.n. twice; rep. from * to end.

14th row: * k.1 t.b.l., y.r.n. twice, k.5, y.r.n. twice; rep. from * to end.

15th row: * k.4, y.r.n. twice, k.1 t.b.l., y.r.n. twice, k.3; rep. from * to end.

16th row: * k.5, y.r.n. twice, k.1 t.b.l., y.r.n. twice, k.4; rep. from * to end.

17th row: * k.6, y.r.n. twice, k.1 t.b.l., y.r.n. twice, k.5; rep. from * to end.

18th to 25th rows: * k.5, k.2 tog., y.r.n. twice, k.1 t.b.l., y.r.n. twice, sl.1, k.1, p.s.s.o., k.4; rep. from * to end.

26th row: before commencing row, slip 1 st. from right-hand needle on to left-hand needle. * sl.1, k.2 tog., p.s.s.o., k.3, y.r.n. twice, k.2 tog., k.1 t.b.l., sl.1, k.1, p.s.s.o., y.r.n. twice, k.3; rep. from * to end.

27th row: before commencing row, slip 1 st. from right-hand needle on to left-hand needle. * sl.1, k.2 tog., p.s.s.o., k.2, y.r.n. twice, k.1, y.r.n. twice, sl.1, k.2 tog., p.s.s.o., y.r.n. twice, k.1, y.r.n. twice, k.2; rep. from * to end.

28th row: before commencing row, slip 1 st. from right-hand needle on to left-hand needle. * sl. 1, k.2 tog., p.s.s.o., k.1, y.r.n. twice, k.3, y.r.n. twice, k.1 t.b.l., y.r.n. twice, k.3, y.r.n. twice, k.1; rep. from * to end.

29th row: before commencing row, k.2 sts. from left-hand needle on to right-hand needle, * y.r.n. twice, k.5, y.r.n. twice, k.1 t.b.l., y.r.n. twice, k.5, y.r.n. twice, sl.1, k.2 tog., p.s.s.o.; rep. from * to end.

30th row: * y.r.n. twice, k.7, y.r.n. twice, k.1 t.b.l.; rep. from * to end.

31st row: * y.r.n. twice, k.9, y.r.n. twice, k.1 t.b.l.; rep. from * to end.

32nd row: * work 2 sts. thus (k.1, p.1) into the 2 y.r.n. of previous row, k.9, (k.1, p.1) into the 2 y.r.n. of previous row, k.1; rep. from * to end.

33rd to 41st rows: k.

42nd row: * y.r.n. twice, (sl.1, k.1, p.s.s.o.) twice; rep. from * to end.

43rd row: * work 2 sts. thus (k.1, p.1) into the 2 y.r.n. of last row, k.2; rep. from * to end.

44th to 47th rows: k., sl. 1 st. from right-hand needle on to left-hand needle at end of last row.

With crochet hook work 1 d.c. into first 4 sts., * 10 ch., 1 d.c. into next 4 sts.; rep. from * to end, 10 ch., 1 s.s. into first d.c. Fasten off.

Work second section exactly as for first section.

Damp and pin out to measurement.

TO JOIN SECTIONS

Attach thread into any loop on last row of first section, 1 d.c. into same loop, 5 ch., 1 d.c. into corresponding loop of second section, 5 ch., 1 d.c. into next loop of first section. Cont. in this manner leaving sufficient opening to insert cushion pad, then complete joining as before, ending with 1 s.s. into first d.c. Fasten off.

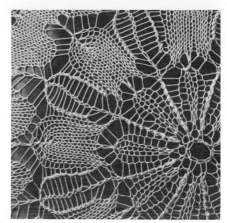

Glossary of terms

Aran The Aran Isles, off the west coast of Ireland, have given their name to the traditional cable stitch patterns used for knitwear which has been made there for many years. The term 'Aran' yarn has come to be applied to the thick yarn (often slightly bulkier than a double knitting) which is used for this type of work. See also **Bainin**.

Asterisk The printing sign frequently used in patterns to save writing out a complex pattern more than once. Thus you may be instructed to work from asterisk to asterisk—in other words, you repeat all the pattern instructions given between the two asterisks.

Bainin Pronounced baw-neen, this is the traditional creamy white yarn used for Aran knitting. The name comes from the Irish word meaning white. Nowadays the yarn can be dyed to many different shades. Although many people still prefer the original creamy yarn, there are many beautiful colourings available in Bainin yarn.

Blocking When knitting is finished it should be pinned out carefully while still in its separate sections, each section drawn gently to its proper shape, and then pressed. This is called blocking; seaming is carried out after blocking.

Bouclé The technical term for yarn which has knops or small slubs in it, and which knits up to a tweedy surface.

Brioche Breton fisherfolk evolved the brioche method of knitting, whereby the yarn is brought forward and then knitted with the actual stitch, so that the fabric has a double texture. The basic rib is attractive and reversible.

Cable, cabling The action of slipping off a group of stitches from the main needle on to a small, double-pointed one, and putting these stitches either to the front or back of the work, and then knitting from the main needle and finally from the small needle; this produces a twisted, rope-like pattern.

Casting off The term for working a final row and eliminating all the stitches in such a way that they will not rip out.

Casting on The term for putting the first row of stitches on to the needle before beginning to work.

Chart The squared pattern from which multi-coloured knitting is often worked. Usually one stitch is represented by one square on the chart. Hence, a design fifteen squares wide comprises fifteen stitches. Each row is represented by a row of squares horizontally.

Circular knitting Tubular work—i.e. knitting in the form of a tube without seams as opposed to normal flat knitting—can be produced either by using a set of four needles, with points at both ends of every needle, or by using a single circular needle. In either case the work in knitted round and round instead of back and forth, as in flat knitting.

Crossover This is a simplified form of cabling. Stitches are twisted by the crossing technique: the second stitch on the left-hand needle is knitted before the first (either from the back or the front depending on the direction in which the stitches are to be crossed) and then the first is knitted. Both are slipped off the needle together.

Decreasing It is often necessary to diminish the number of stitches on the needles, sometimes gradually and sometimes sharply. Various methods are used for this, and usually the method appropriate to a particular pattern will be indicated in the instructions—e.g. cast off 6 sts. at beg. of row, or take 2 tog. at each end of the next and every foll. alt. row.

Fair Isle Traditional multi-colour knitting from the Scottish islands. Bright clear colours are used against a background of white, grey, fawn or brown. The patterns are believed to be Spanish in origin. In a true Fair Isle design, the sequence of patternings is changed all the way up the garment, so no motif is ever repeated. Usually a broad pattern in several colours is alternated with a narrow pattern in only two or three colours. Although an almost limitless number of colours may be used in a Fair Isle pattern normally no more than two colours are ever used in the same row. Nowadays any type of knitting using two or more colours is loosely (and incorrectly) termed Fair Isle.

Four-needle knitting See **Circular knitting.**

Garter stitch A classic stitch pattern where every row is knitted. If every row is purled a similar fabric is produced; this is known as purl garter stitch. To produce garter stitch in circular knitting, knit and purl rounds are alternated.

Gathering As with sewn garments, it is sometimes desirable to have fullness taken in sharply to a much smaller area—for instance, above a cuff. In knitting this is done by working regular decreases right across the row at regular intervals. Thus a bloused effect is created. Alternatively, if the smaller area is worked first, then blousing is achieved by regular increasing across the row.

Gauge Knitting needles are 'gauged' (numbered) according to their size. A gadget called a gauge is available to help you check the size of needles. Gauges are usually made of a lightweight metal or strong plastic. There will be a row of holes or indentations which correspond with needle sizes. Often there is a slot an inch wide as well. With the gauge it is possible to identify the size of any needle, and the slot is a useful tension guide.

Grafting A method of joining two pieces of knitting without making a seam. The two pieces are not cast off but the yarn is threaded on to a sewing needle, and the stitches taken off the knitting needles one by one as the sewing needle is slipped through each. A new row of 'knitting' is thus 'sewn' into the work.

Increasing The term used for putting more stitches on to the needle, either at each end of the work, or actually within the row, depending on the type of shaping required. The finished work will widen according to the rate of increase.

Joining Yarn has to be joined when one ball runs out and a new one is needed, or when a second colour has to be introduced to the pattern. Usually this is done by splicing (see **Splicing**) or by tying one yarn loosely round the other.

Knit One of the two basic stitches used in knitting, and usually abbreviated as 'k.' in patterns. Sometimes however the term is used loosely instead of, more correctly, 'work'—e.g. if a pattern instructs you to 'knit until work is 6 in.' this will probably mean continue in the pattern as already given until work is this length.

Moss stitch A classic stitch pattern which gives a tweedy-textured surface.

Needles Knitting needles are made in pairs for flat knitting, and in sets of four or as single round needles for circular work. Some patterns may call needles 'pins'.

Pattern This can refer either to the entire design for a garment or to a section within it; a special arrangement of stitches taking a certain number of rows may form a complete pattern motif in a design. This will be referred to as the 'pattern' and you may be instructed to work so many patterns before proceeding to the next stage.

Picot hem An edging which is decorative and has a ridged finish. It is knitted or sewn into position.

Pins See **Needles.**

Ply Ply refers to the number of strands used in a yarn—e.g. a two-ply yarn consists of two strands wound together; a four-ply yarn has four strands, and so on. Although generally a four-ply is thicker than a two-ply one this need not necessarily be so since the individual strands may be of any thickness. For instance, a four-ply yarn could be made up from four very thin strands, while a two-ply may consist of two bulky strands.

Purl One of the two basic stitches used in knitting, usually abbreviated in patterns to 'p.'.

Repeat If a pattern motif or group of rows have to be worked more than once in a particular design, or if individual rows have to be worked several times, then instructions are usually given to 'repeat the pattern six times', or something similar. Be careful always to work the correct number of rows or pattern repeats. For instance, if you are instructed to work two rows, and then to 'repeat first and second rows six times', you will work fourteen rows in all.

Rib The repetition of knit and purl stitches, ranged exactly above each other, produces ridged work which has great elasticity. This is called ribbing, and there are various widths of rib which can be produced, depending upon the combination of knit and purl stitches.

Round When circular knitting is being worked, either on four needles or a circular needle, a 'round' of work means the knitting of every stitch once—i.e. from each of the three needles in four-needle work, or completely round the circular needle, so that you are back to the first stitch again.

Row When working two-needle knitting, each time the left-hand stitches have been transferred on to the right-hand needle, that is called an entire row.

Running in The term used for eliminating loose ends of yarn at the edges of the work before, or when, sewing up is done. Each end is threaded on to a sewing needle and carefully worked into the back or edge of the knitting before it is cut.

Scandinavian knitting Multi-colour designs which are similar to Fair Isle, but usually worked in bolder colours. Traditionally Scandinavian patterns are used on ski-wear, husky sweaters and similar garments.

Selvedge The vertical edge of a piece of knitting, often worked with a slipped or knitted stitch so that a ridged edge is formed. This facilitates sewing up, especially when the main fabric is in an open-work pattern.

Slip stitch The action of transferring a stitch from one needle to the other without knitting it. Sometimes this is regularly done with the first stitch in every row, to give a firm edge; sometimes it merely occurs as part of the pattern.

Splicing The action of thinning out two ends of yarn and then rubbing them together to bind them to the thickness of the main yarn. This is the best method for joining in new yarn to a piece of work.

Stitch Each loop on the needle is called a stitch. The term 'stitch' is also applied to different ways of actually working the stitch—e.g. knit stitch, purl stitch, stocking stitch, garter stitch.

Stocking/stockinette stitch A stitch pattern in which rows are alternately knitted and purled, to produce a smooth, flat surface. The reverse is ridged and this is sometimes used as the right side of the fabric, when it is then called reversed stocking stitch.

Tension This is the measurement of the number of stitches and number of rows to each square inch of knitted fabric. The measurement depends on the type of yarn being used, the size of needle, and whether the knitter herself works tightly or slackly. It is important always to check your own tension measurement before beginning a pattern, as the finished size and shape of the garment is entirely dependent on your working to the correct tension measurement throughout.

Turn When shaping occurs in a piece of knitting, it is sometimes necessary not to complete a row, but to work to a certain point in the row, and then to turn and continue work on this first set of stitches only. Simply turn the work round and work from the other side back along the stitches just knitted, leaving the remaining unworked stitches on the right-hand needle. Sometimes the unworked stitches are slipped on to a stitch holder until work is complete on the first set of stitches, and then the yarn is rejoined to the edge of unworked stitches, and they in their turn are worked.

Vandyke patterns A traditional stitch pattern in which V's of stocking stitch are worked on a ground of reversed stocking stitch.

Wool A natural yarn used for knitting all types of garments. Botany wool, from pure-bred Merino sheep, is considered the finest of all wool. From such fleeces the softest wool qualities are spun. Crossbred wool, from crossbred sheep, has a coarser, tougher fibre suitable for the spinning of the harder-wearing qualities of wool.

Yarn This term refers to any spun thread, and can denote either a natural thread such as wool, linen or cotton, or any of the synthetics, such as nylon, Tricel, Terylene, Courtelle and so on.

Acknowledgements

Acknowledgements are due to the following companies who generously gave help with the preparation of this book:

J. & P. Coats Ltd., 155 St. Vincent Street, Glasgow C.2 (Coats patterns in Pattern section, and photographs on pages 34, 164, 165 and 169).

Emu Wools Ltd., Low Street Mills, Keighley, Yorkshire (Emu patterns in Pattern section, and zip-up jacket illustrated on page 18).

John C. Horsfall and Sons Ltd. (Hayfield Wools), Hayfield Mills, Glusburn, Nr. Keighley, Yorkshire.

Lister and Co. Ltd., Providence Mills, Wakefield, Yorkshire.

Martin Mahony and Bros. Ltd., Blarney, Co. Cork (Mahony patterns in Pattern section, and stitch samples in chapter on Aran Knitting).

H. G. Twilley Ltd., Roman Mills, Stamford, Lincolnshire (Twilley patterns in Pattern section, and photographs on pages 6, 7, 29, 46 and 49).

Abel Morrall Ltd. (Aero knitting needles, crochet hooks, Twin-pins and other products).

Knitmaster Ltd. (manufacturers of knitting machines), 30–40 Elcho Street, London S.W.11 (photographs on pages 75, 76, 77, 78 and 79).

Photographs on pages 35, 36, 53, 72, 85, 87, 89, 90, 107, 119 and 135 were taken at **Thatchers Hotel,** East Horsley, Nr. Leatherhead, Surrey.

Ice skates in photograph on page 89 were loaned by **Spires Sports Ltd.,** 60/62 Eden Street, Kingston Upon Thames, Surrey.

Yarn equivalents

Wherever possible, the brand name and weight of yarn quoted in a pattern should be used. Where a particular yarn is not readily available, then select the appropriate general equivalent from the following list. It is essential however that a careful tension check is made before embarking on the pattern—and this applies whether you are using the original brand-name yarn, or an equivalent. Only by achieving the correct tension measurement can you hope to achieve satisfactory results.

J. & P. Coats yarns

Mercer-Crochet No. 20 should be readily available almost everywhere. In USA substitute J. & P. Coats 6/c Crochet Cotton or 3/Mercerised No. 20.

Emu yarns

For Scotch Double Knitting use a standard double knitting.

Hayfield yarns

For Courtier 3-ply Bri-Nylon use a standard nylon 3-ply yarn.
For Nucrêpe use a standard double knitting yarn with a crêpe finish.
For Diane, Gaylon Double Knitting or Croft Double Knitting use a standard double knitting.

Lister yarns

For Lavenda Crisp Crêpe 4-ply use a standard 4-ply yarn with a crêpe finish.
For Lavenda Double Crêpe use a standard double knitting with a crêpe finish.

Mahony's yarns

Baby Berella, Blarney Bainin and Blarney Heatherspun should be readily available almost everywhere. In USA substitute Blarneyspun for Blarney Bainin.

Templeton yarns

For Antler Double Crêpe substitute a standard double knitting with a crêpe finish.

Twilley yarns

Lysbet is a fine cotton yarn; Crysette a medium-weight cotton yarn; and Stalite a slightly heavier cotton yarn: for these yarns substitute cotton yarns of similar weights.
'747' Orlon is an extra-thick Orlon yarn—substitute any bulky synthetic yarn.
For Cortina Super Crochet Wool use a medium-weight wool with a firm twist.

Wendy yarns

For Courtelle Crêpe 4-ply use a standard 4-ply yarn with a crêpe finish.
For Nylonised Double Knitting or Courtellon Double Knit use a standard double knitting (preferably synthetic). For Invitation Crochet Cotton use a medium-weight cotton yarn.

Index

Abbreviations 11, 41
Adapting two needle patterns for circular knitting 58
After-care of knitting 70
All-over diamonds (colour work) 51
Altering the length 70
Alternating cable 30
Angora yarns 5
Aran knitting 40–45
Aran sweaters, children's 105
Aran sweaters, his and hers 149
Argyll-type colour pattern 55
Asterisks 26
Attachments for knitting machines 77

Baby garments—lace-trimmed jacket 85
  —lacy-patterned dress 91
  —layette 80
  —motif-patterned dress 87
Backstitch seam 63
Basic stitches 16
Basket stitch (in Aran knitting) 41
Bathmat, blue 163
Bathmat, pink 163
Bedroom bootees 162
Belted sweater 158
Between-stitch method of casting on 14
Blocking 62
Blarney kiss and cross-stitch rib 42
Blarney kiss (in Aran knitting) 41, 42
Blouse, cotton 120
Blue bathmat 163
Bobble stitch 33
Bootees, bedroom 162
Border strip 51
Bouclé yarns 6
Brackets 26
Butterfly stitch 37
Button bands 64
Buttonholes 68–69

Cable in Aran knitting 40
Cable knitting 29–32, 40
Cable needles 9
Cable-patterned cap 162
Cable-patterned jacket 135
Cap, cable-patterned 162
Cap, Fair Isle 161
Cardigan suit 145
Cashmere yarns 5
Casting off 16, 19

Casting off for circular needle knitting 19
Casting off for four-needle knitting 19
Casting on for circular needle knitting 15, 57
Casting on for four-needle knitting 15
Casting on methods 13–16
Chain stitch 74
Charts, how to work from 52
Checks 50
Chevron lace stitch 38
Chevron sweater 155
Children's garments—Aran sweaters 105
  —cotton jumper in four sizes 102
  —dress with roll collar 98
  —military-style coat dress 95
  —mother and daughter skating dresses 116
  —shorts and pullover 93
  —three-colour dress 100
Circle 60
Circular knitting 8, 15, 19, 56–61
  —casting off method 19
  —casting on method 15, 57
Circular needles 8, 15, 56, 57
Circular stitch patterns 59–61
Classic pullover 152
Classic V-necked sweater 131
Clusters 33–34
Colour knitting 46–56, 58
Colour patterns 48–49
Colour work in circular knitting 58
Continental needle sizes 10
Continental stocking stitch 23
Cork cable and small mock cables 42
Cotton blouse 120
Cotton jumper in four sizes 102
Cotton yarns 6
Crêpe yarns 5
Crochet for edgings 73–74
Crochet hook 10
Crochet medallions (on sweater) 127
Crochet stitches 74
Curving openwork stitch 38
Cushion, oval 164
Cushion, rectangular 166
Cushion, round 168

Decreasing methods 21
Double crochet 74
Double diamond with plait cables 43
Double rib 24
Diamond (in Aran knitting) 41
Diamond lattice pattern 38
Diamonds (colour knitting) 50
Diamonds (twisted stitches) 32

Dress, lacy-patterned 91
Dress, military-style coat 95
Dress, motif-patterned 87
Dress, red, white and blue 139
Dress, three-colour 100
Dress with roll collar 98
Dresses, mother and daughter skating 116
Dropped stitches 28

Edges 39, 65
Eyelet stitch 39

Fair Isle cap 161
Fair Isle stitch sample 52
Fair Isle work 49–50, 52
Fancy diamonds (colour work) 52
Fancy stitch patterns 29–39
Fashion garments—bedroom bootees 162
  —cable-patterned cap 162
  —cable-patterned jacket 135
  —cardigan suit 145
  —classic V-necked sweater 131
  —cotton blouse 120
  —Fair Isle cap 161
  —his and hers Aran sweaters 149
  —lace-up jumper 122
  —mother and daughter skating dresses 116
  —polo-neck sweater with cut-away armholes 130
  —red, white and blue dress 139
  —sleeveless pullover 119
  —striped tunic sweater 133
  —sweater with crochet medallions 127
  —teenage trouser suit 112
  —two-colour waistcoat 110
  —wrap-over jacket 141
Finishing details 62–74
Flat seam 63
Fleur de lys 51
Four-needle knitting—casting off method 19
  —casting on method 15

Garter stitch 23
Grafting 68
Greek key colour pattern 55
Glitter yarns 6
Glossary of terms 170–173

Hems 65–66
Hexagon 61
His and hers Aran sweaters 149
Holding the work (knitting) 12
  —(crochet) 73
Honeycomb cable pattern 31
Honeycomb (in Aran knitting) 41, 43
Horizontal buttonholes 69

Houndstooth 50

Increasing methods 19–21
Invisible method of casting on 15

Jacket, cable-patterned 135
Jacket, lace-trimmed 85
Jacket, wrap-over 141
Joining in new yarn 27
Jumper, cotton, in four sizes 102
Jumper, lace-up 122

Knit stitch 16
Knitted hem 65

Lace-trimmed jacket 85
Lace-up jumper 122
Lacy-patterned dress 91
Lacy patterns 34, 37–39
Ladder of life (Aran knitting) 40
Lattice cable 43
Layette, baby's 80
Left-handed workers 12
Lobster claw and twisted rib 42
Lobster claw (Aran knitting) 40, 42

Machine knitting 75–79
Making up a garment 62–65
Measuring work 27
Medallion knitting 60–61
Medallions 31
Men's garments – belted sweater 158
  – chevron sweater 155
  – classic pullover 152
  – his and hers Aran sweaters 149
Military-style coat dress 95
Mixtures (yarns) 7
Mock checks 51
Mohair yarns 5
Moss stitch 24
Mother and daughter skating dresses 116
Motif-patterned dress 87

Necklines 66–67
Needle gauge 9
Needles 8
Net stitch 37
New yarn, joining in 27

Open cable 31
Opening edges 67
Oval cushion 164

Pattern holders 10
Patterns, how to choose and follow 25
Patterns to make 80–169
Petal stitch 34
Picking up stitches for borders 66

Picot hem 65
Pink bathmat 163
Pip edge 67
Ply 5
Pockets 69
Polo-neck sweater with cut-away armholes 130
Pullover and shorts 93
Pullover, classic 152
Pullover, sleeveless 119
Punch-card knitting machines 78–79
Purl stitch 16

Rectangular cushion 166
Red, white and blue dress 139
Rib patterns 23–24
Round cushion 168
Row counters 9, 77

Scandinavian knitting 49
Selvedges 67
Sewn hem 65
Shaping work 19–21
Shorts, with matching pullover 93
Simple cable 30
Simple stripes 47
Single-bed knitting machines 77
Single rib 24
Sleeveless pullover 119
Slip loop 13
Slip stitch 74
Small buttonholes 69
Spoon (in Aran knitting) 41
Square 61
Squirrel motif (colour work) 55
Stepped diagonal rib 59
Stitch holders 9
Stitch patterns, basic 23–25
Stitch patterns, fancy 29–39
Stocking stitch 23
Stocking stitch, continental 23
Stranding yarn (in colour work) 47
Striped tunic sweater 133
Stripes, simple 47
Stripes, vertical 48
Suit, cardigan 145
Sweater, belted 158
Sweater, chevron 155
Sweater, classic V-necked 131
Sweater, polo-neck, with cut-away armholes 130
Sweater, striped tunic 133
Sweater with crochet medallions 127
Sweaters, Aran, his and hers 149
Synthetic yarns 7

Tape measure 9
Technical problems 27–28
Teenage trouser suit 112
Tension 21–22, 26
Tension (machine knitting) 77, 78

Three-colour dress 100
Thumb method of casting on 13
Tools and materials 5–11
Treble 74
Tree of life (in Aran knitting) 41, 44
Tree of life with twisted rib panels 44
Trellis (in Aran knitting) 41, 42
Trinity stitch (in Aran knitting) 41
Trouser suit, teenage 112
Tubular knitting 61
Twin-bed knitting machines 77
Twisted cable rib 32
Twisted stitches 32–33
Two-colour waistcoat 110
Two-needle method of casting on 14
Two-needle patterns, how to adapt for circular knitting 58

UK needle sizes 8, 10
Undoing stitches 28
USA needle sizes 8, 10

Vandyke stitch 37
Vertical buttonholes 69
Vertical stripes 48

Waistbands 64
Waistcoat, two-colour 110
Washing qualities (yarns) 7
Weaving yarn (in colour work) 47
Weights and measures 10, 11
Wheatear cable 31
Wide rib 24
Wide-set rib (circular knitting) 59
Wide twisted rib 33
Woollen yarns 5
Wrap-over jacket 141

Yarn carrier 77
Yarn equivalents 174
Yarn forward 20
Yarn on needle 20
Yarn round needle 20
Yarn types 5–7
Yarn, using a second time 70
Yarns (machine knitting) 77

Zigzag (in Aran knitting) 40, 44, 45
Zigzags on double moss stitch ground 44
Zigzags with bobbles and small cables 45
Zip fasteners 64